St Antony's/Macmillan Series

General Editors: Archie Brown (1978–1985) and Rosemary Thorp (1985–), both Fellows of St Antony's College, Oxford

Recent titles include:

Amatzia Baram
CULTURE, HISTORY AND IDEOLOGY IN THE FORMATION OF BA'THIST IRAQ, 1968–89

Gail Lee Bernstein and Haruhiro Fukui (*editors*)
JAPAN AND THE WORLD

Archie Brown (*editor*)
POLITICAL LEADERSHIP IN THE SOVIET UNION

Deborah Fahy Bryceson
FOOD INSECURITY AND THE SOCIAL DIVISION OF LABOUR IN TANZANIA, 1919–85

Victor Bulmer-Thomas
STUDIES IN THE ECONOMICS OF CENTRAL AMERICA

Sir Alec Cairncross
PLANNING IN WARTIME

Helen Callaway
GENDER, CULTURE AND EMPIRE

Colin Clarke (*editor*)
SOCIETY AND POLITICS IN THE CARIBBEAN

David Cleary
ANATOMY OF THE AMAZON GOLD RUSH

Roger Cooter (*editor*)
STUDIES IN THE HISTORY OF ALTERNATIVE MEDICINE

Robert Desjardins
THE SOVIET UNION THROUGH FRENCH EYES

Guido di Tella and Carlos Rodríguez Braun (*editors*)
ARGENTINA, 1946–83: THE ECONOMIC MINISTERS SPEAK

Guido di Tella and D. Cameron Watt (*editors*)
ARGENTINA BETWEEN THE GREAT POWERS, 1939–46

Guido di Tella and Rudiger Dornbusch (*editors*)
THE POLITICAL ECONOMY OF ARGENTINA, 1946–83

Saul Dubow
RACIAL SEGREGATION AND THE ORIGINS OF APARTHEID IN SOUTH AFRICA, 1919–36

Anne Lincoln Fitzpatrick
THE GREAT RUSSIAN FAIR

Heather D. Gibson
THE EUROCURRENCY MARKETS, DOMESTIC FINANCIAL POLICY AND INTERNATIONAL INSTABILITY

David Hall-Cathala
THE PEACE MOVEMENT IN ISRAEL, 1967–87

John B. Hattendorf and Robert S. Jordan (*editors*)
MARITIME STRATEGY AND THE BALANCE OF POWER

Linda Hitchcox
VIETNAMESE REFUGEES IN SOUTHEAST ASIAN CAMPS

Derek Hopwood (*editor*)
STUDIES IN ARAB HISTORY

Amitzur Ilan
BERNADOTTE IN PALESTINE, 1948

Hiroshi Ishida
SOCIAL MOBILITY IN CONTEMPORARY JAPAN

J.R. Jennings
SYNDICALISM IN FRANCE

Maria d'Alva G. Kinzo
LEGAL OPPOSITION POLITICS UNDER AUTHORITARIAN RULE IN BRAZIL

Bohdan Krawchenko
SOCIAL CHANGE AND NATIONAL CONSCIOUSNESS IN TWENTIETH-CENTURY
UKRAINE

Robert H. McNeal
STALIN: MAN AND RULER

Iftikhar H. Malik
US–SOUTH ASIAN RELATIONS, 1940–47

Amii Omara-Otunnu
POLITICS AND THE MILITARY IN UGANDA, 1890–1985

Ilan Pappé
BRITAIN AND THE ARAB–ISRAELI CONFLICT, 1948–51

J.L. Porket
WORK, EMPLOYMENT AND UNEMPLOYMENT IN THE SOVIET UNION

Brian Powell
KABUKI IN MODERN JAPAN

Alex Pravda
HOW RULING COMMUNIST PARTIES ARE GOVERNED

Laurie P. Salitan
POLITICS AND NATIONALITY IN CONTEMPORARY SOVIET–JEWISH
   EMIGRATION, 1968–89

H. Gordon Skilling
CZECHOSLOVAKIA, 1918–88
SAMIZDAT AND AN INDEPENDENT SOCIETY IN CENTRAL AND EASTERN
   EUROPE

J.A.A. Stockwin, Alan Rix, Aurelia George, James Horne, Daichi Itô, Martin Collick
DYNAMIC AND IMMOBILIST POLITICS IN JAPAN

Verena Stolcke
COFFEE PLANTERS, WORKERS AND WIVES

Jane E. Stromseth
THE ORIGINS OF FLEXIBLE RESPONSE

Joseph S. Szyliowicz
POLITICS, TECHNOLOGY AND DEVELOPMENT

Jane Watts
BLACK WRITERS FROM SOUTH AFRICA

Philip J. Williams
THE CATHOLIC AND POLITICS IN NICARAGUA AND COSTA RICA

Society and Politics in the Caribbean

Edited by Colin Clarke

University Lecturer in Geography
and Official Fellow, Jesus College, Oxford

M

MACMILLAN

in association with
St Antony's College
Oxford

First published 1991

Published by
MACMILLAN ACADEMIC AND PROFESSIONAL LTD
Houndmills, Basingstoke, Hampshire RG21 2XS
and London
Companies and representatives
throughout the world

Printed in Hong Kong

British Library Cataloguing in Publication Data
Society and politics in the Caribbean. – (St Antony's/Macmillan Series)
1. Caribbean region. Political development
I. Clarke, Colin G. (Colin Graham), *1938 –* II.
University of Oxford, *St Antony's College* III. Series
320.9729

ISBN 0–333–53823–4

677324
Anc

Series Standing Order

If you would like to receive future titles in this series as they are
published, you can make use of our standing order facility. To place a
standing order please contact your bookseller or, in case of difficulty,
write to us at the address below with your name and address and the
name of the series. Please state with which title you wish to begin your
standing order. (If you live outside the United Kingdom we may not
have the rights for your area, in which case we will forward your order
to the publisher concerned.)

Customer Services Department, Macmillan Distribution Ltd
Houndmills, Basingstoke, Hampshire, RG21 2XS, England.

To David Lowenthal,
celebrated Caribbeanist

Contents

Contents

List of Tables

List of Figures

Notes on the Contributors

O. Nigel Bolland is a Professor of Sociology at Colgate University in Hamilton, New York. He studied at the University of Hull and McMaster University and was a Research Fellow at the Institute of Social and Economic Research, University of the West Indies. He is the author of many articles and books on aspects of colonialism and development in Belize and the West Indies, including *The Formation of a Colonial Society: Belize, from Conquest to Crown Colony* (Johns Hopkins University Press, 1977), *Belize: A New Nation in Central America* (Westview Press, 1986), and *Colonialism and Resistance in Belize: Essays in Historical Sociology* (ISER and SPEAR, 1988). He is currently working on a study of the labour movement in the British West Indies in the 1930s and 1940s.

Colin Clarke is a University Lecturer in Geography and an Official Fellow of Jesus College, Oxford. He has taught at the universities of Toronto and Liverpool, where he was Reader in Geography and Latin–American Studies, and he has carried out numerous field investigations in Mexico and the Caribbean. His publications deal with race and ethnic pluralism, urbanization, demography, rural change and politics. He is the author of *Kingston, Jamaica: urban development and social change 1692–1962* (University of California Press, 1975), *East Indians in a West Indian Town: San Fernando, Trinidad, 1930–1970* (Allen and Unwin, 1986), and *Livelihood Systems, Settlements and Levels of Living in 'Los Valles Centrales de Oaxaca', Mexico* (School of Geography, University of Oxford, Research Paper No. 37, 1986); co-author of *A Geography of the Third World* (Methuen, 1983); and co-editor of *Geography and Ethnic Pluralism* (Allen and Unwin, 1984) and *Politics, Security and Development in Small States* (Allen and Unwin, 1987).

Rosario Espinal is an Assistant Professor of Sociology at Temple University in Philadelphia. She has been Visiting Scholar at the Latin American Centre in Oxford, the Kellogg Institute for International Studies at the University of Notre Dame, and the Swedish Institute for Social Research at Stockholm University. Her research deals mainly with the relationship between changes in social structure and political regimes in Latin America. She has written extensively on the

Dominican Republic and is the author of *Autoritarismo y Democracia en la Política Dominicana* (CAPEL, 1987).

Roberto Espíndola lectures in the Research Unit on European–Latin
American Relations at the University of Bradford. He studied law
and political science in Chile and the US. He has taught at the
Catholic Universities of Santiago and Valparaiso and at the University of Essex, and has carried out field research in Chile, the Caribbean and Central America. His current research interests are in the
international relations of the countries of the Caribbean Basin, and
Cuban foreign policy. He was Finance and Commodities Editor of
South magazine, and has covered the Caribbean for the *Sunday
Times*. Currently, he is Editor of *Caribbean Report* and a consultant
for the *Independent*.

Juan M. García-Passalacqua is a political analyst for the newspaper
El Nuevo Día, Channel 11–TV and WKAQ Radio in San Juan. He
holds degrees from the University of Puerto Rico, Tufts University
and Harvard Law School. A former aide to Governors Luis Muñoz
Marín and Roberto Sánchez Vilella, he has held visiting appointments at the Woodrow Wilson International Center for Scholars and
at Yale University. He has published seven books, including *Puerto
Rico: Equality and Freedom at Issue* (Praeger, 1984) and *Crisis
Política en Puerto Rico* (Edil, 1983, 2nd edition).

Michel Giraud, researcher at the Centre National de la Recherche
Scientifique (CNRS) in Paris, is a sociologist. He holds a doctorate in
sociology from the University of Paris–Sorbonne. His main research
interests are in the educational system, migration realities, colour,
cultural identity and class in the French West Indies. He has written a
large number of articles and academic papers on these topics and is
the author of *Races et Classes à la Martinique* (Editions Anthropos,
1979).

Christian A. Girault is a French geographer. He holds a PhD from
McGill University (Montreal), and has published *Le Commerce du
Café en Haiti* (Paris: Editions du Centre National de la Recherche
Scientifique, 1981) and edited the *Atlas d'Haiti* (Centre d'Etudes de
Géographie Tropicale (CNRS) et Université du Bordeaux III, 1985).
He was Senior Associate Member of the Latin American Centre,
St Antony's College, Oxford from 1986 to 1988 and director of the

Franco–British Programme on the Caribbean. Presently he works in Paris on the geo-politics of the Caribbean with RECLUS, a newly established research unit of the Centre National de la Recherche Scientifique.

Jorge Heine is a Senior Fellow at the Centro Latinoamericano de Economia y Política Internacional (CLEPI) in Santiago, Chile, and was formerly Associate Director of the Institute for European–Latin American Relations (IRELA) in Madrid. He holds a PhD from Stanford University and has taught political science at the University of Puerto Rico, Mayagüez and at Inter American University in San Germán, where he also directed the Caribbean Institute and Study Center for Latin America (CISCLA) from 1982 to 1986. He has also been a Visiting Fellow at St Antony's College, Oxford and a Research Associate at the Woodrow Wilson International Center for Scholars (1980–82). His books include *The Caribbean and World Politics: Cross Currents and Cleavages* (co-edited with Leslie Manigat (Holmes & Meier, 1988), *The Puerto Rican Question* (with Juan M. García-Passalacqua: Foreign Policy Association, Headline Series No. 266, 1983) and *Time for Decision: The United States and Puerto Rico* (North-South Publishing, 1983), and *A Revolution Aborted: The Lessons of Grenada* (Pittsburgh University Press, 1990). He is President of the Caribbean Studies Association for 1990–91.

Anthony Payne is a Senior Lecturer in Politics and Director of the Graduate Programme in International Studies at the University of Sheffield. He studied history and politics at Churchill College, Cambridge, and did his postgraduate work at the University of Manchester and the University of the West Indies in Jamaica. He lectured at the Polytechnic in Huddersfield for six years before moving to Sheffield in 1985. His research has dealt mainly with party politics, the political economy of development and international politics in the Caribbean. He is the author of *The International Crisis in the Caribbean* (Croom Helm, 1984); co-author of *Grenada: Revolution and Invasion* (Croom Helm, 1984); co-editor of *Dependency under Challenge: The Political Economy of the Commonwealth Caribbean* (Manchester University Press, 1984) and *Politics, Security and Development in Small States* (Allen and Unwin, 1987); and, most recently, the author of *Politics in Jamaica* (Hurst, 1988).

Tony Thorndike is Professor of International Relations and Head of the Department of International Relations and Politics at the Staffordshire Polytechnic. A graduate of the London School of Economics, he has written and contributed to a number of books and articles on Caribbean political and economic affairs, and published a major study of the Grenadian revolution, *Grenada: Politics, Economics and Society* (Francis Pinter, 1985).

Diego Bautista Urbaneja lectures in political theory at the Central University of Venezuela. He has been Head of the Political Theory Department of the School of Political and Administrative Studies of that University. He was Andres Bello Visiting Fellow and Senior Associate Member at St Antony's College in 1986–87. He specializes in the history and analysis of the Venezuelan political system and has published numerous articles on that subject. He is currently writing a book on Venezuelan democracy. He is also a regular contributor on political affairs to various Venezuelan newspapers.

Acknowledgements

Most of the chapters are based upon papers presented to a seminar I organized at the Latin American Centre, St Anthony's College, Oxford, in summer 1987. I am indebted to Christian Girault and Rosario Espinal, who at that time were visitors to the Latin American Centre, for their close collaboration and advice over the preparation of this book. I also gratefully acknowledge the financial support for the seminar provided jointly by Queen Elizabeth House and the Inter-Faculty Committee for Latin-American Studies at Oxford University, and the editorial help and general encouragement given me by Rosemary Thorp and Alan Angell of St Antony's College. Painstaking help with the proofreading was given by Alina Gruszka, Katie Willis and Aidan Clarke, and Anne Rafique provided admirable editorial services. The book itself contains contributions by geographers, sociologists and political scientists, drawn from the Caribbean and various metropolitan countries, whose mother-tongues are English, French or Spanish, and is dedicated to the geographer David Lowenthal, whose *West Indian Societies* has been an inspiration to us all.

Introduction: Caribbean Decolonization – New States and Old Societies

Colin Clarke

V.S. Naipaul, the Trinidad novelist, has called the Caribbean 'the Third World's Third World', implying that the region lacks an authentic, indigenous heritage, distinct from that imposed by the imperial powers – Spain, Britain, France, Denmark, the Netherlands and, more recently, the US. But the all-embracing nature and sheer length of the colonial impact, coupled to the careful tutelage in metropolitan democratic procedures and values, especially since World War II, have ensured that the Caribbean has become one of the few parts of the Third World where political independence has been accompanied by free elections, multiple parties and liberal democratic freedoms. There is, therefore, in the Caribbean an interesting distinction between new states and old societies; between restrictive social orders founded on slavery and indentured labour, and the current enjoyment, in most but not all societies, of political liberties.

Hispanic control of the Caribbean began in 1492 and was followed by the partitioning of the region by the Spanish, French, British, Dutch and Danish during the seventeenth and eighteenth centuries. US imperial intervention in the Greater Antilles started in the early nineteenth century and culminated in the satellitization of Cuba and annexation of Puerto Rico in 1898 and the purchase of the Danish Virgin Islands in 1917. Hence, each unit's connections – political, economic and intellectual – have been forged almost exclusively with the countries of Western Europe or the US. Soviet collaboration with Cuba since Castro's revolution in 1959 has perpetuated the history of external great power involvement in the Caribbean.

A major feature of Caribbean societies is their insularity and smallness. Not only did these two related characteristics facilitate the early annexation and Balkanization of the Caribbean by distant seaborne empires, but they also help to explain the long period of colonialism, the piecemeal nature of decolonization, and the persistence of very small non-autonomous units. The modal Caribbean

1

society and polity is an island or a collection of islands – though there are some exceptions to this generalization, such as Hispaniola, which contains both Haiti and the Dominican Republic.

The Caribbean, narrowly defined, is occupied by over 30 million people. They live in an archipelago running for more than 2000 km from Cuba to Trinidad (Figure 0.1). Also included in the Caribbean are the three Guianas (French Guiana, Guyana and Suriname) on the shoulder of South America, and Belize in Central America, whose histories link them to the Caribbean rather than to the neighbouring Spanish- or Portuguese-speaking republics. Venezuela, too, experiences – though to a lesser degree – this Caribbean orientation and some of the characteristics of the four Caribbean enclaves; as in their case, its settlement is concentrated on or near to the Caribbean coast, and squeezed, island-like, between the sea and an empty interior.

Caribbean island territories range in size from Cuba, with 110 000 km^2 and about 10 million inhabitants, down to the Grenadines, dependencies of St Vincent and Grenada, each with a few hundred hectares and a handful of residents. Most islands are smaller than Barbados, which has 250 000 inhabitants on a mere 430 km^2. Even Caribbean mainland territories, though big, have small populations: Belize, for example, with 23 000 km^2 has 160 000 inhabitants. It is part of Venezuela's ambiguity as a Caribbean country that it has a population of 18 million and a land area of 912 000 km^2, that stretches inland to the Andes and the Amazon Basin.

This book examines the interrelationships between politics and society in a representative sample of Caribbean units – Anglophone, Francophone and Hispanophone. They include countries that achieved their independence in the nineteenth century – Haiti, Venezuela, Santo Domingo and Cuba; territories of the Commonwealth Caribbean, independent in successive waves since 1962; incorporated or partially incorporated units, such as the *départements d'outre-mer* and Puerto Rico, which are part of France and the US respectively; and the dependencies – minute islands or clusters of islands – that continue a colonial or quasi-colonial relationship with Britain.

Although the Caribbean achieves its regional coherence largely through the historical influence of three interrelated institutions – colonialism, the sugar plantation and slavery, the sugar plantation was installed as *the* mode of production at different time periods in the various islands and mainland enclaves. This, together with the counterpoint between colonialism and independence (or incorpor-

3

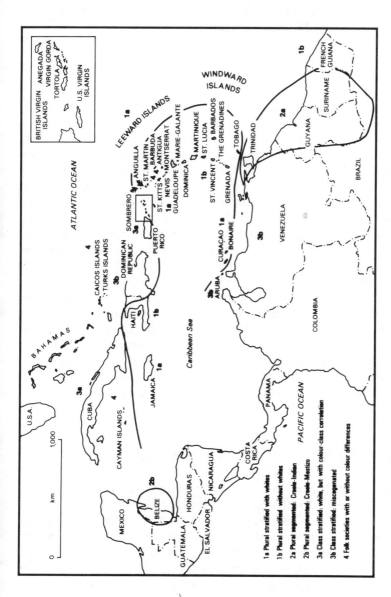

Figure 0.1 Caribbean societies: a typology

ation to the metropole), between slavery and free (or indentured) labour, has produced diverse societies in the Caribbean. It is to the nature of these societies that I turn first, before examining the characteristics of Caribbean states.

THE NATURE OF CARIBBEAN SOCIETIES

There is broad agreement among social scientists that most Caribbean societies are stratified, and that class is involved in forming or reinforcing the social hierarchy. Most analysts also agree that race or colour (skin colour, hair quality, facial features – ranked in 'preference' from Euro to Afro) is deeply involved historically in the social hierarchy, so much so that very few non-Marxists or Marxists write about class alone, but use the term colour–class to define the major strata.[1]

Beyond these generalities, disagreements abound. Is the social hierarchy of white, brown – since race mixing, during colonialism, was commonplace in the Caribbean – and black strata so watertight that the term colour–caste (once used of Haiti) is appropriate?[2] Or are the strata determined principally by class (wealth, status and power) via the occupational hierarchy, with colour reinforcing the rigidity of the system – in Marxist terms 'overdetermining' the class structure?[3] Even more crucially, is class everywhere the primary social differentiator – as Marxists insist – or do other variables, as well as or in addition to colour, such as race (physical appearance) and culture (family, religion, language), displace class into second or third place?[4]

SOCIAL DIFFERENTIATION AND SOCIAL THEORY

The weighting given to class, race, colour and culture depends on the theory of society with which the researcher is working. Marxists place class first, either dismissing the other differentiators as 'false consciousness' or including them as secondary or tertiary differentiators which fragment the labour market but provide little scope for social action separate from class organization.[5] Followers of Weber, like Marxists, envisage classes as products of the capitalist system, but most stress class negotiation rather than class conflict: for them, race, colour and culture (ethnicity) give rise to status groups, but their relationship to the social stratification is dependent upon historical – often political – forces and is not determined solely by the mode of production.[6] Under European imperialism, for example, it might be expected that the 'white race' would take precedence over all others in the stratification, irrespective of class formation internal to itself or of complexities in the non-white population, whether 'indigenous' or 'imported'.

This is the precise point of departure of the pluralists, whose theoretical framework was set out by Furnivall and developed for the Caribbean by M.G. Smith, among others.[7] They argue that superordination and subordination are often politically – not economically – determined; that the distinction between superordinate and subordinate, under such circumstances, is made not on a class basis – as between bourgeoisie and proletariat (capital and labour) – but using racial, cultural or ethnic criteria; and that this differential access to power (and resources) which is politically determined (classically under imperialism) may involve different modes of production and not necessarily capitalism. In short, the pluralists contend that many – but by no means all – societies are stratified into politico-racial (and cultural) sections, with class playing a secondary or tertiary role, either overdetermining the race–culture hierarchy or stratifying, internally, contraposed segments (usually created when whites decolonize and leave the political battleground to contending, co-ordinate racial categories).

All these models sketched in outline above imply social tension, if not conflict. Different from them all is the consensualist school of American sociology that argues that societies develop around shared values.[8] Class stratification and colour–class differentiation, according to this framework, are aspects of the consensus.[9] Whereas the consensualists envisage agreement and shared values encompassing all conditions of men and women, consensus for Marxists occurs crucially within class: through consciousness and organization, the proletarians become a class of themselves, then a class for themselves, at which point they have the capacity for revolution.[10] Weberians also envisage consensus as a within-class or within-ethnic-group characteristic, which is capable of being negotiated on a broader basis; for example, between classes over aspects of consumption.[11] Pluralists, however, interpret consensus as a natural condition only among specific races or cultural groups in a society as distinct from a society-wide condition, but do not predict ways in which a broader consensus (say, inter-ethnic) may emerge. Nonetheless, they do

anticipate that consensus is likely to be greatest among the superordinate stratum. This they interpret as a corporate category that has
achieved internal self-organization to form a corporate group:[12]
subordinate categories generally lack the internal capacity for self-
organization on a continuing basis, though they may achieve it and
create rebellions in the short term.[13] Corporate categories that become corporate groups are analogous to classes of themselves in
Marxist analysis, but pluralists do not envisage corporate groups as
necessarily revolutionary (though Haiti's slaves provide a good example); indeed they may be the precursors of racial–political parties that
compete democratically.[14]

In contrast to Marx, who treats 'the mode of production as a kind
of governing body to the rest of society', Weber suggests that those
non-class

> factors that account for stratification along ethnic or racial lines are
> largely the outcome of historical contingency. The reasons why one
> society was divided along religious lines, another along racial lines,
> and yet another along language lines, could no doubt be made
> intelligible in each particular case. But to offer an historical ac-
> count of how these things came about did not call for the aid of
> some grand 'theory' that purported to explain it all.[15]

> That is precisely what pluralism has attempted to do.

It is my opinon, after more than 25 years of research on the area,
that all four models mentioned so far, Marxist, Weberian, consensualist and pluralist are helpful in explaining the complexity and
diversity of Caribbean societies. Unlike Marxists, however, I do not
see class as universally of primary importance, though it is certainly
significant everywhere, except in the simplest societies. However,
race, colour and culture do not, in my opinion, carry identical weight
throughout the region, whether *vis-à-vis* class or one another.

A TYPOLOGY OF CARIBBEAN SOCIETIES

I conceive of Caribbean societies as divisible into four broad types:
(Figure 0.1): (1) plural-stratified, (2) plural-segmented, (3) class-
stratified, and (4) folk.[16] Smith's ideas about cultural pluralism are
applicable to the first two. Marx or Weber's notions of class are
applicable to the third and to a lesser extent the first, and social

consensus suits the fourth: so each model is powerful in a rather different context.

Each category in the typology is divisible into two sub-types: those societies listed under (a) are the commonest type, while those listed under (b) are racial or colour variants on the class or cultural structures which appear in (a). *Plural-stratified societies* (1) include those with the full stratificational range (a) (Jamaica, the Leeward Islands and the French and Netherlands Antilles) and those that have had that range truncated by the loss of white élites (b) (Haiti, French Guiana and the Windward Islands). *Plural-segmented societies* (2) encompass those with Creole–Indian contrasts (a) (Trinidad, Guyana and Suriname) or Creole–Mestizo differences (b) (Belize); *class-stratified societies* (3) include those that are essentially white, but with a partial colour–class correlation (a) (Cuba and Puerto Rico) and those that have misceginated class stratifications with white–black polarization at the apex and base of the social pyramid, respectively (b) (Dominican Republic and Venezuela). Finally, *folk societies* (4) are tiny primitive socialist communities with a weak resource base. Either they have no major colour differences (a) (Barbuda, black and Saba, white) or they are colour differentiated (b) (Desirade, white–black, and Anguilla, brown–black).

Plural-stratified, class-stratified and folk societies are essentially bi-racial (black–white), while plural-segmented societies are multiracial and include a third racial category.[17] Historically, the plural-stratified society has been key to the evolution of Caribbean social structures. Jamaica during slavery, for example, represented a classic plural-stratified society that in its origins involved ranked cultural sections, legally defined and largely correlated with colour.[18] Most other types of Caribbean society can be related to it, whether bi- or multiracial. The people of the folk societies are similar to Jamaican peasants. Cuba in 1840 (46 years prior to slave emancipation) was more similar to Jamaica – and the rest of the British islands – in 1800 than at any other time in its history (Table 0.1), but the substantial and enduring white presence, fortified by massive white immigration in the early twentieth century, modified the Creole stratification and reduced non-whites to smaller and smaller enclaves in a white, class-based hierarchy. Trinidad in 1834, when British West Indian slavery was abolished, was stratified like Jamaica, but had fewer than 10 per cent of Jamaica's slaves: so, between 1845 and 1917, 144 000 Indian indentured labourers were brought in to work on the nascent

Table 0.1 Slave, free and white populations of Cuba and the British Caribbean compared for the decades leading up to emancipation

	British Caribbean (%)		Cuba (%)		
	1810	1830	1841	1860	1887
White	7.2	6.6	41.4	56.3	67.5
Freedmen	6.6	12.2	15.2	16.2	32.5
Slave	86.2	81.2	43.4	27.5	Slavery abolished 1886: slaves join free coloured group
Total	888 823	843 698	1 007 624	1 389 880	1 631 687

Source: B.W. Higman, *Slave Populations of the British Caribbean 1807–34* (Baltimore and London: The Johns Hopkins University Press, 1984), Table 4.2, p.77, and Franklin W. Knight, *Slave Society in Cuba During the Nineteenth Century* (Madison, Milwaukee and London: University of Wisconsin Press, 1970), p.86.

Note: Slave emancipation was earliest in the British Caribbean (1834) and last in Cuba (1886). British Caribbean whites were always a tiny minority: chronic sex imbalance and out-migration in the early 1800s made their demographic prospects poor without the continuation of colonialism and the plantation. In contrast, the Cuban whites were a large minority in 1841 and became a substantial majority long before emancipation. In both the British Caribbean and Cuba the slaves shrank in number as slave imports were cut off or reduced and pre-emancipation manumission occurred. Even before 1850, Cuba did not have a majority of slaves, unlike the British West Indies in 1810 when more than 85% were enslaved. In contrast with both societies, black slaves in Puerto Rico accounted for no more than 11.4% of the population in 1846, when freedmen made up 39% and whites 50%, while in Santo Domingo (Dominican Republic) on the eve of emancipation in 1794, slaves were 29.1%, freedmen 36.9% and whites 33.9%. See James L. Dietz, *Economic History of Puerto Rico* (Princeton, New Jersey: University of Princeton Press, 1986), p.36, H. Hoetink, *Two Variants in Caribbean Race Relations* (London: Oxford University Press, 1967), p.185, and H. Hoetink, *The Dominican People 1850–1900* (Baltimore and London: The Johns Hopkins University Press, 1982), p.182. These inter-societal differences underpin Hoetink's subsequent observation that 'In the case of the Dominican Republic, an unusually long presugar phase and the presence of a relatively open border with Haiti led to a continuous colour scale on which the darker mixed strata appear to predominate; in Puerto Rico, the lighter-coloured intermediate strata are more numerous; and in Cuba the extreme ends of the continuum appear to be more visible and more numerous than the population in between; see H. Hoetink, '"Race" and Color in the Caribbean', in Sidney W. Mintz and Sally Price (eds), *Caribbean Contours* (Baltimore and London: The Johns Hopkins University Press, 1985), p.68.

sugar estates. An identical process of Creole–Indian segmentation developed over a similar time-period in Guyana and Suriname.

Only one major society type – the class-stratified – correlates with a single imperial system – the Spanish. The other three types of society occur among British, French and Dutch former colonies. More important than imperial regime in determining the social system has been the size of the society, the historical timing of its economic development, the role of the sugar plantation, the system of labour recruitment and control, the size of the black population *vis-à-vis* whites and coloureds, the cultural characteristics of the majority race, and the presence of non-black and non-white populations.

For example, the smallest societies (say under 20 000 population) are folk societies lacking culturally pluralistic features and class stratification, irrespective of whether they were sugar producers in the past or are racially homogeneous today.[19] A major feature of plural-stratified societies, whether truncated by white élite departure or not – and Jamaica since independence in 1962 has been moving rapidly towards the truncated type[20] – is that they were creations of plantation slavery during the seventeenth and eighteenth centuries: black slaves formed the majority, and the culture they practised was syncretic and Creolized. Plural-segmented societies were weakly developed as slave societies and/or had an abundance of potential plantation land when the slave trade in the British Empire was abolished in 1808. Belize is a special case: it developed as a logwood (dyewood)-cutting enclave in Central America, and its black slaves were lumbermen, not canecutters.[21] Segmentation was reflected in urban-based blacks and rural, Spanish-speaking Mestizos and Amerindians.

The class-stratified societies underwent two periods of sugar expansion: the first in the sixteenth century, after which the system of plantation slavery fell into decay as Spanish commercial activity focused on the mainland;[22] the second, during the early nineteenth century, when plantation slavery was reintroduced to Cuba on a substantial scale and very modestly to Puerto Rico, where fewer than 12 per cent were slaves in 1846 when they were most numerous (Table 0.2).[23] Additionally, free-labour plantations were created in the Dominican Republic after 1875.[24] The consequence was that Cuba was a plural-stratified society in 1840 with free whites and enslaved blacks in almost equal proportions, separated by free coloureds (15 per cent). Yet by 1920 the modest increase of blacks and browns in contrast to the enormous influx of white labourers

Table 0.2 Comparison of the Cuban and Puerto Rican populations by race

	Cuba						Puerto Rico			
Year	Population	White	Non-white per cent	Slave per cent	Asiatic	Year	Population	White	Non-white per cent	Slave
1827	311 000	44.2	55.9			1820	230 600	44	56	9.4
1841	418 300	41.5	58.5	43.4		1846	447 900	50	50	11.4
1861	793 500	56.8	43.2	27.5		1860	583 300	51.5	48.5	7.2
1877	988 600	64.9	32.1	20.1	2.9	1877	731 600	56.3	43.7	Emancipation 1873
1887	1 102 900	67.6	32.4	Emancipation 1886	n.a.	1887	798 600	59.5	40.5	
1889	1 052 400	66.9	32.1		0.9	1889	953 200	61.8	38.2	
1907	1 428 200	69.7	29.7		0.6	1910	1 118 000	65.5	34.5	
1919	2 088 000	72.3	27.1		0.6	1920	1 299 800	73.0	27.0	
1931	2 857 000	72.1	27.2		0.7	1930	1 543 900	74.3	25.7	
1943	3 553 300	74.3	25.2		0.4	1940	1 869 000	76.5	23.5	
1953	4 244 000	72.8	26.9		0.3	1950	2 210 703			
1980	10 384 600	66.0	38.0			1980	3 196 500			

Source: Basic percentage distributions for both societies are taken from H. Hoetink, *Two Variants in Caribbean Race Relations* (London: Oxford University Press, 1967), pp.185–6. Slave percentages have been derived from James Dietz, *Economic History of Puerto Rico* (Princeton, New Jersey: University of Princeton Press, 1986), p.36; Franklin Knight, *Slave Society in Cuba* (Madison, Milwaukee and London: University of Wisconsin Press, 1978), p.86; and Rebecca J. Scott, *Slave Emancipation in Cuba* (Princeton, New Jersey: University of Princeton Press, 1985), p.87, Table 10. Information about Asiatics (mostly Chinese) in Cuba is from Anani Dzidzienyo and Lourdes Casal, *The Position of Blacks in Brazilian and Cuban Society* (London: Minority Rights Group, Report No. 7, 1979), p.15, Table 1. The 1980 census figures are quoted in Jean Stubbs, *Cuba: the Test of Time* (London: Latin America Bureau, 1989), p.v.

Note: Cuba and Puerto Rico had similar histories under Spanish colonialism. Neither was a slave society during the nineteenth century, in the British (or French) Caribbean sense, and this was especially true of Puerto Rico, where coffee was more important than sugar during the last decades of the colony. Although they had populations of similar size in 1898, when the US defeated Spain in the Spanish–American War, the massive investment of US capital in the much bigger island of Cuba drew in enormous supplies of labour in the early twentieth century, especially from Spain. By 1930, Cuba's population was twice that of Puerto Rico, and familial links to Spain were strong (and remain so today). After 1898 Cuban immigration policy, as in many other Latin American republics, was to 'whiten' the population and thereby 'civilize' society. Recently there is a great deal of debate about the degree of race prejudice in Cuba and Puerto Rico and, indeed, about the size of the white and non-white populations. Presumably the decline in the proportion of whites in Cuba between 1953 and 1980 reflects élite and middle-class emigration following the Cuban Revolution of 1959. During 1959–62 196 000 left, and the exodus has continued.

(750 000 arrived from Spain between 1900 and 1920 alone) had transformed Cuba into a class-based society in which browns and blacks were accorded middle- and lower-class status, respectively, but were outnumbered by whites in each class.[25] Similar shifts towards a white majority were recorded in Puerto Rico, where miscegenation and the incorporation of light mulattos into the white population, as in Cuba, have played a part in the reduction of the black presence (Table 0.2). In the Dominican Republic, however, whites and blacks form only small minorities, and race mixing has produced a mulatto majority.[26]

SOCIETY TYPE AND GEOGRAPHICAL LOCATION

Certain social and geographical patterns emerge from this analysis. Plural-stratified societies are negroid societies with black majorities and either white or mulatto élites: they are island societies, and encompass the Lesser Antilles plus the two Greater Antilles wrested from Spain in the seventeenth century – Jamaica and Haiti (Figure 0.1). They are classic Creole societies, containing a layering of white, brown and black strata whose order was established in the eighteenth century. They occur in full range or truncated versions, though decolonization is likely to result in truncation becoming the norm. (Historically, truncation has coincided with the disappearance of sugar plantations.)

Plural-segmented societies have one segment (usually the larger demographically) that is Creole, and another which is non-Creole, either brought into the colony for sugar plantation work as in Trinidad, Guyana and Suriname or incorporated in a mainland enclave by pre-existing residence supplemented by in-migration, as in Belize. These societies are all mainland enclaves, except Trinidad, whose underdevelopment in the eighteenth century was due to the persistence of a negligent Spanish colonialism.

The folk societies have evolved into peasant societies since slave emancipation. They fit into the interstices of the Caribbean archipelago and many remain British colonies. But they are common, also, in the Windwards and Leewards, where they have been, and largely continue as, dependencies of larger, adjacent political units – a relationship with which, one after another, they have voiced discontent as decolonization has ensued. These murmurings have been loudest in the Commonwealth Caribbean (especially in Anguilla, which separated itself from St Kitts in 1967, Barbuda, Nevis and

Cariacou), but are echoed in the small units of the Netherlands' and French Antilles, whose decolonization has, in general, been by incorporation into the metropole.[27]

The class-stratified societies are all in the Greater Antilles or on the mainland. Two of them – Cuba and the Dominican Republic – are the largest territories in the Caribbean by population and area. In Cuba and Puerto Rico, 75 per cent of the population is arguably white, and mulattos and blacks – and black culture (*Santaría*) – are subordinate features in social stratification. The Dominican Republic is a mulatto society (locals prefer the term *Mestizo*, which implies an Amerindian rather than a black progenitor) that parades its European heritage and denies its black roots (partly derived from Haiti). Venezuela, though infinitely less dependent on sugar, historically, than the Dominican Republic, is similar in colour–class terms, with Mestizos, in this case, probably outnumbering blacks and mulattos. Although slavery persisted until 1854, no more than 100 000 African slaves were ever imported, and only 12 000 were recognized in the compensation claims of masters.[28]

COLOUR, RACE AND CULTURE

Plural-stratified and most folk societies in the Caribbean are black societies: decolonization implies black or mulatto power (or black and mulatto competition for power). Class-stratified societies are relatively homogeneous white or mulatto societies: blackness, whether in Cuba, Puerto Rico or Santo Domingo is not regarded as 'a problem' – or if it is it is deliberately ignored! Identity in plural-stratified societies must be black, if the long-denigrated masses are to be properly represented; white in the class-based societies. Yet in both types, since they are bi-racial societies, with substantial evidence for miscegenation, the crucial distinctions are of colour not of race.[29]

In plural-segmented societies, however, colour distinctions, though they exist, are relegated to minor significance, and race and culture come to the fore, especially where fierce competition is enjoined in the struggle for power in the decolonizing state. This seems to apply more in the Indian–Creole societies than in Belize, where the prevalence of Catholicism, on the one hand, and Guatemalan claims on the entire territory on the other, may be factors in Creole–Mestizo collaboration.[30]

Plural-stratified and folk societies are Creole societies; plural-segmented societies witness Creole struggle against non-Creole cultures; class-stratified societies have been so transformed from their Creole slave roots that they are in essence culturally homogeneous and the culture of the élite (Hispanic in origin) is substantially shared by the masses – for example, language. Folk societies, by definition, are culturally homogeneous (their culture, unless they are white, is essentially that of the black lower stratum of the bigger hierarchical societies), but plural-stratified societies are problematical in that the culture of the masses is not only 'different' but has been denigrated by the Europe-orientated élite.[31] Decolonization implies de-Europeanization in the plural-stratified societies – it has been most successful in the biggest units, Haiti and Jamaica, so far – and Creole/non-Creole competition in the segmented societies.

To sum up, plural-stratified and folk societies are essentially 'black' societies, plural-segmented societies have a large Indian or Mestizo presence, as well as Creoles (white, brown and black); class-stratified societies are essentially white or, in the case of the Dominican Republic, miscegenated, but it, too, practises a white bias. Indeed, the Dominican Republic is more like Venezuela than its two Spanish-speaking neighbours in having a miscegenated social stratification with white and black (class correlated) extremes, rather than a white population with black and mulatto enclaves, as Cuba and Puerto Rico do.

SOCIETY TYPE AND LABOUR RECRUITMENT

The racial character of each grouping of Caribbean societies conforms to the system of labour recruitment in operation at the particular time it was subjected to the dominant mode of production – the plantation. Plural-stratified (and tiny folk) societies were creations of, or adjuncts to, plantation slavery and involved the differential incorporation of whites, browns and blacks, in rising order of numerical size, as citizens, freemen and slaves: Jamaica, Haiti, the Windwards and Leewards, the French Antilles and French Guiana and most of the Dutch territories fit this model.[32] Plural-segmented societies had similar origins to these stratifications, but subsequently have been complicated by Indian indentured immigration or the inclusion of Mestizo peasant populations. Class-stratified societies were societies with slaves rather than slave societies; in the case of nineteenth-century Cuba and Puerto Rico, they experienced mixed systems of slavery and free labour – or even Chinese indentured labour in the case of Cuba (Table 0.2). In the Dominican Republic, in contrast, the modern sugar plantation was not only a late nineteenth-century phenomenon, but was based on free labour, though this situation was not so very different from Cuba and Puerto Rico where free labourers greatly outnumbered slaves well before emancipation – in 1886 and 1873, respectively.[33] The Dominican Republic is doubly anomalous in the Caribbean: it is the only country without a history of plantation slavery and with extensive race mixing; these circumstances are undoubtedly linked.

So, slavery modally selected and subordinated blacks in perpetuity; indentured labour modally involved Indians (and Chinese) on five-year contracts; but free labour recruitment to Cuban sugar plantations selected whites from the impoverished provinces of Spain, notably Gallicia and the Canary Islands (though as in the Dominican Republic, black Haitians and British West Indian blacks were also drawn in). Each regime chose whichever system was permissible at each point in history; but to simplify, the British, French and Dutch used slavery and indenture to create plural stratified or segmented societies in their Caribbean empires; the Spanish employed slavery, indenture, and, more importantly, free labour; US capital in Santo Domingo, Cuba and Puerto Rico deployed free labour.

The four basic social types recognized in the typology can be ranked from most to least equal: plural-stratified societies are particularly unequal because they involve an hierarchy of colour and cultural differences, as well as class, and there are more barriers to social mobility; plural-segmented societies usually give rise to intersegmental cleavage and competition, with class relegated in significance and individuals categorized as belonging to one 'community' or the other; class-stratified societies are, of course, socially unequal and exploitative, but most individuals' positions are not 'fixed' by racial or cultural characteristics, as in the two previous types, though blacks may still be disadvantaged. Folk societies may be attached to metropoles or to stratified or segmented independent states. Nevertheless, they are internally egalitarian and usually wish to remain so.

SOCIETY TYPE AND DECOLONIZATION

Although all four basic types of society are the products of colonialism, the relationship of the typology to the process of decolonization is by no means simple. From the very outset there was no neat relationship between society and post-colonial polity in the Caribbean. The first colony to become independent in 1804, was a prosperous plural-stratified society – Haiti, where a slave rebellion evolved into a successful war of liberation from the French, debilitated by their own revolution. Haitian slaves secured their freedom and with mulatto freemen captured the state. Since then, however, there has been continual struggle between the upper (mulatto) and lower (black) strata for state control.

Having liberated themselves, the Haitians invaded Santo Domingo in 1822, freed the small population of slaves – they accounted for fewer than 30 per cent of the population of 103 000 in 1794, though an additional 35 per cent were non-white freedmen[34] – and incorporated the former subsistence-orientated Spanish colony into an Hispaniola-wide Haiti. In 1844, emulating Venezuelan independence from Greater Colombia in 1830, the Dominicans rejected Haitian hegemony and declared their sovereignty, only to revert briefly to the Spanish Crown before achieving a third and final independence in 1865. The Dominican Republic's pervasive *mulatización*, combined with a lack of stratified cultures rooted in plantation slavery, undoubtedly facilitated its independence movements; in contrast, Haiti's emergence from slavery involved white genocide and white expulsion.

The third independence in the Caribbean was Cuba's, and it gave rise not only to a civil war against Spain in 1898 but to US intervention. Cuba achieved its formal independence (from the US) in 1902, but remained subservient to its northern neighbour until the abrogation of the Platt Amendment in 1934. In 1898 Cuban blacks had fought side by side with Creole whites against Spaniards, and the class basis of the society already provided the basis for unambiguous nationalism. But while Haiti, which was (and still is) a plural-stratified society, achieved independence early, Puerto Rico, which is class-based (like Venezuela, Santo Domingo and Cuba) remains a 'free associated state' of the US. Haiti is independent but impoverished, yet Puerto Rico is essentially a colony, and deeply penetrated by US capitalism and federal services, against which the local independence movement can make little headway.[35]

All the remaining plural-stratified and segmented societies have been decolonized constitutionally by imperial consent since World War II, either by the grant of full independence, as in the case of the former British territories, or by their incorporation into the mother country (French Antilles), or via their association with the mother

country (the Netherlands' Antilles). All these methods of decolonization have been endorsed by the United Nations.

A TYPOLOGY OF POLITICAL REGIMES

Depending upon the nature of the regime, Caribbean polities may be
grouped into four categories. (1) 'Colonial' states, which operate
political systems that are either overseen by, or are integrated with,
an external power. They include Puerto Rico and the US Virgin
Islands (US), Martinique, Guadeloupe and French Guiana (France),
the Netherlands Antilles (Netherlands) and the Cayman Islands,
British Virgin Islands, Montserrat, Turks and Caicos Islands and
Anguilla (Britain). (2) Independent states based upon liberal-
democratic values. Virtually all the Commonwealth Caribbean units
belong to this category, namely Jamaica (independent in 1962),
Trinidad and Tobago (1962), Barbados (1966), Grenada (1974),
St Lucia (1979), Dominica (1979), St Vincent (1979), Belize (1981),
Antigua and Barbuda (1982) and St Kitts and Nevis (1983), plus
Venezuela and the Dominican Republic. (3) Leftist-socialist units
include Cuba, Guyana (1964) and Suriname (1975), leaving (4)
conservative-authoritarian states as a residual category with Haiti.
These assignments are by no means fixed, however.

When World War II ended in 1945, only three Caribbean island
states were independent – Haiti, the Dominican Republic and Cuba:
all either were or were about to become dictatorships. So when the
British, French and Dutch began to decolonize, either by liberating
or incorporating their territories, a major preoccupation was the
establishment of democracy. In pursuit of this objective, the British
tried to create an inter-island federation which would incorporate
more checks and balances than was feasible in a unitary state – as well
as providing a vehicle for small-island decolonization. It was the
failure of this policy after the break-up of the colonial federation
(1958–62) that created the first phase of independence (1962–66), the
second stage of independence from the holding status of associate
statehood (1974–83), and the recognition by Britain of a residual and
continuing category of five dependencies.

But if imperial hegemony in the British Caribbean was rapidly
dissipated between 1958 and 1983, so too was the right-wing character of political control in Cuba, the Dominican Republic and Venezuela. In 1959 the Batista dictatorship in Cuba was overthrown by

Fidel Castro's guerilla movement, and within three years – following US blockade and an abortive CIA-backed invasion, Castro declared the country Marxist. Trujillo, the dictator of the Dominican Republic, was gunned down in 1961, thus paving the way for political polarization, military upheaval, US intervention, and a painful process of democratic recovery, a path along which Venezuela, too, has travelled since Jiménez was ousted in 1958.

Prior to the break-up of the West Indies Federation, the major problem territory for the British was British Guiana, led by the Marxist, Cheddi Jagan, with majority Indian support. Between 1961 and 1966, when Guyana became independent under Forbes Burnham, the CIA destabilized the Jagan government as a prelude to communal rioting, and Britain eventually introduced proportional representation to undermine single-party rule. After 1968, Creole control was established using electoral malpractice; and in the early 1970s Burnam declared Guyana a socialist co-operative republic.[36] Moreover, Grenada, the first of the associated states to become independent, experienced a left-wing coup in 1979, after which the People's Revolutionary Government aligned itself with Cuba and began to socialize the public sector.[37] A year later, a coup in Suriname stimulated similar developments.

The US invasion of Grenada following Bishop's assassination in 1983 is a timely reminder of the continuing dependence of the Caribbean on the major world powers and of the fluidity of the typology of societies and states presented above. While the social structure of Caribbean societies can be swiftly modified by out-migration (for example, of upper-class whites from post-revolutionary Cuba or from Jamaica during Michael Manley's democratic-socialist government (1976–80), so their political regimes can be modified by decolonization, revolution (Cuba), coup (Grenada and Suriname), invasion (by the US in the Dominican Republic and Grenada) or assassination (Dominican Republic 1961). Furthermore, since the mid-1980s, both Guyana and Suriname have modified their anti-capitalism, while retaining crucial elements of their authoritarian regimes.

Clearly, the unchanging authoritarian political culture of Haiti has much to do with its achievement of independence via slave insurrection more than a century and a half before constitutional decolonization became the norm. In Haiti, cultural pluralism has provided excellent opportunities for social control – witness 'Papa Doc' Duvalier's use of Vodun priests as political informers.[38] The switch from conservative-authoritarianism to leftist-socialist orientations in Cuba is not so surprising. Early-twentieth-century democracy in Cuba was fragile, the class structure provided a potential basis for socialism, and there were few racial or cultural impediments to Castro's guerrilla revolution.[39] The Dominican Republic might have followed Cuba's trajectory in 1965, but the US intervened militarily to prevent it happening and to create a long, but so far fairly successful, transition to democracy.

EXPLAINING REGIME TYPE

Comparison between the social and political typologies reveals a poor fit between them. Plural-stratified societies are independent or incorporated (French and Netherlands Antilles): most are liberal-democratic, but Haiti is conservative-authoritarian. Plural-segmented societies are all independent, but are spread between liberal-democratic (Trinidad and Tobago and Belize) and left-socialist states (Suriname and Guyana). Class-stratified societies are dependent (Puerto Rico) or independent left-socialist (Cuba) or liberal-democratic (Dominican Republic and Venezuela). Folk societies are dependencies of various kinds, and democratic.

Correlations between the political typology and former imperial systems are equally imperfect. Colonies and integrated territories belong to the former British, French, Spanish or Dutch empires. Independent, liberal-democratic states tend to be ex-British but include two former Spanish colonies, the Dominican Republic and Venezuela. Left-socialist republics include Cuba (Spanish), and, until recently, Guyana (British) and Suriname (Dutch). The only remaining conservative-authoritarian regime, Haiti, was French until 1804.

Levels of economic development or modernization are no more explanatory of regime type. The most advanced economies are those of Venezuela, Puerto Rico, Cuba, the Dominican Republic (all Spanish-speaking), plus Jamaica, Trinidad and Tobago, Barbados and some of the British dependencies, Martinique and Guadeloupe (French) and the Netherlands Antilles. Most are democratic states or incorporated units, though Venezuela and the Dominican Republic are transitional from authoritarian pasts – as is Cuba, which is socialist. At the other extreme of development, the ex-British Windwards and Leewards are poor but democratic; Haiti is poor but autocratic; Guyana and Suriname are poor and formerly socialist, though both seem to be liberalizing, largely for economic reasons.

It is perhaps logical, given the colonial history of the Caribbean, that the timing and method of decolonization should have had such a major impact on the territories. Irrespective of society type, those units that have undergone late twentieth-century constitutional decolonization from Britain, France and the Netherlands seem far more imbued with democratic values than their predecessors that achieved independence violently. With independence, local political élites have emerged to develop (often neo-colonial) economic strategies, and to project a new image of their societies. But given the constraints of smallness, economic dependence and entrenched social inequality, it is not surprising that in most Caribbean societies – Cuba under Castro and Grenada under Bishop excepted – politics have rarely set about changing the social order. Instead, the social order has imposed limits to political organization and in general has ensured that conservative programmes have prevailed.

The interplay between politics and society, society and politics across the units eludes easy generalization. What can be said, however, is that all Caribbean states bear the traces of extreme social inequality based upon differences of race, class and culture, but that the relationships between these variables and political organization and electoral processes depend upon historical and geographical circumstances, coupled to the leadership and managerial skills of the population. That democratic forms of government are so prevalent, however, must in large measure be attributed to the Caribbean's north-west European inheritance and, in the case of Puerto Rico and the Dominican Republic, to US influence.

ORGANIZATION OF THE BOOK

This is the first book to be devoted to the relationship between society and politics across the three major linguistic groups of the Caribbean – English, French and Spanish. It examines all five of the Greater Antilles – Cuba, Haiti, the Dominican Republic, Puerto Rico and Jamaica, most of the Lesser Antilles – Trinidad and Tobago, the south-eastern Caribbean states, with a separate chapter on Grenada, the two French insular departments, and the two mainland states of Belize and Venezuela, which are, respectively, Central American and Caribbean, and South American and Caribbean.

While all the Hispanic units are often treated as part of Latin America, it is Venezuela which is clearly most marginal to the Caribbean region, although it has a lengthy Caribbean coastline and considers itself to be a major actor in Caribbean affairs.

I have divided the book into three parts: (I) independent parliamentary democracies (Jamaica, Trinidad and Tobago, the south-east Caribbean states, Grenada, the Dominican Republic and Venezuela); (II) independent authoritarian regimes (Haiti and Cuba); and (III) territories under metropolitan control (the French Antilles and Puerto Rico). The independent authoritarian regimes have been sub-divided into (a) regimes in which democratization has been frustrated (Haiti); and (b) communist regimes (Cuba).

In the independent parliamentary democracies and British territories under metropolitan control (the chapter on the south-eastern Caribbean treats them together), citizens enjoy the full range of civil liberties, trades unions are often linked to political parties (indeed, parties have frequently been created by unions and vice versa), the military is not involved in politics, and fair elections are held at constitutionally prescribed intervals. However, in those territories under non-British metropolitan control, local parties are either affiliates of metropolitan equivalents (Puerto Rico) or are totally synonymous with them (Martinique and Guadeloupe).

Since the fall of the Duvalier dictatorship in 1986, after a period of 30 years, Haiti's transition to democracy, though widely demanded locally, has been frustrated by the army and the *tontons macoutes* (security volunteers). The 1987 elections were abandoned in bloodshed, the 1988 presidential poll was rigged by the military, President Manigat was subsequently expelled, and since then two factions of the army in turn have held power after palace coups. In Haiti, with its long history of militarism going back to the independence wars, 'the man on horseback' is once again the political arbiter.

Cuba's nationalist revolution against the Batista dictatorship in 1959 was carried out by a guerilla group led by Fidel Castro. After the US-backed invasion of the Bay of Pigs in 1961, Castro declared the revolution Marxist, and the Cuban economy, once an adjunct of the US economy, is now highly dependent (though more advantageously so) on Soviet oil supplies and sugar purchases. Cuba has militarized civilian society to defend the state (which has also given it the capacity to intervene in armed struggles in Black Africa), but press censorship, informing on the disaffected, and general social control (notably through counter-revolutionary Committees for the

Defence of the Revolution), and the absence of non-communist parties and free trade unions, indicate Cuba's extensive curtailment of civil liberties by the standards of the parliamentary democracies.

This framework apart, I have not attempted to impose any particular approach on the authors, each of whom is an authority on the subject matter of his or her chapter. Some contributors have emphasized the political at the expense of the social, and vice versa; some acknowledge the reciprocal relationship between the two. Some have focused more sharply on elections, others have emphasized the evolution of political culture. Many have adopted an historical slant, taking independence or some other critical change as the starting point of an essentially chronological treatment.

A Weberian class and status (race and culture) framework is used by most contributors, implicity. This works well for the class-based societies (Cuba, Santo Domingo, Venezuela and Puerto Rico), and is satisfactory for Jamaica, the French Antilles, and the south-eastern Caribbean states, though it is interesting to note the stress given to cultural differences in the Haitian chapter (Chapter 8). In this latter category of societies, which I have described as hierarchical pluralities, it is important to keep class, colour and cultural analysis in play. Provided it is, perhaps it doesn't matter which model is adopted, though it does seem analytically desirable in a comparative book of this type to separate the Jamaican- from the Cuban-type of society with their very different historical development and distinctive associations (or dissociations) between class, colour and culture.

In contrast, class analysis is of only limited value in understanding the politics of Belize and Trinidad and Tobago. Each is recognized by the contributors as a segmented plurality, but while it is possible to extrapolate the alignments between race and party in Trinidad, it is not feasible to do so in Belize.

Finally, it is important to bear in mind that class, culture and race (or colour) are ultimately society-specific in their significance. Even the cultural distinctions so typical of Jamaica – such as Creole speech versus accented but standard English – are muted in the Leeward Islands; class in Trinidad, because of its greater economic diversification, is much more complex than in, say, Belize; and to be black is a very different experience in tiny Barbuda compared to Haiti or Cuba. The explanation for this diversity, as I have argued above, is to be found in the size of the societies and the differential historical incidence of the key institutions that have moulded the Caribbean. Listed in chronological sequence, they are colonialism, forced labour recruitment for the plantations and decolonization. Over time, politics and society in the Caribbean have been deeply interwoven and they continue to interact in complex ways.

NOTES

1. Pioneer non-Marxist sociological works use the term colour–class; see Fernando Henriques, *Family and Colour in Jamaica* (London: Eyre and Spottiswood, 1953), and Lloyd Braithwaite, 'Social Stratification in Trinidad: a preliminary analysis', *Social and Economic Studies*, Vol. 2, Nos 2 and 3 (1953), pp.5–175. For more recent Marxist approaches, see Ken Post, *Arise Ye Starvlings: the Jamaican Labour Rebellion of 1938 and its Aftermath* (The Hague: Martinus Nijhoff, 1978), especially pp.77–158; Aggrey Brown, *Colour, Class and Politics in Jamaica* (New Brunswick, New Jersey: Transaction Books, 1979); and George Beckford and Michael Witter, *Small Garden Bitter Weed: Struggle and Change in Jamaica* (London: Zed Press, 1982). An outstanding example of a Marxist work which largely ignores racial or colour components of society is W. Richard Jacobs and Ian Jacobs, *Grenada: El Camino hacia La Revolución* (México: Editorial Katun, 1983). For a non-Marxist work that emphasizes affluence and poverty over colour see Carl Stone, *Class, Race and Political Behaviour in Urban Jamaica* (Kingston: Institute of Social and Economic Research, 1973).
2. The term 'caste' is used by J. Lobb, 'Caste and Class in Haiti', *American Journal of Sociology*, Vol. 46 (1940), pp.23–34, and by James G. Leyburn, *The Haitian People* (New Haven: Yale University Press, 1941). A more recent author prefers to use social class, but adds, 'The colour factor, together with strong regional loyalties, complicates the picture': see David Nicholls, *From Dessalines to Duvalier: Race, Colour and National Independence in Haiti* (Cambridge: Cambridge University Press, 1979), p.10.
3. Stuart Hall, 'Pluralism, Race and Class in Caribbean Society', in *A Study of Ethnic Group Relations in the English-speaking Caribbean, Bolivia, Chile and Mexico* (Paris: UNESCO, 1977), pp.150–82.
4. The primacy of culture over class – and race – has been strongly advocated by M.G. Smith in numerous publications, for example, *The Plural Society in the British West Indies* (Berkeley: University of California Press, 1965); 'Race and Stratification in the Caribbean', in M.G. Smith, *Corporations and Society* (London: Duckworth, 1974), pp.271–346, and *Culture, Race and Class in the Commonwealth Caribbean* (Mona: Department of Extra-Mural Studies, University of the West Indies, 1984).
5. David Harvey, *Social Justice and the City* (London: Edward Arnold, 1973); a flexible Marxist position, on the other hand, is portrayed in Ken Post, *op. cit.*

6. Frank Parkin, *Max Weber* (London and New York: Tavistock Publications, 1982), p.96.
7. J.S. Furnivall, *Colonial Policy and Practice: a Comparative Study of Burma and Netherlands India* (London: Cambridge University Press, 1948); M.G. Smith, *The Plural Society in the British West Indies* (Berkeley, Los Angeles and London: University of California Press, 1965). M.G. Smith's plural hypothesis has been used by social geographers, for example, David Lowenthal, *West Indian Societies* (Oxford and London: Oxford University Press, 1972) and Colin Clarke, *Kingston Jamaica: Urban Development and Social Change 1692–1962* (Berkeley and Los Angeles: University of California Press, 1975) and *East Indians in a West Indian Town: San Fernando, Trinidad, 1930–1970* (London: Allen and Unwin, 1986). It also provides the implicit framework for Bridget Brereton's *Race Relations in Colonial Trinidad* (London and New York: Cambridge University Press, 1979).
8. Talcott Parsons, *The Social System* (London: Tavistock, 1952).
9. The approach of Henriques, working on Jamaica, and Braithwaite, on Trinidad (*op. cit.*), is consistent with the consensualist model.
10. Karl Marx and Friedrich Engels, *Selected Works* (London: Lawrence and Wishart, 1972).
11. Parkin, *op. cit.*, p.93.
12. M.G. Smith, *Corporations and Society* (London: Duckworth, 1974) and Colin Clarke 'Pluralism and Plural Societies: Caribbean Perspectives', in Colin Clarke, David Ley and Ceri Peach (eds), *Geography and Ethnic Pluralism* (London: Allen and Unwin, 1984), pp.51–86.
13. The Haitian Revolution, the Caribbean's only successful slave rebellion, is a case in point, though the uprising was not confined to slaves.
14. As in the case of Trinidad and Guyana. For Trinidad, see Chapter 2 of this book. For Guyana see especially Leo A. Despres, *Cultural Pluralism and National Politics in British Guiana* (Chicago: Rand McNally, 1967) and J. Edward Greene, *Race vs Politics in Guyana* (Jamaica: Institute of Social and Economic Research, University of the West Indies, 1974).
15. Parkin, *op. cit.*, p. 96.
16. This is a modification of David Lowenthal's five-fold categorization of West Indian societies which divides folk societies into those that are homogeneous and differentiated by colour, but omits the class-based Hispanic units; see David Lowenthal, *West Indian Societies* (Oxford and London: Oxford University Press, 1972), pp.78–9.
17. M.G. Smith, *Culture, Race and Class in the Commonwealth Caribbean* (Kingston: Department of Extra-Mural Studies, University of the West Indies, 1984), pp.37–45.
18. Clarke, 'Pluralism and Plural Societies', *op. cit.*
19. For example, M.G. Smith, *Kinship and Community in Carriacou* (New Haven and London: Yale University Press, 1962), John Y. Keur and Dorothy L. Keur, *Windward Children* (Assen: Vangorcum, 1960), and David Lowenthal and Colin Clarke, 'Common Lands, Common Aims: the Distinctive Barbudan Community', in Malcolm Cross and Arnaud Marks (eds), *Peasants, Plantations and Rural Communities in the Caribbean* (Guildford and Leiden: Department of Sociology University of

Surrey and Department of Caribbean Studies of the Royal Institute of Linguistics and Anthropology, 1979), pp.142–59.

20. Special tabulations of the 1960 and 1982 censuses in my possession reveal that Kingston's white population has been reduced by 90 per cent since independence. The Chinese have recorded a similar reduction, as have the Jews; see Carol S. Holzberg, *Minorities and Power in Black Society: the Jewish Community of Jamaica* (Lanham, Maryland: North-South Publishing, 1987), pp.248–9.

21. O. Nigel Bolland, *Colonialism and Resistance in Belize: Essays in Historical Sociology* (Benque Viejo del Carmen, Kingston, Jamaica and Belize City: Cubola Productions, Institute of Social and Economic Research, University of the West Indies, and the Society for the Promotion of Education and Research, 1988).

22. Eric Williams, *From Columbus to Castro: the History of the Caribbean 1492–1969* (London: André Deutsch, 1970), especially pp.23–57.

23. That is black slaves, according to James L. Dietz, *Economic History of Puerto Rico: Institutional Change and Capitalist Development* (Princeton, New Jersey: Princeton University Press, 1986), Table 1.7, p.36.

24. Jose del Castillo, 'The Formation of the Dominican Sugar Industry: from Competition to Monopoly, from National Semiproletariat to Foreign Proletariat', in Manuel Moreno Fraginals, Frank Moya Pons and Stanley L. Engerman (eds), *Between Slavery and Free Labour: the Spanish-Speaking Caribbean in the Nineteenth Century* (Baltimore and London: The Johns Hopkins University Press, 1985), pp.215–34.

25. Hugh Thomas, *Cuba or the Pursuit of Freedom* (London: Eyre and Spottiswood, 1971), p.1120.

26. The incorporation of mulattos into the majority white population in Puerto Rico and Cuba, in contradistinction to their association with the black population in the US and their separate status in the British, French and Dutch West Indies, has been discussed by H. Hoetink, *Two Variants in Caribbean Race Relations* (London: Oxford University Press, 1967). Frank Tannenbaum reports that the Dominican Republic had 13 per cent of its population white and 19 per cent black in the early 1940s in *Slave and Citizen: the Negro in the Americas* (New York: Vintage Books, 1946), p.7.

27. For detailed accounts of small island dissention refer to Colin Clarke, 'Political Fragmentation in the Caribbean: the case of Anguilla', *Canadian Geographer*, Vol. 15 (1971), pp.13–29, and David Lowenthal and Colin Clarke, 'Island Orphans: Barbuda and the Rest', *The Journal of Commonwealth and Comparative Politics*, Vol. 18, No. 3 (1980), pp.293–307.

28. The figure of 100 000 slave imports is given in Angelina Pollak-Eltz, 'Slave Revolts in Venezuela', in Vera Rubin and Arthur Tuden (eds), 'Comparative Perspectives on Slavery in New World Plantation Societies', *Annals of the New York Academy of Sciences*, Vol. 292 (1977), pp.439–45. For information on Venezuelan emancipation and declining slave numbers see Leslie B. Rout Jr, *The African Experience in Spanish America: 1502 to the Present Day* (Cambridge: Cambridge University Press, 1976), pp.250–1. Rout cites an estimate of 30.7 per cent for the

black and mulatto population of Venezuela in 1940.

29. For a discussion of black and mulatto competition for power in an independent Caribbean state, Haiti, see Nicholls, *op. cit.* Good examples of anti-black sentiment in the Hispanic Caribbean are given by Harry Hoetink, 'The Dominican Republic in the Nineteenth Century: Some Notes on Stratification, Immigration and Race', in Magnus Morner (ed.), *Race and Class in Latin America* (New York and London: Columbia University Press, 1970), pp.96–121, especially pp.114–21, and for pre-revolutionary Cuba by Thomas, *op. cit.*, pp.1115–26. The beginning of the movement to adjust Jamaican nationalism to a post-independence black identity is described by Rex Nettleford in *Mirror Mirror: Identity, Race and Protest in Jamaica* (Kingston: William Collins and Sangster, 1970), in *Caribbean Cultural Identity: the Case of Jamaica* (Kingston: Institute of Jamaica, 1978), and in his edited book, *Jamaica in Independence*: Essays on the Early Years (Kingston: Heinemann Caribbean, and London: James Currey, 1989). More relaxed race relations in post-revolutionary Cuba, are, however, reported in Peter Marshall, *Cuba Libre: Breaking the Chains* (London: Victor Gollancz, 1987).

30. For studies of race and politics in Trinidad and Guyana see Selwyn Ryan, *Race and Nationalism in Trinidad and Tobago: a study of de-colonization in a multi-racial society* (Toronto: University of Toronto Press, 1972), Leo A. Despres, *Cultural Pluralism and National Politics in British Guiana* (Chicago: Rand McNally, 1967) and J. Edward Greene, *Race vs Politics in Guyana* (Jamaica: Institute of Social and Economic Research, University of the West Indies, 1974). For a review of the social history of Belize see Bolland, *op. cit.*

31. In addition to the two books by Rex Nettleford cited above, an excellent account of the denigration of blacks by whites and blacks' internalization of the evaluation is given in a classic book by Madeline Kerr, *Personality and Conflict in Jamaica* (London and Kingston: Collins and Sangster's Book Stores, 1963; 1st edition 1952).

32. The most complete study of these plural-stratified and segmented societies to date is David Lowenthal's excellent comparative volume, *op. cit.* Because of lack of space, little attention in this introduction is given to the emergence of the free people of colour. Those who are interested should consult David W. Cohen and Jack P. Greene (eds), *Neither Slave Nor Free: the Freedmen of African Descent in the Slave Societies of the New World* (Baltimore and London: The Johns Hopkins University Press, 1972) and Gad J. Heuman, *Between Black and White: Race, Politics and the Free Coloreds in Jamaica, 1792–1865* (Westport, Connecticut: Greenwood Press, 1981).

33. The crucial role of slaves in the maintenance of the sugar industries of Cuba and Puerto Rico, as their numbers declined in the run up to emancipation, is discussed thoroughly in Rebecca J. Scott, *Slave Emancipation in Cuba: the Transition to Free Labour, 1860–1899* (Princeton, New Jersey: Princeton University Press, 1985) and Dietz, *op. cit.*

34. H. Hoetink, *The Dominican People, 1850–1900: Notes for a Historical Sociology* (Baltimore and London: the Johns Hopkins University Press, 1982), p.182.

35. For a controversial treatment of Puerto Rico see Raymond Carr, *Puerto Rico: a Colonial Experiment* (New York and London: New York University Press, 1984). The most comprehensive account of Puerto Rican society is still Julian H. Steward *et al.*, *The People of Puerto Rico: a Study in Social Anthropology* (Chicago and London: University of Illinois Press, 1972; 1st edition 1956).
36. Colin Baber and Henry B. Jeffrey, *Guyana: Politics, Economics and Society* (London: Frances Pinter, 1986).
37. Tony Thorndike, *Grenada: Politics, Economics and Society* (London: Frances Pinter, 1985).
38. Michel S. Laguerre, *Voodoo and Politics in Haiti* (London: Macmillan, 1989), p.108.
39. Thomas, *op. cit.*

Part I
Independent Parliamentary Democracies

1 Jamaican Society and the Testing of Democracy

Anthony Payne

INTRODUCTION

As a professional political scientist I am almost duty-bound to conduct an enquiry into the relationship between politics and society in
Jamaica by emphasizing the political aspect of that equation. Viewed
in comparative Caribbean terms, the distinctive feature of Jamaican
politics is undoubtedly the country's long-standing commitment to at
least a working form of democracy. I take it, therefore, that what
needs to be explained in this context is the nature of Jamaican
democracy and that the question before us is the extent to which its
development has been socially determined. This chapter thus begins
by presenting brief profiles of Jamaican society and politics in the
post-War era and then proceeds to consider the interaction of these
two dimensions in the crisis years of the 1970s – a phase of Jamaican
history which I have delineated as the 'testing' of the country's
democracy. Finally, it addresses the central analytic theme of this
study by means of a discussion of the competing merits of social and
political explanations of Jamaica's experience of democracy.

THE SOCIO-ECONOMIC SETTING

Modern Jamaican society cannot be understood without locating its
origins in the plantation history of the island which brought thousands of black slaves from Africa to work in the cane fields and left
them without adequate means of support when nineteenth-century
emancipation, free trade and competition destroyed the system of
sugar monoculture. Some ex-slaves established themselves as independent peasants, usually on poor land, and grew either food for the
domestic market or new primary products for export, such as bananas; others continued to work as wage-labourers on the diminished
number of plantations. The economy was not significantly restruc-
tured until after World War II, when it began to acquire its modern

31

shape. Bauxite production began in 1952 and grew swiftly to an output of 1 million tons by 1953 and 6 million tons by 1958; tourism was developed as a further valuable earner of foreign exchange; and many light industrial plants were established on the island as a result of the policy, adopted by successive governments during the post-War period, of offering a range of incentives to overseas investors. By these various means the Jamaican economy was able to grow throughout the 1960s by an average of nearly 6 per cent annually.[1]

Yet despite this apparently creditable achievement, the economy remained weak and dependent in several ways. Domestic agriculture stagnated in this period and was the source of continuing poverty in rural areas. Income distribution was more uneven than ever; the share of the poorest 40 per cent of the population in personal earned income declined from 7.2 per cent in 1958 to 5.4 per cent in 1968. Illiteracy, poor housing and unemployment thus remained the lot of vast numbers of Jamaicans. In fact, the level of unemployment and underemployment in the society increased hugely, doubling from 12 per cent to 24 per cent during the very period of fast economic growth. The higher wage rates paid in the new mineral and manufacturing sectors encouraged people to forsake low-paid agricultural employment in the hope of finding work in these industries, even though the capital-intensive character of most of the imported technology meant that few jobs were created in these areas. The expanding sectors generally forged very limited links with other parts of the economy. A substantial amount of sugar was still shipped in a raw state, although it was technically and commercially feasible to refine it on the island; most of the bauxite mined was exported as ore despite the advantages to Jamaica of processing it locally; the manufacturing sector consisted largely of 'screwdriver' operations, heavily dependent on the import of raw materials and partly finished components; and the tourist industry, notorious for its failure to integrate itself with local agriculture, was itself partly responsible for Jamaica's growing imports of foodstuffs. The overall effect was accurately described as 'a form of perverse growth.'[2]

Much of the explanation of the flaws inherent in this pattern of growth lay in the nature of the foreign control to which the Jamaican economy was still subject at the end of the 1960s. The island's leading sugar estates were owned by a large British company, the bauxite industry was in the hands of four US and Canadian corporations, and many hotels were parts of foreign businesses. Banks and insurance companies, a large section of the communications network and even a number of basic public utilities (including the electricity and telephone services) were also foreign-owned. Only in the manufacturing sector were most firms in majority local ownership, although the distinction between a family firm and the branch plant of a foreign company was hard to discern in practice. As a Jamaican economist pointed out, 'a family firm may manufacture a metropolitan product under a franchise, the clauses of which are so detailed that the metropolitan enterprise is determining almost all the major managerial decisions – raw and intermediate materials procurement, capital equipment, marketing methods, accounting formats and even employment policy.'[3] What is certain is that in Jamaica, as in so many other parts of the Caribbean, the generation of economic growth in the 1950s and 1960s was fuelled primarily by the inflow of private foreign capital in the cause of development, but was ultimately lost to the local economy via profit repatriation and the various other well-known aspects of intra-company transfer pricing.[4]

The flawed nature of the economic development experienced in Jamaica after the War produced a discordant class system. At the top of the social hierarchy it fostered the emergence of a local capitalist class allied in a subordinate role to foreign capital. This class was initially based on ownership of land and control of the colonial distributive trade through import/export agencies and commission houses, but succeeded in adjusting its role in the economy in the 1960s by moving, somewhat reluctantly, into local manufacturing, generally on behalf of former suppliers. It grew into a tightly knit clique, not extending much beyond 21 family groupings and focused on just five interrelated 'super-groups', the Ashenheims, the Desnoes-Geddes, the Harts, the Henriques and the Matalons, who between them occupied more than one-third of the available directorships in the corporate economy[5] and did extremely well financially out of the post-War growth of the Jamaican economy. Other social groups also benefited, though to a lesser degree. The educated middle class took advantage of the growing numbers of professional and managerial positions being established both in the private and public sectors, and the unionized sector of the working class was able to bargain effectively for improvements in wages and working conditions. This latter group comprised craftsmen, technicians and production workers throughout industry and commerce, but also included some unskilled manual and service workers in such key growth industries as bauxite.

Set against the numerically small groups which had gained from the

Jamaican economic boom of the 1950s and 1960s were much larger sections of the people who had suffered both relatively and absolutely. Under the dual pressure of modernization and the market, many peasants were forced off the land, emigrating to Kingston where they swelled the ranks of the urban poor and unemployed. Wage levels for many casual workers and domestic servants within the urban economy were such that even employment did not lead to any escape from poverty. The unemployed lived in appalling conditions, somehow existing below official subsistence levels. By the late 1960s they numbered some 150 000, approximately a third of the population of Kingston, the country's capital and only major city. Of these, at least one-third can be said to have comprised of a *lumpenproletariat*, permanently detached from the labour market. The latter survived mainly through petty and organized crime, gambling, prostitution and trade in illegal commodities such as *ganja*. Many were involved in Rastafarianism – a highly visible but largely unorganized movement united only around a few quasi-religious beliefs such as the divinity of former Emperor Haile Selassie of Ethiopia.

Exacerbating this polarized class structure was the question of race. According to figures derived from census data for 1961, 91.4 per cent of the population were either fully or partly of African ancestry and thus considered black, 1.7 per cent were East Indian, 0.6 per cent Chinese, 0.8 per cent European white and 5.5 per cent some other category.[6] Yet the Jamaican capitalist class was characterized by an almost complete absence of blacks and a preponderance of Jews, local whites, Lebanese, Syrians and Chinese.[7] At the other end of the social spectrum it was almost exclusively blacks who were poor, unemployed and living in the West Kingston ghetto. As Gordon Lewis wrote, the grim reality of Jamaican life in the mid-1960s was 'of a racial separatism, undeclared yet virulent, that infected every nook and cranny of interpersonal and inter-class relationships, based on a social system characterized by strongly entrenched class–colour correlations'.[8] Class conflicts did not run exactly parallel to racial cleavages, but the links were too close for the tensions not to be readily apparent and occasionally felt.

THE POLITICAL SETTING

For the first two decades after the introduction of universal suffrage in 1944, Jamaica's political system succeeded so well in containing the explosive implications of this social structure that the country gained something of a reputation for political stability. Party, rather than class or race, was developed as the primary collective frame of reference for the politically conscious in Jamaica.[9] At the centre of the political system were two competing political parties, the People's National Party (PNP) and the Jamaica Labour Party (JLP). Formed as institutional expressions of the contrasting styles of their founding leaders, Norman Manley and Alexander Bustamante, neither party sought to build up a distinct class base or to concern itself with serious mass politicization. Rather, they developed into electoral machines,[10] led and dominated by educated professionals who acted as brokers and bargainers in an attempt to assemble multiple-class coalitions that could contain the divergent interests of all social strata. Thus each party was financed by prominent members of the local capitalist class, serviced by trade unions run primarily as 'vote-catching annexes',[11] and defended in the ghettoes by political gangs drawn from the *lumpenproletariat* itself. At the same time, party leaderships paid homage to the official myth of the multiracialism of Jamaican society, well symbolized by the national motto of 'Out of Many One People'.

The resulting system impeded the formation of either class or racial solidarity among the large, massively under-privileged sector of the population. As Carl Stone put it, 'it may seem to be a gross oversimplification to suggest that the alliances reflect grand conspiracies on the part of the privileged strata to manipulate and control the manual classes . . . [yet] . . . the effect of the strategy produces such a result.'[12] Accordingly, the positions of the two parties gradually converged – especially in the mid-1950s – until they differed only on a small range of issues, none of them threatening the common strategy of multiple-class, multiracial electoral appeals. In fact, the only issue of significance on which they diverged in this period related to the creation of a West Indies Federation as the vehicle in which the various small colonies of the English-speaking Caribbean might jointly travel the road to political independence. The Federation came into being in 1958, but was never accepted by the JLP and was brought to an effective end in September 1961 as a result of a referendum held in Jamaica in which the JLP campaigned vigorously and successfully against continuing membership. Yet, even after this bitter battle, the two parties again quickly came together in the cause of achieving separate political independence for Jamaica. The simple truth was that their leaders shared a common stake in the acquisition of state power and the general stability of Jamaican political life and were ready to work together to suppress the dissemination of disruptive political messages, especially those which might alarm important external economic and political forces.

Therefore, despite superficial similarities to the political norms of Western liberal democracy, what actually emerged in Jamaica – both before and especially after the advent of independence in August 1962 – was a clientelistic style of politics rooted in the particular pattern of economic development experienced in the country. The low level of employment made available by the highly capital-intensive strategy of industrialization meant that the possibility of working for the state and its various departments, boards and corporations became ever more crucial as a source of livelihood. A patronage tradition developed in which political support was exchanged for the material benefit of a job or even a home. In this way, mass participation in the political system was directly related to the welfare value of party politics. To insure against penetration of the system by a radical third alternative feeding on the material disaffection of the opposition party's clients, the opposition was traditionally allowed unofficial access to a minority portion of the available state largesse. Social discontent was thereby reduced and channelled against the party in office, not against the political system itself, underlining again the role of partisan politics in containing a revolutionary expression of political alienation. In view of the absence of serious discussion of differing socio-economic or ideological alternatives, democratic participation in Jamaica was limited to judging which party élite was most likely to maximize the welfare of each individual and his family.

For all the seeming vitality of Jamaican democracy in this period it is obvious that the quality of mass involvement in politics was very low. The role of the poorer ranks of the party coalitions was simply to act as an accurate mirror of current mass grievances, thereby enabling the political and business leaders to devise more adeptly the techniques of symbolic accommodation which were the basic stuff of political presentation in an élitist society where, as James Mau showed in the mid-1960s, the upper and middle classes were fearful of violent uprisings and rebellious behaviour on the part of the poor and unemployed.[13] The electorate responded on the whole, not to the policy content of contrasting PNP and JLP programmes of development, but to the different styles and attributes of the respective party leaderships – a 'darkened theatre audience that alternatively applauds and hisses the actors on the national stage'.[14] As a system it was far from fragile, having established firm roots in the hearts and minds of the majority of the urban mass public, and yet the feeling persisted that it was intrinsically vulnerable to the incursion of a form of politics prepared to articulate, rather than mask, the class and racial cleavages of Jamaican society.

THE 'TESTING' OF JAMAICAN DEMOCRACY 1968–80

The first real test of the extent of the vulnerability of Jamaican democracy to such new types of radical politics came in October 1968 when the summary expulsion from the country of the black-power activist and university lecturer, Dr Walter Rodney, provoked a major outbreak of rioting and violent protest on the part of the unemployed and the *lumpenproletariat*.[15] What the Rodney riots showed was that there existed in Jamaican society a reservoir of antagonism to the status quo sufficiently strong to seize the opportunity provided by a student demonstration to come out on to the streets of Kingston and virtually take over the centre of the city for an afternoon and evening. The mode of economic development of the country had generated the discontent and the conventional party political system had eventually failed to contain it. Although the speed with which the riots were dissipated suggested that the Jamaican social and political system was still far from the point of collapse, they were nevertheless a chilling warning of what might occur if attempts were not made to address the social failings of the Jamaican political economy and draw the poor, the unemployed and the *lumpenproletariat* back into the mainstream of democratic politics.

The way forward was pointed out by Norman Manley when in November 1968, right at the end of his political career, he told his party that, whereas the mission of his generation had been to achieve the goal of political independence, the task of the next was to proceed to social and economic renewal.[16] The mantle was taken up by his son, Michael, when he assumed the party leadership in the following year. Under his guidance the PNP proceeded to establish itself as the vehicle for the legitimate aspirations of the poor, black people of Jamaica. It voiced the discontent arising from the joblessness, victimization, coercion and corruption which were increasingly features of the governing JLP's period of office in the late 1960s and cleverly associated itself with the symbols of black racial identity by embracing sympathetically the culture of Rastafarianism and the protest implicit in reggae music. Michael Manley was himself projected to the electorate as a populist leader in the image of the biblical figure of Joshua, successfully building up around his personality a massive expectation of change which brought the PNP a sweeping victory in the general elections of 1972.[17]

The general 'people orientation' of the campaign, although real and indeed vivid, did not prejudice either the party's traditional multi-class coalition or its familiar agnosticism on matters of ideology. Stone's post-election survey confirmed both the cross-class nature of PNP support and the non-ideological nature of its appeal.[18] However, on agreeing to become party leader three years earlier, Manley had apparently indicated to his supporters that he was willing to do so only with the proviso that his selection would involve a clear ideological differentiation of the PNP from the JLP.[19] Although it was not made public at the time, the PNP did begin a major internal discussion of its ideology as soon as the 1972 election was won. This process bore fruit in September 1974, when, at the annual PNP conference, Manley enunciated the party's new commitment to a 'democratic socialism' that was flexible and undoctrinaire, stood for the 'equality of man', and held that 'human beings are moral and capable of acting together to achieve common purposes'.[20] Nevertheless, his tone was conciliatory, and the subsequent detailed statements confirmed that the model the party had in mind was moderate and completely non-Marxist in character.

While these changes were occurring within the PNP, the JLP remained demoralized by defeat; few formal statements of policy were made, and a struggle began to wrest the leadership away from Hugh Shearer, the retiring prime minister. By late 1974 this had been won by Edward Seaga, who thus assumed the post just as his opponents were declaring their commitment to socialism. He responded to the ideological challenge by branding the new doctrine as a covert form of communism. The term 'socialism/communism' became his favourite form of description for it. These attacks had little immediate impact on public opinion, but they did indicate one of the main weapons which the JLP under Seaga intended to use against the government. After many years of avoiding the issue, ideological battle had been joined in Jamaican party politics.

This change, which was a major adjustment of post-War norms in the country, was also reflected in the emergence of a third party on the political scene – the communist Workers' Liberation League (WLL), formed in December 1974 under the leadership of Trevor Munroe, a lecturer in politics at the University of the West Indies campus in Jamaica. To begin with, the WLL was highly critical of the PNP, taking the view that the party basically represented the interests of the 'national bourgeoisie' and that the decision 'to dust off the old slogans of bourgeois socialism' was only designed 'to harness and channel the rising revolutionary consciousness of the masses [and] restrain them from taking a left, democratic course'.[21] By the end of 1975, however, the continued development of socialist initiatives by the Manley government, the opening of cordial relations with Cuba and the JLP's deployment of anti-communist propaganda combined with other factors to persuade the WLL to change its line and adopt a position of 'critical support' for the PNP. Thereafter it played an increasingly important role in maintaining leftward pressure on the Manley government.

In the light of these developments, it was not surprising that the 1976 election should have been characterized by a more intense level of mobilization and ideological conflict. The PNP was fired by its growing confrontation with local capital and what it interpreted as externally inspired 'destabilization'. The latter was real: although a 'smoking gun' was never found, the weight of evidence makes it likely that the CIA was at work, in league with the JLP, the conservative-minded *Daily Gleaner*, and opposition businessmen and trade unionists, to undermine the elected government of Jamaica. Yet the implications of 'destabilization' have often been exaggerated. The key point about the 1976 campaign is that the PNP had deepened its commitment to democratic socialism since 1974 and had begun to address the difficult question of class struggle. There is no doubt, too, that it succeeded in arousing an unprecedented degree of national fervour to its cause. Previous efforts to build up the party at the grassroots level were vindicated as cadres (including some WLL personnel) emerged to plan and organize campaign activities all over the island. Public meetings were held frequently and attended by huge numbers – the rally in Montego Bay at which Manley announced the date of the election reportedly attracted a crowd of around 100 000 people. The PNP's message was thus transmitted mainly by face-to-face means, which enabled it to offset the extensive media advertising which the JLP's closer connections with the local capitalist class enabled it to enjoy. In sum, the JLP could match neither the intensity of the PNP's ideological conviction nor the extent of its popular mobilization, and it went down to predictable and resounding defeat.

The pattern of the vote revealed considerable changes in the social base of the two main parties since 1972. Both enjoyed mass support from black Jamaica (for the society had become progressively more black because of white emigration during the course of the 1970s), but, despite winning 57 per cent of the vote, the PNP no longer represented the majority of people of all classes. Its support among capitalists and the middle class all but disappeared, but was more than displaced by gains among the working class and the unemployed.[22] The effects of the ideological intensification of Jamaican politics had been to polarize class voting patterns, leaving the PNP very much the party of the lower social classes and the JLP as the party of the upper end of the social system. The old multi-class politics of the 1950s and 1960s had, to all intents and purposes, been destroyed. There was also a new and noticeable generational aspect to the results relating to the youth vote. This was more important than normal in 1976 because of the lowering of the voting age to 18 since the previous election. Stone again has shown that the PNP enjoyed a 2 to 1 lead over the JLP among voters under 30 years of age,[23] a tribute in good part to the youthful element in society which it had brought into active participation in politics.

What has to be understood is that, as a result of the process of mobilization and the changing nature of its support base, the PNP had become a quite different political party from the old days. The right mostly had been prepared to accept the populist flavour of Manley's early embrace of democratic socialism, but they undoubtedly bridled at the growing ascendancy of the left in the heady and euphoric period that immediately followed the election victory. Although the left was always more articulate, the right or moderate wing of the party was the more numerous, especially in the parliamentary group. It was, however, divided among itself, especially on the critical matter of economic management, and was reluctant to challenge Manley himself. Nevertheless, accelerating economic difficulties, and the decision in April 1977 to seek assistance from the International Monetary Fund (IMF), provided the moderates with the opportunity to begin their fight back. The evidence suggests that the months leading up to the party conference in September 1977 were ones of great internal bitterness within the PNP as the left was forced into retreat. In the end, the moderate wing of the PNP successfully reasserted itself, but at the price of undermining much of the coherence and vitality that had enabled the party to dominate Jamaican politics so completely from the early 1970s onwards.

True to the see-saw character of Jamaican party democracy, as the PNP began to divide and weaken, the JLP at last began to recover, not merely from its defeat in the 1976 election but from its original loss of office back in 1972. The number and range of its verbal attacks on the government increased, embracing issues of economic management, the Cuban/communist threat, movement towards a one-party state and alleged breaches of human rights. Seaga broke new ground by taking his campaign abroad and trying to win foreign allies in his attempt to undercut support for the PNP. Perhaps most important of all, however, the party moved to renovate its own organization. The JLP leadership had eventually come to realize that the rules of the political game in Jamaica had changed during the period of the PNP's ascendancy and that, as a consequence, no party could win office without an effective capacity for political mobilization. In the last few months of 1977 it founded auxiliary organizations for women, farmers and 'higglers'; revitalized its youth organization, *Young Jamaica*, and for the first time instituted area councils to strengthen party machinery. Although the JLP's mobilization capacity was not immediately transformed by these moves, the essential groundwork had been laid.

In fact, all the essential elements of the next contest between the parties had been put in place by the end of 1977. The remaining years of the Manley government up to the election of October 1980 merely saw an extension and deepening of trends already identified. Left–right divisions in the PNP continued, but as the social and political costs of the IMF connection began to be felt, it was the right which was placed on the defensive and the left that again began to take the initiative. The symbolic issue became the return of leading left-wing activist, Dr D.K. Duncan, to the post of PNP general secretary, which was eventually achieved at the 1979 conference. His reappointment inspired a brief attempt within the party to work out a viable 'non-IMF' economic strategy for the government; but the truth was that the PNP was already irreparably damaged by past divisions in the face of crippling economic problems. For its part, the JLP heightened its anti-communist rhetoric, continued to strengthen its organization by trying to get its trade union affiliate involved in more political action, and flexed its new mobilization capacity in a number of mass demonstrations, notably over the gas prices of January 1979 when Kingston and several other towns were virtually brought to a halt. Finally, the WLL, transmuted in August 1978 into the Workers' Party of Jamaica (WPJ), only further complicated the picture by announcing in mid-1979 that it was prepared to extend its policy of 'critical support' for the PNP into an actual alliance. The PNP was taken by surprise and the moderate element within it was embarrassed; the JLP revelled in the provision of more ammunition for its anti-communist campaign, especially as it was obvious by 1980 that informal collaboration was taking place between the PNP left and the WPJ.

The high levels of tension and mobilization generated over the preceding years made the 1980 election the most violent ever in Jamaica.[24] Between February and October some 600 people were killed in political conflict. In June there was also revealed an attempted plot against the PNP government by some officers in the Jamaica Defence Force which the high command of the army itself nipped in the bud. The election nevertheless took place following a careful and impartial enumeration of the voters' register and the result showed a massive swing to the JLP, which won 59 per cent of the vote and an extraordinary 51 of the 60 seats in parliament. The shift of opinion affected all classes, giving the JLP a majority in all the main social categories, although without entirely reversing the closer class alignment of 1976. Turnout was a record 77 per cent of eligible voters, again revealing the extent of the popular politicization which had been brought about in this highly charged phase of Jamaican political development.

CONCLUSION

By contrast, the conduct of politics in the 1980s has been characterized by what can only be described as restraint. That is not to say it was uneventful or not at times turbulent, but it is to recognize that leading politicians in both major parties understood how close the Jamaican democratic system had come to collapse in 1980. The PNP's boycott of the snap election called by Edward Seaga in December 1983 and its consequent absence from the Jamaican parliament damaged the system less than had been anticipated. The PNP called repeatedly for the holding of proper elections once the issue which had prompted its boycott, the preparation of a new voters list, had been resolved, but it never sought to use its public support, as testified by its regular lead in opinion polls throughout the second half of the 1980s, to make the country ungovernable. It preferred, it seemed, to wait, and win the next election as and when it was called by Seaga under the normal terms of a five-year parliament beginning at the end of 1983. Indeed, Manley himself was wont to say that he was more concerned with the conduct of that election than the result. In this spirit, a code of conduct was signed by Manley and Seaga on behalf of their parties in August 1988 and the election finally held in February 1989. It was won easily by the PNP, thereby confirming the Jamaican tradition that no party is ever given more than two consecutive terms in office by the electorate, but more importantly perhaps it passed with relatively little violence. Thirteen people only were killed, which was a low figure by past local standards, especially as the governing party was changing, with all the attendant implications for jobs and patronage.

Clearly, on the evidence described, the quality of democracy in Jamaica leaves much to be desired and, even as it stands, needs to be constantly protected from unscrupulous leaders, trigger-happy gunmen and ambitious soldiers. The maintenance of democracy in developing societies is hard work, but it can be said that, by and large, Jamaica has toiled effectively in its cause. Powerful forces favouring democracy have been forged in the country, not least by a people who have become attached to their own electoral tradition. Jamaica still very much counts as a democracy, especially when discussed in a broader Caribbean context. Fear and tyranny have not held sway, as in Haiti; prime ministers have not been put up against a wall and murdered, as in Grenada; elections have not been blatantly rigged, as in Guyana. All in all, given the pressures, especially those between 1968 and 1980, it has been quite a heroic performance.

How is it to be explained? Theories of democracy range widely and often do not make clear where definition ends and theorizing begins. Those theories that emphasize 'regime performance', satisfaction of popular demands and economic well-being do not shed much light on the Jamaican experience, much of which has revolved around the containment of social dissatisfaction. On stronger ground are theories which draw attention to the capacity of cross-cutting social cleavages to contribute to democratic stability by moderating the intensity of politics. Jamaicans generally possess a number of politically relevant affiliations (class, race, generation, party) which pull them in conflicting directions and reduce the zero-sum character of political conflict. The decline of a local plantocracy by the time of independence also removed from the Jamaican scene one of the most powerful anti-democratic forces at work in other parts of the Third World. Even so, it is hard to be persuaded that socio-economic factors predetermine the nature of Jamaica's democracy.

Political factors must constitute the bulk of the explanation of the emergence of a democratic system. In this context the crucial consideration was Jamaica's experience of British colonialism. In a recent analysis of the prospects for further democratization in different parts of the world, Samuel Huntington quoted the observation that 'every single country in the Third World that emerged from colonial rule since the second world war with a population of at least one million . . . with a continuous democratic experience is a former British colony'.[25] As he further noted, the effectiveness of British rule in encouraging democratic development appears to depend on the duration of that rule before independence. Whereas in most of Africa British colonialism lasted less than a century, Jamaica was part of the British Empire for over 300 years. The colonial legacy was long and deep. It left behind a respect for authoritarianism, but also an awareness of the possibilities of democracy. The preparation for democratic self-government was also more elaborate and sustained in Jamaica than in many other British colonies where independence came with a rush.

The importance of all this is not to say that Britain left Jamaica with a perfect set of democratic institutions – the illusion of 'Westminster in the sun'. Similar inheritances collapsed quickly enough in other ex-British colonies. Rather, it is to suggest that Britain socialized a generation of Jamaicans into broadly democratic values. English-speaking, colonially educated, the recipients of élite scholarships from Jamaica College to Oxford, Cambridge and London, the beneficiaries of other training programmes in Britain – what else could the Jamaican élite become but would-be parliamentary democrats, especially since they grasped the fact that political independence granted on these terms would not bring them down from the top of the tree socially and economically? The result was that, at independence, local leaders who genuinely believed in democracy took responsibility for its preservation and continued the process of education and dissemination into the next generation.

It is this élite, incorporating politicians, civil servants, judges, army officers, journalists, university teachers and others, which has been mainly responsible for the maintenance of that degree of openness and competitiveness which the Jamaican political system possesses.

The political crisis of 1980 was its greatest test to date. The democratic system was under genuine threat in a highly politicized situation. Yet Manley did not rig the election in order to stay in power; the JLP stopped short of inciting a complete breakdown of law and order; the Jamaica Defence Force caught the conspirators in its midst; and a team of honourable public servants was put together to preside over voter registration. Democracy came close to collapsing, but did not do so. What the Jamaican experience reveals, above all, is that the democratic commitment of political leaders does have a significant impact on the prospects for stable democracy. With certain individual exceptions, the leadership of the modern Jamaican state has felt the necessary attachment to the democratic system and has displayed an adherence to the rules of the game, even, albeit waveringly, in times of stress and at the expense of sectional political goals. In the final analysis, this has been the factor which has made the critical difference in underpinning the country's formal democratic structures.

Looking into the future, the role of the political élite nevertheless still remains crucial, especially as the first post-independence generation, largely schooled in Britain, is ageing and being replaced by younger men and women educated either in the region or in the United States. The latter applies especially to the Jamaica Defence Force whose links with the US have been greatly expanded during the Reagan/Seaga years. Yet, for the moment, the evidence of the February 1989 election encourages the belief that the political leadership of the country, in which both Manley and Seaga must now count as men at the end of their careers, may still possess enough of the ideology of liberal democracy to want to fight to preserve its existence in Jamaica.

NOTES

1. For a full discussion, see O. Jefferson, *The Post-war Economic Development of Jamaica* (Kingston: Institute of Social and Economic Research, University of the West Indies, 1972).
2. *Ibid.*, p.285.
3. S. de Castro, *Tax Holidays for Industry: Why we have to Abolish them and How to do it* (Kingston: New World Publications Pamphlet No. 8, 1973), p.6.

4. See N. Girvan, *Foreign Capital and Economic Underdevelopment in Jamaica* (Kingston: Institute of Social and Economic Research, University of the West Indies, 1971).

5. S. Reid, 'An Introductory Approach to the Concentration of Power in the Jamaican Corporate Economy and Notes on its Origins', in C. Stone and A. Brown (eds), *Essays on Power and Change in Jamaica* (Kingston: Jamaica Publishing House, 1977), pp.15–44.

6. O.C. Francis, *The People of Modern Jamaica* (Kingston: Department of Statistics, 1963), pp.1–5.

7. Reid, *op. cit.*, p.25.

8. G.K. Lewis, *The Growth of the Modern West Indies* (New York: Monthly Review Press, 1969), p.191.

9. For a fuller account, see C. Stone, *Class, Race and Political Behaviour in Urban Jamaica* (Kingston: Institute of Social and Economic Research, University of the West Indies, 1973).

10. P.D. Robertson, 'Party "Organization" in Jamaica', *Social and Economic Studies*, Vol. 21 (1972), pp.30–43.

11. Lewis, *op. cit.*, p.179.

12. Stone, *op. cit.*, p.46.

13. J.A. Mau, *Social Change and Images of the Future: A Study of the Pursuit of Progress in Jamaica* (Cambridge, Mass.: Schenkman, 1968).

14. Lewis, *op. cit.*, p.190.

15. See Anthony Payne, 'The Rodney Riots in Jamaica: The Background and Significance of the Events of October 1968', *The Journal of Commonwealth and Comparative Politics*, Vol. 21 (1983), pp.158–74.

16. See R. Nettleford, *Mirror Mirror: Identity, Race and Protest in Jamaica* (Kingston: Collins Sangster, 1970), p.167.

17. See O. Senior, *The Message is Change* (Kingston: Kingston Publishers, 1972).

18. C. Stone, *Electoral Behaviour and Public Opinion in Jamaica* (Kingston: Institute of Social and Economic Research, University of the West Indies, 1974), pp.55–8.

19. See E.H. and J.D. Stephens, *Democratic Socialism in Jamaica: The Political Movement and Social Transformation in Dependent Capitalism* (London: Macmillan, 1986), p.62.

20. *Jamaica Daily News* (16 September 1974).

21. T. Munroe, 'The New Political Situation', *Socialism!*, Vol. 1, No. 6 (1974), p.8.

22. See C. Stone, *Democracy and Clientelism in Jamaica* (New Brunswick, New Jersey: Transaction Books, 1980), pp.159–73.

23. *Ibid.*, p.168.

24. For a discussion, see A.M. Waters, *Race, Class and Political Symbols: Rastafari and Reggae in Jamaican Politics* (New Brunswick, New Jersey: Transaction Books, 1985), pp.199–247.

25. See S. Huntington, 'Will More Countries become Democratic?', *Political Science Quarterly*, Vol. 99 (1984), p.26.

2 Society and Electoral Politics in Trinidad and Tobago

Colin Clarke

INTRODUCTION

The distribution of political power in the Commonwealth Caribbean has been transformed since World War II by the introduction of adult suffrage. White élites, previously entrenched behind restrictive property franchises, have seen their electoral advantage disappear, and only a few individual whites have been successful at the polls, usually because of their backing by recently created, anti-colonial parties. Everywhere, coloured (brown) and black political élites have emerged to fill the legislative and executive vacuum created by the departure or demise of Creole and expatriate whites.

Caribbean electoral politics in the 1960s – as decolonization produced four independent states and six states in association with Britain – were dominated by the brown, educated, articulate middle stratum, who saw themselves as the heirs of the ruling class.[1] The black masses were bystanders, called upon every half decade to validate the democratic system by voting at a general election. Yet despite political demotion and emigration, the social, and above all, economic power of the whites remained intact into independence. Brown politicians, steeped in British values, proved unable to re-model the social order – even in those rare instances when they wished to do so. However, in Trinidad, as in Guyana, the social consequences of colour distinctions, which are so typical of Caribbean Creole societies, have been reduced in the face of non-Creole opposition, and black and coloured politicians have had to compete for electoral support with parties based on culturally distinct social segments of Indian origin.[2]

Trinidad's democracy has been vitiated by demography. The two-party system, so appealing to Britain before Trinidad's independence in 1962, has been little more than a front for competition between the two racially defined social segments. Vera Rubin noted that 'the

so-called racial politics may then be actually seen as . . . urban
politics versus rural politics – opportunities for Hindus versus opportunities for Creoles as both Negroes and East Indians now are in
open competition for the political positions which have been vacated
by the British.'[3] Nevertheless, most nationwide Trinidad political
parties have sponsored multiracial slates for election: and each has
denied making an appeal to race, however much individual candidates may have done so. In Trinidad, racism is an out-group vice,
rarely an in-group virtue.

The fact remains, however, that government and opposition in
Trinidad, since adult suffrage was introduced in 1946, have been
decided by racial blocks of majority (Creole) and minority (Indian)
status, and that only since 1986 have Indians escaped from their
beleaguered position and shared power through an electoral alliance
with black or brown parties. This chapter examines the major features of Trinidad's plural social structure, their spatial expression,
and their implications for political party formation and racial block
voting for constituency. It outlines the evidence for racial voting,
dividing the years 1946–86 into five time-periods. Attention is then
focused on non-racial issues that are of importance in Trinidad's
electoral politics – the economy, class and ideology, the trade unions,
and culture. Finally, a brief assessment is made of the current
multiracial government and of the general problem that segmental
pluralism poses for political alignments in Trinidad and other similar
territories in the Caribbean.

SOCIETY, SPACE AND 'INDIAN' RACE

Trinidad and Tobago (1 056 000 population in 1980) – a two-island
unitary state – is located in the south-eastern Caribbean, off the coast
of Venezuela. Colonized by Spain from 1498 to 1797, Trinidad was a
British possession for more than 150 years, and Tobago was added to
it for administrative purposes in 1889. Since World War II, Trinidad's
black political élite, while imbued with a multiracial ethic, have
generally denied the cultural pluralism of their society. 'All o' we is
one', runs a local saying, a point of view that is elaborated by Dr Eric
Williams, the late prime minister, in his history of the, then, recently
independent state:

> [I]n Trinidad, the Negro, the Indian, the French and the Spaniard,
> English and Portuguese, Syrian and Lebanese, Chinese and Jew,

all have messed out of the same pot, all are victims of the same subordination, all have been tarred with the same brush of inferiority. Divergent customs and antipathetic attitudes have all been submerged in the common subordinate status of colonialism.[4]

However, this emphasis on equality and harmony fails to conceal the island's divisions: differences of race, class, colour and culture have had a long and complex history in Trinidad, and each defines important elements in the social structure.

The principal feature of Trinidad's society is the dichotomy between Creole and Indian. The term 'Creole' has a special meaning in Trinidad. It excludes the Indian population, together with the small Carib, Syrian, Portuguese and Chinese minorities. Creoles may be white, brown or black, and phenotype correlates with cultural and socio-economic stratification. Creoles account for about 58 per cent of the population of Trinidad and Tobago: the breakdown by colour groups is whites 0.9 per cent, browns 16.3 per cent, blacks 40.8 per cent.

Stratification of the Creole segment was effected during slavery, under the influence of white sugar planters and administrators. Slave emancipation in 1834–38 removed the legal distinctions between strata but left the old social hierarchy intact. Within less than a decade, Indian indentured labourers were brought into the island to work on the sugar estates (144 000 over the period 1845–1917). Their descendants, often known locally as East Indians, now account for about 41 per cent of the island's population. However, this element is also divided, and comprises Hindus (24.9 per cent of Trinidad's total population), Moslems (5.9 per cent) and Christians (9.7 per cent).

Creoles and Indians constitute co-ordinate segments, each internally stratified by class or occupation, often in conjunction with colour, religion or caste. Race segments Indians and Creoles; religion reinforces this distinction and further divides Indians into Hindus, Moslems and Christians; caste is a Hindu phenomenon that has only minor implications for Christian Indians; shades of colour are important to Creoles but only of minor significance for Indians. Among the various aspects of stratification, only class is common to all the major racial and religious categories.[5]

Class, as reflected in the occupational stratification, places Creoles and Indians in parallel ranking systems. The Creole upper class, originally white, but with brown and black admixtures, consists of planters, merchants, industrialists, professionals, politicians, and senior civil servants; the middle class, typically brown but now increasingly darkened by educational mobility, contains civil servants

and local government officers, white-collar workers in the private sector (including banking and insurance), teachers, and nurses; the lower class, largely black, involves manual workers in industry (notably oil), urban service sector employees, including the majority of policemen, domestic servants, shop workers and marginal casual labourers (the unemployed and underemployed of the capital and other towns).[6]

Among Indians the upper class is characterized by businessmen, landowners and professionals; the middle class by local government officers, teachers, nurses, retailers, and private-sector white-collar workers – many of whom commute daily to the towns from villages in the sugar belt; the lower class by manual workers in the sugar industry, the cultivators of peasant plots, urban service-sector workers and domestic servants. Distinctions between Creoles and Indians hinge partly on the urban location of the former and rural residence of the latter, but also involve finer-grained occupational distinctions: carpenters are traditionally black, while road haulage businesses and cinemas are largely in Indian (Hindu) hands.[7]

It may be argued that Trinidad's is a class structure, with multi-racial and multi-cultural groupings in each of the three hierarchical strata. However, the salience of Creole–Indian social pluralism and its reinforcement by religion, the persistence of endogamy and of social networks based on race confirm that class is of secondary or tertiary significance as a social differentiator in this society. And racial segregation at the national scale fits this latter interpretation.

In addition to the neighbouring island of Tobago, which is a political dependency with an almost entirely black population, Trinidad throughout the second half of the twentieth century has been divided into five racial zones[8] (Figure 2.1). The western sugar belt and its subsidiary rice-growing areas (Figure 2.2), lying between Port of Spain, the capital, and San Fernando (Figure 2.3), together with the Naparimas around San Fernando and the sparsely populated south-west peninsula, are predominantly Indian. Port of Spain and its associated conurbation stretching along the Eastern Main Road towards Arima, contained more than 250 000 inhabitants in 1960, over 90 per cent of whom were Creole. San Fernando, with a population of 40 000 at that date, is the only other town of note.[9] Almost three-quarters of its inhabitants were Creole, but Indians formed a sizeable minority (25.7 per cent) – the largest proportion that Indians achieved in any urban settlement of note. The north and east of Trinidad are rural and sparsely populated, largely with blacks,

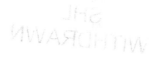

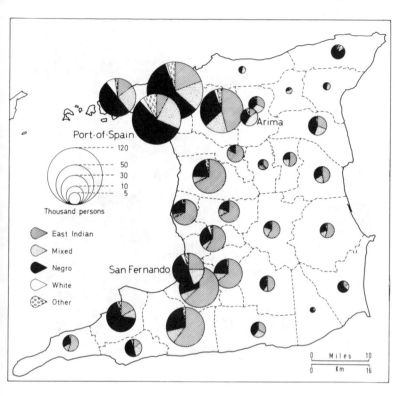

Figure 2.1   Trinidad, 1960: race and colour

except for Nariva where there is a pocket of Indians. By far the most
racially heterogeneous locality is the central uplands, where mixed
communities of blacks and Indians subsist by small-scale cultivation
supplemented with cocoa farming.[10]

The outstanding feature of the spatial pattern was the contrast
between town-dwelling Creoles and rural Indians. Whites, coloureds,
blacks and Chinese were only weakly segregated from one another at
the national level (Table 2.1), and the three Indian groups were
tightly aligned. Christian Indians (Catholic in the north and Presbyterian in the south) were more urbanized than Hindus and Moslems,
resided in close proximity to Creoles of mixed ancestry, but segregated themselves moderately from blacks. Indian isolation supported
a distinctive way of life and leadership. Naipaul noted:

Living by themselves in villages, the Indians were able to have a

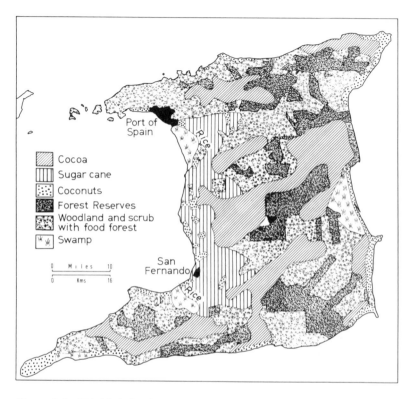

Figure 2.2   Trinidad: land use

Table 2.1   Indices of dissimilarity between racial and religious groups in
Trinidad in 1960

	White	Mixed	Negro	Hindu	Moslem	Christian East Indian	Chinese
White	—	26.0	30.2	58.4	54.5	40.2	25.0
Mixed		—	18.2	53.3	42.1	28.4	26.5
Negro			—	52.9	41.3	38.8	23.9
Hindu				—	16.1	32.5	62.5
Moslem					—	22.3	52.8
Christian East Indian						—	43.3
Chinese							—

Source: 1960 census, using district boundaries.

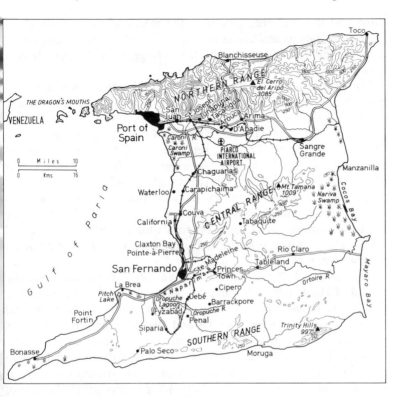

Figure 2.3   Trinidad: place names

complete community life. It was a world taken up with jealousies
and village feuds; but it was a world of its own, a community within
the colonial society, without responsibility, with authority doubly
and trebly removed. Loyalties were narrow: to the family, the
village. This has been responsible for the village headman type of
politician the Indian favours, and explains why Indian leadership
has been so deplorable, so unfitted to handle the mechanics of
party and policy.[11]

Indians and blacks were separated socially and spatially, both
through British design and their own mutual consent. Sharp distinctions between white overseers and black or Indian gangs, and between Indian field-hands and black factory workers typified
nineteenth-century sugar estates. Blacks denigrated the Indians as
slaves, and scorned them as scabs who depressed wages and levels of

living and thus put free labour at the mercy of the planter class. Moreover, Indians and blacks internalized white racist stereotypes of one another. Indians abused blacks as 'niggers' and blacks hurled back the epithet 'Coolie'.

Thus when Indians began to organize in the late nineteenth century, they eschewed multiracial working-class alliances for racially exclusive bodies – the East Indian National Association in Princes Town and the East Indian National Congress in Couva, both Christian-dominated. Political representation, too, was conceived along racial lines. The first Indian nominee to the Legislative Council, George Fitzpatrick, who took his seat in 1912, spoke out mainly on matters of significance to the Indian population.[12] So strong was Indian fear of erosion of the Indian way of life that in 1922 they reacted to British and Creole proposals for constitutional advance with a plea – which was refused – for proportional or communal representation.[13]

By the late 1920s Trinidad's Indian intellectuals favoured the revival of Hindi and Urdu, and the politically minded had launched the Young Indian Party. During the depression, however, several Indians, notably Hosein, Roodal and Rienzi, began to forge links with black politicians and trade unionists.[14] They aspired to a multiracial, socialist, independent society, whose ideals, for a while, were embodied in Cipriani's Trinidad Labour Party. Adrian Cola Rienzi (Krishna Deonarine), the most outstanding Indian political figure of the 1930s, analysed social problems in classical Marxist rather than racial terms, though somewhat dogmatically: 'only the dictatorship of the working class, guided by revolutionary determination and socialist philosophy can solve the contradictions and create a new social order that shall bring science and society into harmony and shall make mankind the master of the wealth that human industry and ingenuity have created'.[15]

Electoral success for the Trinidad Labour Party was out of the question, since barely 6 per cent of the population qualified for the vote. However, the world economic depression followed by the Italian invasion of Ethiopia fanned labour agitation and black protest, and in the late 1930s Rienzi and Roodal committed themselves to the black-led Butler Party.[16] In October 1936 Butler demanded better accommodation and wages for oil and sugar workers. Within a year labour riots, with a strong anti-white and anti-imperialistic tenor, which were eventually suppressed by the British military, put Butler in jail, and it was left to Rienzi, a barrister, to create the

Oilfield Workers' Trade Union (OWTU) and the All Trinidad Sugar Estates and Factory Workers' Union (ATSEFWU) – still the largest and most important labour organizations in the island.[17]

However, during the late 1930s and early 1940s, groups once more polarized along ethnic lines. Indian areas returned Indian candidates to the Legislature on the restricted franchise and Creoles voted for Creoles.[18] Rienzi was slowly absorbed into the island's legal élite and in 1944 left active politics. The Creole-dominated Legislature, on the eve of the introduction of universal adult suffrage in 1946, had to be compelled by Britain – at the instigation of Rienzi – to remove a restriction requiring Indian voters, alone, to prove their literacy in English.[19] The scene was set for a more pernicious bout of racial politics, this time based on 'one man one vote' and a multi-party democratic system, with the Indians fearful of the future and reluctant to endorse transfers of power to the Creole majority.[20]

RACE AND THE ELECTORAL PROCESS

Pre-war expressions of racial sentiment carried over into the first election held under adult suffrage in 1946. An appeal to race was a relatively simple, though inflammatory, means of drumming up electoral support. 'Then', in Naipaul's words, 'the bush lawyers and the village headmen came into their own, not only in the Indian areas but throughout the island. Then the loudspeaker van reminded people that they were of Aryan blood. Then . . . the politician, soon to be rewarded by great wealth, bared his pale chest and shouted "I is a nigger too!".'[21]

Division of the population into homogeneous racial and religious regions provided ample scope for vote-selling by constituency. Naipaul explores how, in one of his character's words, 'election bringing out all sort of prejudice to the surface'.[22] The novelist's Hindu candidate calculates: 'it have eight thousand votes in Naparoni. Four thousand Hindu, two thousand Negro, one thousand Spanish, and one thousand Muslim. I ain't getting the Negro vote and I ain't getting a thousand Hindu votes. That should leave me with five thousand.'[23]

Thirty-five years after 1946, the majority of Trinidad's Creoles and Indians still supported rival political parties: no government until 1986 had ever been formed with substantial Indian (particularly Hindu) backing. All six elections after 1955 were won by the Creole-dominated People's National Movement (PNM), created and led until his death in 1981 by Dr Eric Williams. What is the evidence for racial voting? What parties contested the elections on what platforms (other than racial affiliation)? How and why was the PNM defeated in 1986? To answer these questions I have divided Trinidad's recent electoral history into five periods: steps towards responsible government, 1946–56; the coming of independence and the struggle for segmental dominance, 1956–61; Creole hegemony and Creole patronage, 1961–71; crisis and recovery, 1971–81; breaking the mould of racial politics, 1981–86.

STEPS TOWARDS RESPONSIBLE GOVERNMENT

The 1946 election resulted in a tie between the multiracial Butler Party (though Butler himself lost to Gomes in Port of Spain) and the black radical United Front (three seats each) with two seats going to the Trades Union Council and Socialist Party, and one to an Independent.[24] Four of the nine elected were Indians, representing sugar-belt constituencies, and many people 'lamented the fact that race had played such a decisive role. . . . It was feared that adult suffrage had merely served to politicize and harden the cleavages in the society'.[25]

Although the 18-member Legislature contained three Crown officials and six nominated members who acted as a counterweight to the elected element, the Indians were alarmed at the prospect of further political evolution towards responsible government in the Executive Council.[26] Kumar warned, 'I do not think we should invite the possibilities of a political party which might gain a slight majority at an election, controlling the whole colony and entirely over-riding the interests of the other portion that might find itself with a small minority.'[27] The East Indian National Congress sent a memorandum to the British Colonial Office, protesting at their vulnerability, and 'Hindu pundits went up and down the country warning their flock that they would be politically and culturally swamped by the Negro majority if self-government was granted',[28] but to no avail. Britain approved an Executive Council of nine, with four nominated members: the elected element had a majority if they were united on an issue.

The 1950 election, therefore, was a crucial one, and Butler's emerged as the most successful party, taking six seats, four with

Indian representatives, out of 18 (seven *in toto* had Indian victors), in
a skilful return to the 1930s blend of 'sugar and oil'.[29] Although they
formed the largest single group in the Legislative Council, the
Butlerites were not given even a token seat on the Executive Council
on which Gomes, Bryan and Joseph were to figure prominently as,
respectively, ministers of labour, agriculture and education. Butler's
Indian allies, reacting against his lack of patronage, moved away
from him and cast in their lot with the People's Democratic Party
(PDP) formed in 1953 by Bhadase Maraj, the sugar union boss and
the head of the orthodox Hindu organization, the Sanathan Dharma
Maha Sabha.[30]

By 1955 the PDP seemed poised for power, but the election was
delayed for a year to allow a new constitution to be framed. In
January 1956 Dr Eric Williams created the People's National Movement, the charter of which demanded a full ministerial system with
self-government in internal affairs, and advocated sound economic
management, together with improvements in housing, health and,
most crucially, education. While this programme received widespread support among the black lower class, Williams's opinions on
denominational education, birth control and the press alienated the
Catholic Church and the white establishment. The upshot was that
the PNM snatched victory by a single seat margin (13 out of 24), with
the PDP (5 seats), Butler Party (2 seats), Trinidad Labour Party–
Caribbean National Labour Party (2 seats), and Independents
(2 seats) trailing in its wake.[31] Several 'old-time' politicians – Gomes
and Joseph, Chanka Maharaj and Kumar – disappeared from the
political scene.[32]

The PNM polled only 39 per cent of the vote cast, and scraped to
victory largely because the sympathies of the electorate in many
constituencies were divided among numerous candidates. Moreover,
the PNM fielded successful Indian candidates in two key (statistically
and racially) marginal constituencies – Kamaluddin Mohammed in
St Joseph and Dr Winston Mahabir in San Fernando West: both were
to become cabinet ministers. Mohammed (Moslem) and Mahabir
(Christian) excepted, successful PNM candidates were all Creole,
while the PDP representatives were without exception Indian, and
represented sugar-belt constituencies.

Although the PNM had won a majority of the elected seats, the
Legislative Council still contained five nominated members and two
appointed officials. The PNM insisted it would govern alone or go
into opposition, and the governor and British secretary of state for

the colonies responded by helping the PNM to a working majority. Kumar's 1946 warning was forgotten; Williams was allowed to name two of the nominated members and was guaranteed that the other three would not be hostile to the PNM. Moreover, the governor declared that the votes of the two appointed officials would be available to the PNM government (giving it 17 votes in normal circumstances) – a very different treatment from that received by Butler in 1950. Butler was thought of as an anti-colonial rabble-rouser and radical with no detailed programme, whereas the Oxford-educated Williams was regarded (by the liberal governor but not by white Creoles) as a sound reformer devoted to constitutional decolonization.

INDEPENDENCE AND THE STRUGGLE FOR SEGMENTAL DOMINANCE

Williams had originally intended the PNM to be not only nationalist and reformist, but also multiracial, and to include Indians, whether Christian, Moslem or Hindu. The electoral results for 1956 do indeed show that urban, middle-class Christians and Moslems sided with the PNM in San Fernando and some of the suburbs of Port of Spain. However, the very existence of the PDP as a political arm of ortho-dox Hinduism – an outstanding example of cultural pluralism being projected into organized politics – ruled out the possibility of Hindu support for the PNM, and drove Christians and Moslems into the PNM's open arms.[33] Williams's anti-colonialism appealed to non-white Creoles just as it alienated whites, but the PNM in power represented nothing more radical than 'brown man' government. The defeated Gomes observed of the PNM, 'within the Party itself, the middle-class elements are in the ascendancy. . . . The choice of certain persons for ministerial positions and other plums indicate quite clearly that while the rump of the Party remains proletarian, its entire personality is being controlled by elements from higher social strata.'[34] However, racial hostility between black Creoles and Hindu Indians engendered by the 1956 campaign persisted through the next quinquennium, and served to conceal the middle-class nature of the PNM's leadership and policies. To the PNM, as Ivar Oxaal observed, 'the East Indian . . . pseudo-party . . . represented a gift from the gods'.[35]

The final colonial phase, 1956–61, was one of intense segmental competition to achieve control. 'The conflict between the two political groups was fierce and hysterical, and at times the community seemed on the brink of war. This was especially true in 1960–61 when preparations were being made for the pre-independence elections and the constitutional settlement upon which independence was to be based.'[36] The period witnessed the establishment of a West Indies Federation and the holding of a federal election in 1958, the Trinidad element of which was won by the Democratic Labour Party (affiliated to the opposition groups); a bitter struggle between the PNM government and the US over the naval base at Chaguaramas, which was required for the federal capital; and the withdrawal of Jamaica from the Federation after a referendum in 1961, leading in turn to the independence of Trinidad and Tobago as a unitary state, and the collapse of the federal experiment.

As a result of the DLP's victory by six seats to the PNM's four in the federal election in Trinidad, Williams attacked the Indians, branding them as a 'recalcitrant and hostile minority'.[37] Henceforth, rank-and-file Christians and Moslems, in retaliation, would turn their backs on the PNM and vote 'Indian'. In this they were facilitated by the 1957 merger between the PDP, the Trinidad Liberal Party and the Party of Political Progress Groups to form the Democratic Labour Party (DLP) of Trinidad and Tobago (an affiliate of the Federal DLP), for they would no longer be supporting a purely Hindu party. In fact, the DLP was essentially an Indian–white alliance, which greatly simplified the drawing up of the battle lines for the 1961 election.

Meanwhile, Williams was projecting his charismatic personality among the black masses by giving open-air lectures at the 'University of Woodford Square' in central Port of Spain, where he held his listeners spellbound as he denounced white Creoles in 'Massa day done', and attacked US neo-colonialism in 'From slavery to Chaguaramas'.[38] Oxaal notes that:

> [T]he image of Williams as a racial messiah was not limited to the black lower class, although it was strongest there, but could be found in the Creole middle class as well. Among members of the latter, however, the belief in personal and collective salvation through Dr Williams often shaded over into a more secular variant of the True Believer in which the *rationality* and *honesty* of the Doctor were so fervently espoused as to occasion the willing surrender of independent judgement and will, associated with an

intense hostility to any form of criticism, direct or implicit, of the
political leader.[39]

As the 1961 general elections approached, with a new constitution
which would give full internal self-government, it was clear that the
DLP badly needed a more sophisticated leader than the now sickly
Bhadase Maraj; someone who could capture the popular imagination
and compete with Williams at 'doctor politics'. Such a man the
Indians found in Dr Rudranath Capildeo, a lecturer in mathematics
at University College, London. The PNM, for its part, approached
the elections with caution. In 1956 it had won with only a minority
vote; in 1958 it had been defeated; and after 1960 it was faced with an
articulate DLP leader.[40]

But the PNM was mindful, above all, that the key to its defeat in
1958 had been the way in which the constituency boundaries had
been drawn: almost half its voting strength was concentrated in the
capital city, and the rest distributed in such a way that it could easily
have been swamped by the Indian vote. So the key to its victory in
1961 lay in its control – as government – of the electoral boundaries'
commission. It steadfastly refused the DLP's request for a neutral
commission of persons from the West Indies or the UK; instead it
ensured that the one DLP member was confronted by four PNM
parliamentarians or supporters.

> In the countryside there was strong evidence to substantiate the
> DLP's claim that the PNM had herded as many Indian voters as
> was possible into constituencies which they could not possibly win,
> and had extracted from such areas large blocks of Negro voters
> who were then recombined into new constituencies. Ten of the
> thirty constituencies contained populations which were more than
> 50 per cent Indian. The DLP won them all. . . . The evidence
> certainly suggests that the cartography [Figure 2.4] was undertaken
> with the electoral returns of the previous election in mind.[41]

The 1961 general election was the most bitterly fought in Trinidad's colonial period, perhaps of all campaigns up to the present.
Whereas only 52.9 per cent had turned out in 1946, the figure rose to
70.1 per cent in 1950, 80.1 in 1956 and 88.11 in 1961: the electorate
was deeply politicized as the co-ordinate socio-racial segments were
organized into electoral groups. The PNM took 58 per cent of the
vote, an enormous improvement over their 1956 result, and 20 seats
to the DLP's 10.[42] Once more the urban–rural split underpinning

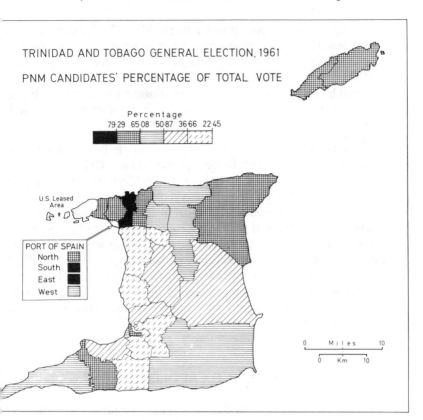

Figure 2.4 Trinidad and Tobago general election, 1961: PNM candidates, percentage of the total vote by constituency

Creole–East Indian polarization was in evidence (Figures 2.1 and 2.4), though the DLP was to argue that the result had been rigged not only by the gerrymandering of constituency boundaries but by the use of pre-programmed voting machines.[43]

Ideology hardly entered into the election: it was a straightforward competition between black and brown versus Hindu and white made manifest in the personal rivalry of the intellectual champions of each major racial group – Dr Williams and Dr Capildeo. This point is exemplified by Albert Gomes in one of his inimitable observations.

The truth is that Dr Williams and his party have been zig-zagging along the political road since 1956, alternately driving to the Left and to the Right – until 1960, a year that marks a definite turn to the Right with the ruthless unloading of Mr. C.L.R. James and the *detente* with the Americans over Chaguaramas. . . . Any suggestion that the election is a battle between the forces of progress (PNM) and those of reaction (DLP) is a convenient fiction invented by Dr Williams. . . . In an ideological sense, this is a battle between Tweedledum and Tweedledee, both of whom are driving hard on the Right.[44]

The influence of race and cultural affiliation can be estimated from the characteristics of the successful candidates. Only two of the PNM's 20 seats were held by Indians – both Moslems: similarly, two of the DLP's ten legislators were Creole, but three Indians were Christian and one Moslem. However, at least three out of the four Hindu representatives of the DLP were Brahmins (the highest of the four Hindu varnas) and this shows how high caste was projected via the Maha Sabha on to the national political stage. Of the 12 PNM cabinet places, two went to Moslems, two to whites and eight to black/brown legislators: for the second time Hindus were not represented in the government – soon to become the government of an independent state.

CREOLE HEGEMONY AND CREOLE PATRONAGE

The 1961 election over, Williams declared Trinidad's intention to seek sovereignty outside the West Indies Federation. With Jamaica's withdrawal, Trinidad and Tobago was not willing to shoulder the economic burden of the grant-aided Windwards and Leewards: '1 from 10 leaves none', in Williams's immortal words – though for a time it looked as though the PNM might seek to incorporate willing neighbours in a unitary state, thereby boosting its black population. Despite the fears of a racial war in Trinidad, an independence constitution was negotiated with the British, though it involved compromise on the part of both government and opposition.[45] Capildeo warned, 'It is easy to let slip the dogs of war; it is impossible to return to the positions before they were unleashed.'[46]

The first years after independence were characterized by optimistic neo-colonial development based on oil, sugar and light manufacturing and by the generally weak opposition mounted in the House of Representatives by the DLP, whose leader spent much of the year lecturing in London. PNM hegemony determined that national culture was essentially Creole culture, and Creoles tended to regard Indian political activity – much of which was, admittedly, negatively critical – as 'refractory if not treasonable'.[47]

A more authoritarian tone began to enter into government activities. In 1965 the trades union movement was disciplined by the Industrial Stabilisation Act; C.L.R. James, the famous Trinidad Marxist and former associate of Prime Minister Williams as editor of the PNM's weekly, *The Nation*, was placed under house arrest; and a Commission of Inquiry into Subversive Activities was set up. When the 1966 general election duly produced 24 seats for the PNM to 12 for the DLP on a 65.79 per cent turnout, many believed that the voting machines had been used to shore up the DLP and to eradicate additional parties like the Liberal Party (8.88 per cent of the vote) and C.L.R. James's radical Workers' and Farmers' Party (3.46 per cent), both of which had sprung from discontent with the DLP.[48] Racial bifurcation of the electorate was by now convenient to Creole and Indian political leaders alike. Formerly well-known politicians such as Victor Bryan, 'Buzz' Butler and Lionel Seukeran, who were detached from the two parties which controlled the racial vote, were ousted.

Material expectations, which had been raised by party politics, the media and independence, could not be satisfied either by modest economic growth or by the government's purchase, in the late 1960s, of Shell's oil assets and acquisition of a substantial share of the sugar industry. Unemployment more than doubled between 1960 and 1970, by which time it was 13 per cent; moreover it was heavily concentrated in the poorer, Creole sections of Port of Spain.[49] Discontent at the end of the first decade of sovereignty hinged not on Creole–Indian stress, but on a factor missing from the late 1950s and 1960s, namely, black proletarian disaffection from brown, middle-class government.

Trinidad was ripe for crisis when the international student disturbances of 1968 meshed with US black-power riots and the two, in combination, were projected onto the urban scene by students at the Trinidad campus of the University of the West Indies.[50] Black-power disturbances, involving student activists at the St Augustine campus and marginalized urban blacks in San Fernando and Port of Spain, led to the declaration of a state of emergency in February 1970, at the very point when unionized oil and sugar workers were entering the fray.[51] Part of the – largely Creole – Defence Force sympathetic to black power mutinied, and control was re-established by the government only because of the loyalty of the coastguard (which blocked the road from the barracks to the capital) and the police.[52]

These events split the Creole segment along its lines of latent internal cleavage and broke the PNM's control of marginalized urban blacks. Fearful that the black-power outburst might engulf them, for that is how Indians reacted to the black protesters' symbolic march to Chaguanas,[53] and frustrated by a decade of what they saw as Creole gerrymandering of electoral boundaries and fixing of voting machines, the DLP took no part in the 1971 elections, so that the PNM won all 36 seats with a 33 per cent turnout and only 28 per cent of the electorate voting for them.[54] No white candidates were sponsored, for the first time in a Trinidad general election, though the power base of the PNM 'had come to rest more and more on the old, the fair-skinned and the established'.[55]

The low turnout certainly dispelled DLP criticism of rigged voting machines – why should the PNM fix such a low level of popular support? However, if Creole hegemony was weak on legitimacy and democracy (there was no opposition), the Indians were in no position to expose their opponents. Internecine strife, never totally absent from the DLP, had broken out in 1969 when Capildeo was replaced as party leader by Vernon Jamadar. Bhadase Maraj claimed that, as he had handed over the leadership to Capildeo in 1960, he was the logical successor, The party split; the majority of MPs accepted Jamadar's leadership; and Maraj fought the 1971 election with his newly created Democratic Liberation Party, but polled only 12.6 per cent of the votes cast and did badly even in sugar-belt constituencies.[56]

Jamadar's problems were just beginning when he replaced Capildeo as leader of the official DLP. In 1970, his 'new' DLP joined forces with the Action Committee of Dedicated Citizens (ACDC), created earlier that year by the Tobagonian A.N.R. Robinson, who had resigned as finance minister in the Williams's cabinet because of the PNM's misunderstanding and mishandling of the black-power crisis. But Robinson unilaterally pulled the DLP out of the 1971 election, and Jamadar, fearful of Maraj's competition in the sugar belt, eventually joined the boycott.

The total crisis of the late 1960s and early 1970s seemed so large that one contemporary political commentator confidently predicted, 'the Williams era is coming to a close'.[57] The faltering economy, rising unemployment, black power and Indian disaffection seemed likely to usher in a new political regime. Why did the PNM continue in government for 15 more years after 1971?

CRISIS AND RECOVERY

If continuity immediately after 1971 was only to be expected, since there was no formal opposition in the House of Representatives and the PNM in the person of Eric Williams guaranteed stability and security for Creoles and Indians alike, the longer-term recovery, economically, was totally unexpected, and had little to do with the policy adopted by the government. It was entirely due to chance discoveries of oil and natural gas off the Atlantic Coast of Trinidad, coupled to windfall profits after 1973, generated by OPEC price increases. Williams announced his withdrawal from public life, but rapidly agreed to continue in office as the price of oil quadrupled.[58]

Williams's retention of the prime minister's office, plus his re-distributive policy based on the oil boom, gave the PNM an excellent chance of regaining control over lower-class blacks and staying in power. In the 1976 elections, the first after Trinidad and Tobago became a republic, the two DLP factions were obliterated in a 55.8 per cent turnout, leaving the PNM with 24 seats and 54 per cent of the popular vote in the first election at which the age limit was 18.[59] The United Labour Front (ULF), a coalition of the radical forces which had operated in 1970–71, backed by a formal alliance of the four major trade unions which had collaborated during the bitter struggle for higher wages in 1975, the Oilfield Workers' Trade Union, the All Trinidad Sugar Estates and Factories Workers' Trade Union, the Transport and Industrial Workers' Union and the Island-Wide Cane Farmers' Trade Union, displaced the DLP as the opposition, but the compact was transitory, and the party's voting strength and eventually its leadership, devolved upon the Indians.[60] The ULF's ten seats coincided almost exactly, spatially, with the 12 taken by the DLP in 1966.[61] Tapia, a radical-intellectual party, got none.

The 1981 election, the first for 20 years without voting machines, was held shortly after Eric Williams's death in office, and repeated the 1976 results in their essentials (both had a 56 per cent turnout).[62] The oil-propelled boom, and the replacement of Williams by George Chambers as the PNM leader, resulted in a 26 to 8 seat victory for the Creole government over Panday's ULF, with Tobago, as in 1976, falling to A.N.R. Robinson's Democratic Action Congress. (Tobago was Robinson's bailiwick and potentially separatist.)

For the purpose of the election, the 'opposition parties', the ULF and DAC, plus Lloyd Best's Tapia – had formed the Alliance, 'a political instrument that at once attempted to accept and to transcend the separate interests that went to make up the organization'.[63] For, whereas the ULF was based, electorally, on the Indian sugar belt, the DAC drew its support from black Tobago, which resented Trinidad's neglect, while Tapia was not only urban and radical, but black. In short, the supporters of each party in the Alliance were very different from one another racially.

In addition to the PNM and the Alliance, a new party was formed to contest the election, the Organization for National Reconstruction (ONR) headed by Karl Hudson-Phillips, a former attorney general and (like Robinson) once heir-apparent to Williams in the PNM.[64] The ONR was unable to capture a single constituency in Trinidad's first-past-the-post system, but it polled 22 per cent of the votes (against the PNM'S 52.6 and the ULF's 15.1), and made substantial gains in the residential districts of suburban Port of Spain, known locally as the East–West Corridor, and San Fernando. The ONR was typified as a party of defectors, 'a crossover party comprising professionals and businessmen of all races – Blacks, Indians, Whites, Chinese, Syrians and so on with minimal grassroots support'.[65]

This pattern of crossing over encouraged La Guerre to surmise that 'the decline in the race factor which started in 1966 is causing voters to reassess their traditional alignments. The very character of the constituencies has undergone change. This is why the ONR was able to halt the advance of the PNM in the East–West Corridor and to make inroads into rural and East Indian constituencies.'[66] But, as we have seen, there is no evidence that race declined in significance after 1966, though culture or religion seem to have done so. Indeed, the reason why the ONR made headway in rural East Indian districts in 1981 was due to limited black penetration of the sugar belt where suburban residential districts were established from the late 1960s. In short, racial voting by blacks continued – but in a novel context. It is essential, therefore, to approach with scepticism La Guerre's prediction that 'although race has not been banished, its importance in succeeding national elections is likely to be much less significant than it was in preceding years.'[67]

BREAKING THE MOULD OF RACIAL POLITICS

After the mid-1970s the PNM was able to present itself to prosperous Indians of all religions as the guarantor of the status quo, and to ameliorate intersegmental relations by expanding government patronage in the shape of subsidies, tax relief and the generation of employment.[68] As its electoral position returned to the high degree of security it achieved in the early 1960s – but with lower turnouts – so its capacity for buying off crises expanded. Trinidad's GDP increased nine-fold between 1970 and 1980, and unemployment dropped to 9 per cent.[69] Oil revenues were used to create service employment among the urban unemployed and to subsidise the loss-generating and nationalized sugar industry: hence proletarian blacks and Indians benefited from PNM government largesse.[70]

However, oil revenues flagged after 1983, and investments in iron and steel, petrochemicals and fertilizers made by the PNM in the more optimistic 1970s were unable to sustain economic growth at the inflated level to which all Trinidadians – especially urbanites – had become accustomed. Sensing popular discontent with the PNM government, and with allegations of corruption, including drug smuggling, being bandied about, the Alliance and the ONR established a strategic collaboration during the 1983 local government elections and routed the PNM.[71] In 1985 the National Alliance for Reconstruction was established under the leadership of A.N.R. Robinson, an umbrella movement embracing the ULF, DAC, Tapia and the ONR, an amalgam of radical and conservative, Indian and black groups.

The result of the 1986 election, with a 64 per cent turnout, was the virtual destruction of the PNM as a parliamentary force (they held on to only three seats, two in Port of Spain and one in San Fernando), the defeat of Prime Minister Chambers, and the first change of government since independence. With 33 out of 36 seats and 67 per cent of the vote (Figure 2.5) the NAR received an overwhelming mandate to govern. Robinson became prime minister and named Basdeo Panday, leader of the ULF as his deputy. East Indians could claim for the first time 'is we government'.

But had race ceased to be a crucial factor in the election? Obviously, the NAR was a multiracial, multi-party alliance. Yet it was above all an alliance of racially based, race-voting parties. Out of the 33 NAR seats, ten were held by Indian representatives: eight of these constituencies were in the sugar belt, one was in Nariva, a long-established Indian stronghold, and only one (at Tunapuna)

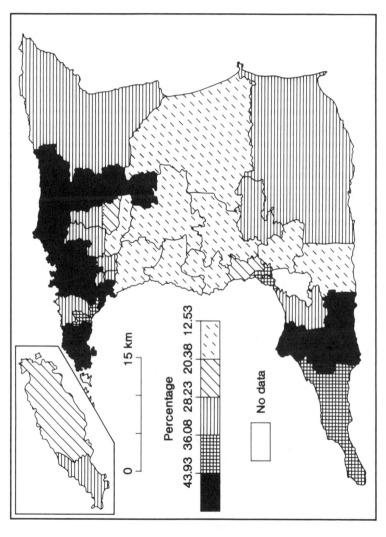

Figure 2.5   Trinidad and Tobago general election, 1986: PNM candidates, percentage of the total vote by constituency

represented a traditional Creole constituency. In other words, virtually the same 8–10 constituencies returned NAR Indians as returned ULF or DLP candidates in the past.[72]

If the 23 NAR Creole victors are added to the three PNM, it is found that they represented essentially the same 26 constituencies held by the PNM in 1981.[73] It seems likely that the ONR and DAC, by capturing the Creole urban vote, and that of Tobago, could have ousted the PNM without Indian support: that they had that support guaranteed success, and created a genuine platform for Creole–Indian collaboration *within* the government. But it was achieved through racial voting for candidates who were known to represent political parties with distinct racial associations.

DISCUSSION

Despite the proclivity to racial voting going back to 1946 and the formation of the PDP as an exclusively Hindu party in the early 1950s, Trinidad has nonetheless been fortunate that a diversified and growing economy post World War II, based on sugar and oil, enhanced by windfall profits in world markets during the 1970s, ameliorated intersegmental tensions both during the period of decolonization from 1946 to 1962 and the crucial decade following the black-power riots and mutiny of the Defence Force in 1970.

Nonetheless, it is important to note that economic stagnation and rising unemployment in the 1960s spelled discontent and disruption among those least able to survive through subsistence farming – urban black marginals. Similar economic problems associated with low world market prices for sugar and oil, currently beset the NAR government, as state coffers are emptied and its powers of patronage decline: it may be expected that class tensions, generally muted compared to the clamour of segmental clashes, will once more come to the fore.[74]

At the beginning of this chapter I pointed out that despite some specialization by occupation and industry, Creoles and Indians are each internally stratified by class. I have also shown that race and ethnicity (especially Hinduism), not class, have been the organizing frameworks for politics in Trinidad. This does not mean, however, that class has played a negligible role within segments or that solidarity between classes across the Creole–Indian divide has been totally absent.

Political competition between Creoles and Indians to fill the power vacuum created by white decolonization resolved itself into a struggle between middle-class browns and blacks versus middle-class and upper-class Hindus (mostly Brahmins) using, respectively, the voting strength of the black proletarians and the Indian lower classes (and castes). Divide and rule satisfied the competitors for post-colonial power as much as it had British imperialists: class tension, the advocacy of social or Marxist ideology, and demands for radical or revolutionary change recurred but were contained.

There was a tendency for the higher classes to deviate from the political norm for their segment.[75] Upper-class white Creole disaffection from the PNM was particularly noticeable and many in the 1950s and 1960s were allied to the DLP. There was also a tendency for upper- and middle-class Indians to support the PNM either openly or clandestinely.[76] After independence in the 1960s this was largely with a view to seeking access to patronage and via patronage resources – educational scholarships and government contracts, for example; after the black-power disturbances many middle-class Indians voted for security under the PNM or abstained (as the low turnouts probably imply); following the oil boom, Indians of all classes benefited from PNM welfare or patronage provision.[77]

Class solidarity between the segments has been much more sporadic than across-class solidarity or inter-class manipulation within segments, and has involved working-class collaboration between blacks and Indians – classically oilfield workers and canecutters. The first important occasion in modern times when it was manifest was during the 1937 labour disturbances. It was also the objective of the abortive march to Chaguanas and the general strike of 1970; it was the basis for the foundation of the ULF – but in that instance black working-class support was soon withdrawn. Ironically, the NAR does not involve a single class within two racial segments, but an across-the-board 'federation' of Creoles and Indians: it is composed of an unholy alliance of the radical, working-class ULF and the conservative, middle-class ONR, and combines races and classes in a potentially very unstable fashion.

Although the disturbances of 1937 led to the creation of Trinidad's two key trade unions, organized labour has not been directly involved in politics in the way it has in Jamaica, Antigua or Grenada. While Maraj was president general of the Maha Sabha, political organizer of the PDP and labour leader (of the Sugar Workers' Union), there was no formal link between the PDP and the union:

likewise, the Trades Union Congress generally gave support to the PNM, and Williams nominated trades unionists to the Senate after 1961, but no formal link was sought or achieved.[78]

The impact that the trades unions have attempted to have has not been through collaboration with existing parties, but by inter-union compacts in confrontation with the established parties – especially the party forming the government: hence the involvement of the OWTU and the Sugar Workers' Union in the 1970 general strike, and their creation of a new party, the ULF, in 1976.[79] As the latter developed into an Indian party, so it became dependent on the Sugar Workers' Union, and Panday, like Maraj in the 1950s, was leader of both party and union – but, unlike Maraj, not of orthodox Hindus via the Maha Sabha, though Panday, too, was a Brahmin.

This has represented a major break in the politics of the Indian segment. Hinduism, while it has flourished since the oil boom, has not been the basis for political organization, though it has reinforced and redefined a sense of Indian identity.[80] 1970 represents more of a watershed in Indian than Creole politics: it killed the DLP and the Maha Sabha's direct involvement in politics. Likewise, the role of cultural categories such as the Christian Indians and Moslems has declined. In 1956 Christian and Moslem voters were attracted to the PNM platform by candidates of their own religion, and by their perception that the PDP was a Hindu party. Their wish to distance themselves from the Hindus disappeared after Williams's attack on all Indians.[81] Henceforth, Moslem leaders would continue to attempt to deliver the Moslem vote to the PNM in return for patronage, but increasingly after 1960 Moslems and Christians voted (with Hindus) for the DLP,[82] and after 1976 for the ULF and NAR (or abstained). Even so, the last PNM cabinet still had one Moslem (Kamaludin Mohammed) and one Presbyterian Indian (Errol Mahabir), and the former had served continuously in government for 30 years. Since 1960 race has played an increasingly important differentiating role *vis à vis* culture, though the 1986 NAR cabinet has been the first ever to contain Hindus!

CONCLUSION

The chapter demonstrates the persistence of racial voting in Trinidad throughout the period of universal adult suffrage. For the most part this has involved voting for the party of one's race rather than for individual candidates of one's race, though the two have often coincided. Even in 1986, when the multiracial NAR displaced the Creole PNM with a landslide victory and its race-party components, such as the ONR and ULF, were not overt, Indians voted for Indian candidates of ULF persuasion.

Religion declined in political significance between 1960 and 1980 as the racial boundary between the PNM and the Indian parties was ever more sharply defined. This secularization of politics facilitated inter-party co-operation among the opposition and the creation of the Alliance in 1981 and the NAR in 1985. However, there is no sign that the decline in the importance of religion has been matched by the increased salience of class, though the sacking by Prime Minister Robinson of his deputy, Panday, and two other Indian (ULF) members of the cabinet in dispute with him over the 1988 budget, which favoured the rich against the poor, clearly has both class as well as race implications.[83]

Looking back over the last 40 years, politics have mirrored Trinidad's plural-segmented society and, in turn, exacerbated racial tensions between Creoles and Indians. But this was not the only feasible outcome. In Belize, in Central America, as Nigel Bolland demonstrates elsewhere in this book (Chapter 3), similar vertical cleavages between Creoles and Spanish-speaking Mestizos have given rise to two parties, each with multiracial support. But here the outside threat of Guatemalan annexation, coupled to the integrating role of the Catholic Church, may have encouraged inter-racial collaboration. In Guyana, on the South American mainland, on the other hand, the Indian majority has fared less well than the Indian minority in Trinidad. Although they formed the government in the last years of British colonialism, throughout independence they have been systematically disadvantaged by Creoles, and elections have been rigged using overseas and proxy voting.[84]

Trinidad stands mid-way between these two other cases of Caribbean segmental pluralism. Westminster-style democracy has ensured electoral victory for the Creole majority for four decades, with the Indian minority enjoying full civil liberties.[85] Currently Trinidad follows the Belizean model of multiracial government with strong consociational overtones (as of 1989 there were five Indians to 13 Creoles in the Alliance cabinet),[86] but the socio-political situation undoubtedly contains the dynamic potential for regression to racial politics or even gravitation towards the Guyanese pattern of Indian oppression.

ACKNOWLEDGEMENT

The author wishes to express his gratitude to the Nuffield Foundation for a grant towards fieldwork in Trinidad in 1985, during which much of the material in this chapter was collected.

NOTES

1. C.L.R. James, *Party Politics in the West Indies* (Port of Spain, 1962), pp.130–9.
2. M.G. Smith, *Culture, Race and Class in the Commonwealth Caribbean* (Kingston, Jamaica: Department of Extra-Mural Studies, University of the West Indies, 1984).
3. V. Rubin, 'Culture, Politics and Race Relations', *Social and Economic Studies*, Vol. 11 (1962), pp.433–55, quotation on p.453.
4. E.E. Williams, *History of the People of Trinidad and Tobago* (Port of Spain: Peoples National Movement Publishing, 1962), p.280.
5. C.G. Clarke, *East Indians in a West Indian Town: San Fernando Trinidad, 1930–1970* (London: Allen and Unwin, 1986).
6. L. Braithwaite, 'Social Stratification in Trinidad', *Social and Economic Studies*, Vol. 2 (1953), pp.5–175; and F.S. Braithwaite, 'Race, Social Class and the Origins of Occupational Elites in Trinidad and Tobago', *Boletín de Estudios Latinoamericanos y del Caribe*, Vol. 28 (1980), pp.13–30.
7. W. Dookeran, 'East Indians and the Economy of Trinidad and Tobago', in J. La Guerre (ed.), *Calcutta to Caroni: The East Indians of Trinidad* 2nd revised edn (St Augustine, Trinidad: Extra Mural Studies Unit, University of the West Indies), pp.63–73.
8. J. Augelli and H.W. Taylor, 'Race and Population Patterns in Trinidad', *Annals of the Association of American Geographers*, Vol. 20, No. 2 (1960), pp.123–38.
9. C.G. Clarke, 'Pluralism and Stratification in San Fernando, Trinidad', in B.D. Clark and M.B. Gleave (compilers), *Social Patterns in Cities* (London: Institute of British Geographers, Special Publication No. 5, 1973), pp.53–70.
10. C.G. Clarke, 'Scale Factors and Ethnic Patterns in Trinidad', *Geographical Society Journal* (University of Liverpool), Vol. 4 (1976), pp.30–4.
11. V.S. Naipaul, *The Middle Passage* (London: André Deutsch, 1962), p.82.
12. G. Tikasingh, 'Toward a Formulation of the Indian View of History: the representation of Indian opinion in Trinidad, 1900–21', in B. Brereton and W. Dookeran (eds), *East Indians in the Caribbean* (New York and London: Kraus International), pp.11–32.

74

Colin Clarke

13. *Ibid.*
14. S. Ryan, 'The Struggle for Afro-Indian solidarity in Trinidad and Tobago', *Trinidad and Tobago Index*, Vol. 4 (1966), pp.3–28.
15. B. Samaroo, 'Politics and Afro-Indian relations in Trinidad', in J. La Guerre (ed.), *Calcutta to Caroni* (London: Longman, 1974), pp.84–97; quotation, originally from Adrian Cola Rienzi, *The Beacon* (1932), p.87.
16. W.R. Jacobs 'The Politics of Protest in Trinidad: The Strikes and Disturbances of 1937', *Caribbean Studies*, Vol. 17, Nos 1–2 (1977), pp.5–54.
17. S.D. Ryan, *Race and Nationalism in Trinidad and Tobago: a Study of Decolonization in a Multiracial Society* (Toronto: University of Toronto Press, 1972), pp.44–69.
18. J.G. La Guerre, *The Politics of Communalism: the Agony of the Left in Trinidad and Tobago 1930–55* (Trinidad: Pan Caribbean Publications, 1982), p.30.
19. B. Samaroo, 'The Making of the 1946 Trinidad Constitution', *Caribbean Studies*, Vol. 15, No. 4 (1976), pp.5–27.
20. La Guerre, *op. cit.*, p.44–6.
21. Naipaul, *op. cit.*, p.83.
22. V.S. Naipaul, *The Suffrage of Elvira* (London: Andre Deutsch, 1958), p.136.
23. *Ibid.*, p.52.
24. Trinidad and Tobago, *Report on the Legislative Council General Election 1946* (Port of Spain, 1947).
25. Ryan, *op. cit.*, p.77.
26. J. La Guerre, 'The General Elections of 1946 in Trinidad and Tobago', *Social and Economic Studies*, Vol. 21 (1972), pp.184–203.
27. Ryan, *op. cit.*, pp.82–3; quotation originally in Hon. Ranjit Kumar's minority report appended to the *Report of the Constitutional Reform Committee* (Port of Spain, 1946).
28. *Ibid.*, p.83.
29. Trinidad and Tobago, *Report on the Legislative Council General Elections 1950* (Port of Spain, 1954).
30. J. La Guerre, 'The General Elections of 1950 in Trinidad and Tobago', *Social and Economic Studies*, Vol. 29 (1980), pp.321–35.
31. Trinidad and Tobago, *Report on the Legislative Council General Elections 1956* (Port of Spain, 1958).
32. For a personal account of Albert Gomes's experience, see his autobiography, *Through a Maze of Colour*, (Port of Spain: Key Caribbean Publications, 1974), p.166.
33. Y.K. Malik, *East Indians in Trinidad: A Study in Minority Politics*, (London, New York, Toronto: Oxford University Press, 1971).
34. Ryan, *op. cit.*, p.168; original quotation from Albert Gomes in *Trinidad Guardian*, 11 November 1956.
35. I. Oxaal, *Black Intellectuals Come to Power* (Cambridge, Massachusetts: Schenkman, 1968), p.183.
36. Ryan, *op. cit.*, p.171.
37. E.E. Williams, *Inward Hunger: the Education of a Prime Minister* (London: Andre Deutsch, 1969), p.275.

38. P.K. Sutton (compiler), *Forged from the Love of Liberty: Selected Speeches of Dr. Eric Williams* (Trinidad: Longman Caribbean, 1981).
39. I. Oxaal, *Black Intellectuals Come to Power* (Cambridge, Massachusetts: Schenkman, 1968), p.101.
40. G.K. Lewis, 'The Trinidad and Tobago General Elections of 1961', *Caribbean Studies*, Vol. 2, No. 2 (1962), pp.2–30.
41. Ryan, *op. cit.*, p.245.
42. Trinidad and Tobago, *Report on the General Elections 1961* (Trinidad and Tobago, 1965).
43. K. Bahadoorsingh, *Trinidad Electoral Politics: the Persistence of the Race Factor* (London: Institute of Race Relations, 1968).
44. Ryan, *op. cit.*, p.275 fn.; quotation originally in Albert Gomes, *Trinidad Guardian*, 19 November 1961.
45. A.N.R. Robinson, *Patterns of Political and Economic Transformation in Trinidad and Tobago* (Cambridge, Massachusetts: Institute of Technology Press, 1971).
46. Ryan, *op. cit.*, p.336; quotation originally in Rudranath Capildeo, *Statesman*, 19 August 1962.
47. D. Lowenthal, *West Indian Societies* (London: Oxford University Press, 1972), p.175.
48. Trinidad and Tobago, *Report on the Parliamentary General Elections 1966* (Port of Spain, 1967).
49. S.S. Goodenough, 'Race, Status and Urban Ecology in Port of Spain, Trinidad', in C.G. Clarke (ed.), *Caribbean Social Relations* (Liverpool: Centre for Latin-American Studies, University of Liverpool, Monograph Series No. 8, 1978), pp.17–45.
50. I. Oxaal, *Race and Revolutionary Consciousness* (Cambridge, Massachusetts: Schenkman, 1971); S. Craig, 'Background to the 1970 Confrontation in Trinidad and Tobago, in S. Craig (ed.), *Contemporary Caribbean: a Sociological Reader* (Port of Spain: Susan Craig, 1981) Vol. 2, pp.385–423.
51. P.K. Sutton, 'Black Power in Trinidad and Tobago: the Crisis of 1970', *Journal of Commonwealth and Comparative Politics*, Vol. 21 (1983) pp.115–32.
52. L. Best, 'The February Revolution', in D. Lowenthal and L. Comitas (eds), *The Aftermath of Sovereignty* (Garden City, New York: Doubleday, 1973), pp.306–29.
53. D.G. Nicholls, 'East Indians and Black Power in Trinidad', *Race*, Vol. 12 (1971) pp.443–59; see also J. La Guerre, 'Afro-East Indian Relations in Trinidad and Tobago', *Caribbean Issues*, Vol. 1 (1974), pp.49–61.
54. E. Greene, 'An Analysis of the General Elections in Trinidad and Tobago 1971', in Trevor Munroe and Rupert Lewis (eds), *Readings in Government and Politics of the West Indies* (Mona, Jamaica: Department of Government, University of the West Indies, 1971), pp.136–45: see also Trinidad and Tobago, *Report on the Elections to the House of Representatives 1971* (Port of Spain, no date).
55. Ryan, *op. cit.*, p.482.
56. E. Greene, 'An Analysis of the General Elections in Trinidad and

Tobago 1971', in Munroe and Lewis, *op. cit.*, pp.136–45.
57. Ryan, *op. cit.*, p.337.
58. C.D. Parris, 'Trinidad and Tobago – September to December 1973', *Social and Economic Studies*, Vol. 30 (1981), pp.42–62.
59. S.D. Ryan, 'Trinidad and Tobago: the General Elections of 1976', *Caribbean Studies*, Vol. 19, Nos 1 and 2 (1979), pp.5–32; see also *Trinidad and Tobago, Report on the Elections to the House of Representatives 1976* (Port of Spain, no date).
60. S. Ryan, 'The Disunited Labour Front', supplement to *Caribbean Monthly Bulletin* (Rio Piedras, Puerto Rico, no date).
61. S.D. Ryan, 'Trinidad and Tobago: the General Elections of 1976', *Caribbean Studies*, Vol. 19, Nos 1 and 2 (1979), p.26; original observation in Lloyd Best, *Sunday Guardian*, 19 September 1976.
62. J. La Guerre, 'The General Elections of 1981 in Trinidad and Tobago', *Journal of Commonwealth and Comparative Studies*, Vol. 21 (1983) pp.133–51; see also Trinidad and Tobago, *Report on the Parliamentary General Elections 1981* (Port of Spain, no date).
63. La Guerre, *Ibid.*, p.144.
64. S. Ryan, 'The Church that Williams Built: Electoral Possibilities in Trinidad and Tobago', *Caribbean Review*, Vol. 10, No. 2 (1981), pp.12–13, 45–6.
65. J. La Guerre, 'The General Elections of 1981 in Trinidad and Tobago' *Journal of Commonwealth and Comparative Studies*, Vol. 21 (1983), p.152; original quotation in J. Hackett, *The Express*, 11 November 1981.
66. La Guerre, *Ibid.*, p.154.
67. *Ibid.*
68. P. Sutton, 'Trinidad and Tobago: Oil Capitalism and Presidential Power', in A. Payne and P. Sutton (eds), *Dependency under Challenge* (Manchester: University of Manchester Press, 1984), pp.43–76.
69. J.M. Sandoval, 'State Capitalism in a Petroleum-Based Economy', in F. Ambursley and R. Cohen (eds), *Crisis in the Caribbean* (Kingston, Port of Spain and London: Heinemann), pp.247–68.
70. S. Ryan, E. Greene and J. Harewood, *The Confused Electorate: a Study of Political Attitudes and Opinions in Trinidad and Tobago* (St Augustine, Trinidad: Institute of Social and Economic Studies, 1979).
71. K. Yelvington, 'Vote Dem Out: the Demise of the PNM in Trinidad and Tobago', *Caribbean Review*, Vol. 15, No. 4 (1987), pp.8–33.
72. S. Ryan, E. Greene and J. Harewood, *The Confused Electorate: a Study of Political Attitudes and Opinions in Trinidad and Tobago* (St Augustine, Trinidad: Institute of Social and Economic Studies, 1979), p.156.
73. S. Ryan, 'Political Change and Economic Reconstruction in Trinidad and Tobago', *Caribbean Affairs*, Vol. 1, No. 1 (1988), pp.126–60, see specially p.139.
74. D. Pallister, 'Carnival Mood Evaporates as Crisis Starts to Bite', *The Guardian* (London), 4 March 1988.
75. C.G. Clarke, *East Indians in a West Indian Town: San Fernando, Trinidad, 1930–70* (London: Allen and Unwin, 1986), p.140
76. P.C. Hintzen, 'Bases of Elite Support for a Regime: Race, Ideology and

Clientelism as bases for Leaders in Guyana and Trinidad', *Comparative Political Studies*, Vol. 16, No. 3 (1983), pp.363–91.

77. P. Hintzen, 'Ethnicity, Class and International Capitalist Penetration in Guyana and Trinidad', *Social Economic Studies*, Vol. 34, No. 3 (1985), pp.107–63; see also P. Hintzen and R. Premdas, 'Race, Class and Development: Toward an Explanation of Poverty and Repression in Less Developed Countries', *Plural Societies*, Vol. 15 (1984), pp.193–219.

78. R. Ramdin, *From Chattel Slave to Wage Earner: a History of Trade Unionism in Trinidad and Tobago* (London: Martin, Brian and O'Keefe, 1982).

79. *Ibid.*

80. S.A. Vertovec, 'Hinduism and Social Change in Village Trinidad', (Oxford University D.Phil.thesis, Faculty of Anthropology and Geography, 1988).

81. E.E. Williams, *Inward Hunger: the Education of a Prime Minister* (London: Andre Deutsch, 1969), p.275.

82. C. Clarke, 'The Political Ecology of a Town in Trinidad', in W. Peter Adams and F.M. Helleiner (eds), *International Geography 1972* (*International Geographical Union*, Montreal, 1972), pp.798–81.

83. *Caribbean Insight*, Vol. 11, No. 3 (1988), p.1.

84. C. Baber and H.B. Jeffrey, *Guyana: Politics, Economy and Society* (London: Pinter, 1986).

85. For an appraisal by Trinidadians of the first quarter century of independence see the recently published S. Ryan (ed.), *Trinidad and Tobago: An Independence Experience* (St Augustine, Trinidad: Institute of Social and Economic Research, University of the West Indies, 1988), and Ryan's *The Disillusioned Electorate: The Politics of Succession in Trinidad and Tobago* (Port of Spain: Inprint Caribbean, 1989).

86. I am indebted to my colleague Dr Tony Lemon of the School of Geography, Oxford University, for pointing this out to me.

3 Society and Politics in Belize

O. Nigel Bolland

INTRODUCTION

Belize is an anomalous society.[1] On the one hand, it is singular among Caribbean societies because of its Central American location; on the other hand, despite its location, it is rarely included in discussions of Central American politics and societies. Belize's historical connections – cultural, economic and political – have been largely with the Anglophone Caribbean, and there can be no doubt that Belize is part of the Caribbean 'socio-cultural area',[2] yet the country's future may well lie in closer relations with its immediate neighbours. Perhaps given this position, Belize may be able to play a special role as a link between Central American and Caribbean societies.[3] At any rate, the culturally and racially pluralistic nature of the society, which includes a large proportion of Creole or Afro-Belizeans, the persistence of colonialism until very recently, the liberal-democratic nature of the political system, and the increasingly pervasive influence of the United States, are features that Belize shares with many other Caribbean nations.

POPULATION, PLURALISM AND ECONOMIC DEVELOPMENT

Belize, unlike most Caribbean societies, is quite sparsely populated. About 160 000 people are distributed in a country of 22 963 km^2 of land, or about twice the size of Jamaica (Figure 3.1). While the overall popluation density is only about seven persons per km^2, some districts are much more densely populated than others and there is a high degree of urban concentration. Belize District contains over one-third of the total population (Table 3.1).

Since about 1930, over half the population has been living in the seven largest towns, which, in order of decreasing size, are Belize City, Orange Walk Town, Corozal Town, Dangriga, San Ignacio,

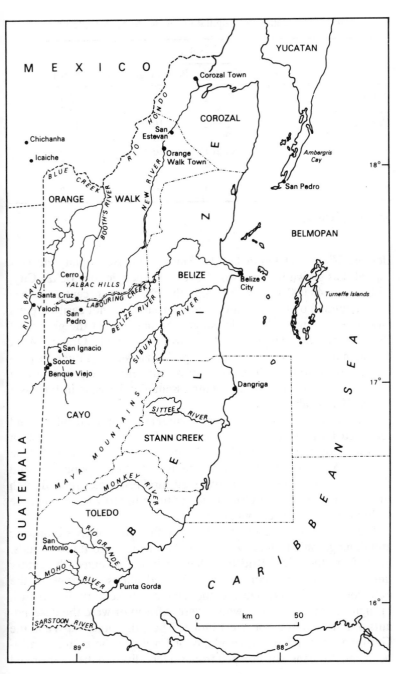

Figure 3.1 Districts and major settlements of Belize

Table 3.1   Density of population in Belize by district, 1980

| District | Population | | Density per km² |
	Number	Percentage	
Belize	50 801	35	12.1
Cayo	22 837	16	4.3
Corozal	22 902	16	12.3
Orange Walk	22 870	16	4.8
Stann Creek	14 181	10	6.5
Toledo	11 762	8	2.5
Total	145 353	100	6.3

Source: Census, 1980.

Benque Viejo and Punta Gorda. Since 1970, Belmopan, the new capital, has grown into a town of over 3000 people, but Belize City, with about 40 000 people, remains the chief urban centre. Belize City, bounded by the sea and swampy ground, cannot easily expand and is very congested. While emigration has limited the growth of Belize City and Dangriga, other towns, especially Orange Walk Town, have been growing quite rapidly. However, rather surprisingly, urbanization has decreased in recent years, the proportion of the population living in towns being essentially the same in 1980 as it was in 1931 (Table 3.2).

Almost half the population lives in rural areas, in small villages and scattered farms in the north, along the Belize River and Western Highway, on the coast south of Dangriga, and in southern Toledo District. Much of the country remains very thinly populated and there are considerable underdeveloped rural resources. Indeed, with suitable development, Belize could continue to grow for a long time without becoming overpopulated.

The patterns of settlement in Belize reflect the colony's economic and demographic history, which may be divided into three periods. First, from the initial British settlement in the seventeenth century until the 1840s the economy was focused almost entirely on the extraction of timber. During the eighteenth century the British brought in slaves, most of whom were African or were the descendants of Africans from the West Indies. The indigenous Maya and the Garifuna, who are the descendants of Caribs of the eastern Caribbean and Africans who escaped from slavery, lived in the interior and

Table 3.2 Population of Belize City and the six next largest towns, 1881–1980

Date	Belize City	Six next largest towns, total	Urban total	Urban total as percentage of population
1881	5 767	4 930	10 697	39.0
1891	6 972	4 948	11 920	37.9
1901	9 113	6 627	15 740	42.0
1911	10 478	7 862	18 340	45.3
1921	12 423	9 077	21 500	47.4
1931	16 687	9 730	26 417	51.4
1946	21 886	11 186	33 072	55.8
1960	32 867	15 901	48 768	53.9
1970	39 050	25 701	64 751	54.0
1980	39 771	35 381[a]	75 152	51.7

[a] Includes Belmopan.
Source: Censuses of 1946, 1960, 1970, 1980.

in southern coastal communities, respectively. The British settlers and their slaves, along with a growing free black and coloured population, lived chiefly in the town that was established at the mouth of the Belize River. Until the middle of the nineteenth century this town resembled little more than a trading post attached to a massive timber reserve. The population fluctuated in this period, but by 1845 there were about 10 000 persons in the settlement, less than 4 per cent of whom were white.[4]

The second period began in 1848 when thousands of Mestizo and Maya refugees from the Caste War of Yucatan began settling in the northern and western districts. The 1861 census recorded over 25 000 people in Belize, 57 per cent of whom were foreign-born. While the timber trade declined and the colonial economy commenced a century of stagnation, many of the more recent immigrants developed agriculture, including for a while some sugar production. By the end of World War II the population of Belize had doubled (Table 3.3).

The third period, from 1946 to the present, has been characterized by an accelerated rate of population growth and a diversification of the economy. Since a net emigration from Belize has taken place this century, the high growth rate has resulted chiefly from natural increase, due in particular to a dramatic decline in the infant mortality rate. Though the birth rate remains high, the average annual

O. Nigel Bolland

Table 3.3 Total population of Belize, 1790–1980

Date	Total population
1790	2 656
1803	3 959
1806	3 526
1816	3 824
1823	4 107
1826	4 163
1829	3 883
1832	3 794
1835	2 543
1839	2 946
1841	8 235
1845	9 809
1861	25 635
1871	24 710
1881	27 452
1891	31 471
1901	37 479
1911	40 458
1921	45 317
1931	51 347
1946	59 220
1960	90 505
1970	119 934
1980	145 353

Sources: O. Nigel Bolland, *The Formation of a Colonial Society* (Baltimore and London, Johns Hopkins University Press 1977), p.3; Census of 1980.

rate of population increase has declined, from just over 3 per cent between 1946 and 1960 to just under 2 per cent since 1970.

A decline in the export of such forest products as mahogany and chicle in the 1930s and 1940s resulted in an economic crisis, social dislocation and the emergence of modern politics in Belize.[5] The production of sugar and citrus expanded in the 1950s, and the value of sugar and citrus exports has exceeded that of forest products since 1959. Belize also exports a considerable quantity of seafood, including fish, lobsters, conch and shrimp, and several other agricultural products, such as corn, rice, red kidney beans, beef, poultry and honey, have become well-established. Tourism, meanwhile, remains on a small scale and most of Belize's light industries, which are oriented chiefly towards the domestic market, are small.

Despite these developments, the Belizean economy has not kept pace with the growth in the labour force. Unemployment has increased in recent years and was officially estimated to account for 14.3 per cent of the labour force in 1980, *before* the recent recession and a major crisis in the sugar industry. Presently, the unemployment rate is probably between 20 and 25 per cent. The problem is especially acute in Dangriga and Belize City. Moreover, underemployment is widespread as only about two-thirds of the people counted as employed actually work full-time.

One important consequence of this pattern of economic development and unemployment has been the migration of thousands of Belizeans, mostly young, urban and black, to the United States. Estimates of the number of Belizeans who have moved to North America, chiefly for economic reasons, vary between 20 000 and 80 000. In other words, perhaps as many as a third of all Belizeans now live in North America, and their remittances to relatives at home constitute an important contribution to the national economy. The number of immigrants has also increased in recent decades. The proportion of the population that was foreign-born increased from 8 per cent in 1960 to 11 per cent in 1980, due to the immigration of thousands of Mennonites, Mexicans and Central Americans. Most recently, an influx of immigrants, many of them refugees from the strife in Guatemala and El Salvador, is estimated to amount to about 25 000 persons.

The net result of these patterns of emigration and immigration is a change in the racial/ethnic proportions of the population, a change that has recently become one of the major political issues in the country. The people of Belize, as indicated above, are the product of diverse migrations, chiefly during the last two centuries, so there is nothing unusual about these recent developments. What is remarkable is the degree to which public opinion is conceiving of the 'alien' issue, as it is called, as something of a scapegoat for the nation's problems.[6] In this small, heterogeneous state that has a developing but still weak sense of nationalism,[7] existing racial prejudices and ethnic stereotypes could be used by unscrupulous politicians to develop factional support. There is widespread concern in the new nation about the proliferation of racial and ethnic associations and the so-called 'imbalance' that is perceived to be developing as a result of the migration patterns. This sense of 'imbalance' implies the existence of a perception that racial/ethnic proportions in the population have achieved a degree of stability during the last century or so, and consequently that any disturbance of this 'balance' is some-how subversive of Belizean society, traditionally conceived.

The 1861 census suggests that there were 18 per cent Maya, 38 per cent Mestizo, 31 per cent black or coloured (Creole), 7 per cent Garifuna and 4.5 per cent white, the remainder being East Indian, Chinese or not stated.[8] Some Maya and Mestizos returned to the Yucatan after the Caste War, while other Maya, both Kekchi and Mopan, came to Belize from Guatemala in the late nineteenth century. The 1980 census reports that Creoles constitute about 40 per cent of the population; Mestizos, 33 per cent; Garifuna, 8 per cent; Maya, 7 per cent; white, 4 per cent; Kekchi, 3 per cent; East Indians, 2 per cent; and small groups of Chinese and Arabs are also present.[9] Most of these 'groups' are themselves the result of considerable mixtures, of course, including the Creole, the Mestizo and the Garifuna. There is substantial intermarriage between Mopan and Kekchi Maya, and the East Indians are largely 'creolized'. It would be an oversimplification to conceive of these groups as static, because changing historical forces, particularly economic and political forces, have been and continue to be the sources of dynamic ethnic redefi-nitions.

Nevertheless, some factors, such as language, are significant markers of ethnic categorization and are often used in Belize as a short-hand for identifying groups, such as 'Spanish' and 'Creole'. Creole[10] is the first language of a little over one-half the people and Spanish is the first language of just under one-third. The remainder grow up speaking a variety of languages, including Garifuna, German and Maya. Belize is a mosaic of languages, with Creole as the first language for nine out of ten people in Belize District but for less than one in five people in Corozal and Orange Walk Districts, where Spanish is the primary language of about 70 per cent of the popu-lation. Since English is the official language and the medium of instruction in schools, many Spanish, Maya and Garifuna speakers can also speak English. Perhaps one-third of the population is bi-lingual, and many people are multilingual, but there also are many monolingual Creole speakers. Creole, which is increasingly the lingua franca of Belize, especially among the youth, is itself absorb-ing Spanish and North American influences.

Another ethnic marker that both defines and overlaps communities is religion. Anglicans, Methodists and Baptists were among the first to create churches in Belize, but today they account for only 12 per cent, 6 per cent and 1 per cent of the population, respectively. The first modern Catholic church was established in 1851, following the influx of refugees from Yucatan, and today the Catholic Church is a national institution, uniting 62 per cent of the population. The Church has grown because it has gained adherents among the Creoles as well as the Garifuna, Maya and Kekchi. The Mennonites, constituting the fourth largest religious community in Belize, mostly keep their congregationalist Protestantism to themselves, but Pentecostal and Adventist churches are growing, with adherents among various ethnic groups.

The present geographical distribution of racial/ethnic groups reflects their settlement patterns when they entered the country: two-thirds of the Creoles live in Belize District, the Mestizos are largely in the north, the Garifuna in coastal communities in the south, and the East Indians in rural Toledo and Corozal, where they were brought to work on sugar plantations in the nineteenth century. Several of the larger towns have a predominant ethnic character. For example, Belize City is 76 per cent Creole, Dangriga is 70 per cent Garifuna, and Orange Walk Town is 69 per cent Mestizo. It is among some villages, however, that we find the strongest ethnic identity, such as the Mennonite communities in Cayo and Orange Walk Districts, and the Kekchi villages in Toledo District. Neighbouring communities may be ethnically quite distinct, as, for example, Creole Placentia and Garifuna Seine Bight in Stann Creek District. However, despite this pattern of community settlement, a considerable amount of dispersal, with increasing ethnic interaction, also takes place. The Garifuna, for example, though only 8 per cent of the population, are present in every part of Belize, rural and urban, and in the towns of San Ignacio and Punta Gorda there are representatives of every ethnic group of Belize (Table 3.4).

Some authors have simplified the social structure of Belize by linking together several of these racial and ethnic groups into larger segments or 'complexes'. For example, M.G. Smith has written of the 'cleavage' between the 'Negro–white Creole and the Spanish–Indian Mestizo' segments of what he conceived as a 'plural society', divided 'culturally, linguistically, and by race'.[11] He predicted in 1965 that, as national autonomy increased, 'this cleavage will tend to deepen'.[12] More recently, Smith has categorized Belize as a 'complex multiracial society' in which a 'Creole hierarchic plurality' is combined with a 'basic division into contraposed segments that differ in race, culture, numbers, political status, economic interests, religion, and in other ways',[13] but he made no attempt to document or analyse

Table 3.4 Population by ethnicity and district, 1980

District	Population (number)	Ethnic group (percentage)							
		Creole	East Indian	Garifuna	Kekchi	Maya	Mestizo	White	Other/not stated
Belize	50 801	75.1	1.5	3.2	0.1	0.7	13.1	1.1	5.1
City	39 771	76.0	1.5	3.5	0.1	0.3	12.2	0.9	5.5
Rural	11 030	71.8	1.5	2.3	0.1	2.1	16.4	1.6	4.1
Cayo	22 837	31.0	1.1	1.9	0.4	4.6	49.0	8.0	3.8
Belmopan	2 935	56.8	3.2	9.3	0.1	0.5	22.9	3.9	3.3
San Ignacio	5 616	28.1	1.5	1.2	0.5	1.0	59.0	1.1	7.6
Rural	14 286	26.9	0.4	0.7	0.4	6.9	50.5	11.6	2.5
Corozal	22 902	16.9	2.9	2.3	0.3	13.8	58.4	1.7	3.7
Town	6 899	30.5	1.8	3.2	0.0	0.0	59.2	0.3	5.0
Rural	16 003	11.1	3.3	1.9	0.4	19.7	58.0	2.2	3.4
Orange Walk	22 870	11.3	0.2	2.3	0.2	6.8	64.5	13.5	1.1
Town	8 439	19.7	0.4	5.1	0.0	3.8	68.9	0.2	1.9
Rural	14 431	6.4	0.2	0.6	0.3	8.6	61.9	21.3	0.7
Stann Creek	14 181	32.9	2.0	45.6	0.2	5.2	10.5	0.5	3.0
Dangriga	6 661	21.6	1.4	70.0	0.0	0.3	1.8	0.4	4.5
Rural	7 520	43.0	2.7	23.7	0.4	9.7	18.3	0.5	1.7
Toledo	11 762	11.9	8.6	12.7	31.5	25.4	5.9	1.0	3.0
Punta Gorda	2 396	23.6	4.4	48.3	1.1	3.3	8.9	0.9	9.9
Rural	9 366	9.0	9.6	3.4	39.3	31.1	5.1	1.0	1.3
Total	145 353	39.7	2.1	7.6	2.7	6.8	33.1	4.2	3.7

Percentages may not add to 100 due to rounding error.
Source: Census, 1980.

the social structure. C.H. Grant, who did attempt to analyse the social structure, oversimplified it by distinguishing between the 'Creole and Mestizo complexes', the former including whites, Creoles and Garifuna, and the latter consisting of Spanish, Mestizo and Maya.[14] When so many Creoles and Garifuna share Catholicism with Mestizo and Maya, and when Creole-speaking people have different racial antecedents and belong to various religious denominations, the distinction between these so-called 'complexes' is too simple by far. Such attempts to classify and group together the various peoples of Belize by static racial and cultural attributes, which in fact are both changing and overlapping to a considerable degree, hinders our understanding of the dynamics of Belizean culture.

As most of the peoples of Belize, including the Creoles, Mestizos and Garifuna, are the result of social interaction and cultural synthesis, it is unreasonable to assume that these historical processes have ceased and that Belizean people are now fixed in unchanging ethnic groups and social identities as if they lived under glass cases in a museum. The process of creolization, for example, which created a new culture out of African and European roots in the eighteenth and nineteenth centuries,[15] has not ceased. The processes of national assimilation and cultural synthesis, which may well have accelerated in recent decades, continue to change social identities and redefine ethnic boundaries. Moreover, we should acknowledge the existence of 'multiculturalism', that is, the ability of people to practise or participate in more than one cultural tradition, and to share an overarching national identity with people of different ethnic identities.

Interaction between the various ethnic groups, which for a long time was inhibited by ethnic segmentation in the labour process and by the related settlement patterns, has increased in the last half century, with the expansion of national communications by road, radio and telephone, and with almost universal participation in educational institutions and in the democratic political system since the early 1950s. Such increasing interaction gives rise to more cross-fertilization of culture and the emergence of new syntheses, as well as stimulating cultural revitalization movements.

In sum, while it is clear that Belize will remain racially and culturally pluralist, we should not adopt a plural society model which makes these 'cleavages' hard and fast and underestimates the importance of economic factors and class interests. So far at least, politics and social conflicts in Belize have not become institutionalized on the basis of social pluralism, as M.G. Smith's model predicts.[16] Rather than race and ethnicity, the key issues that have dominated Belizean politics for nearly 40 years have been the prolonged process of constitutional decolonization that delayed independence until 1981 and the vicissitudes of a very dependent economy.

Two major changes have taken place in the economy since World War II. One has been the shift, previously mentioned, from forestry to agriculture as the basis of the economy, and the other has been the re-orientation of control from Britain to the United States, which has accelerated recently. The dominance of the mahogany and chicle trade was reflected in the monopoly position of the Belize Estate and Produce Company (BEC) which, since its formation in the nineteenth century, had been the chief landowner and business enterprise in Belize.[17] Until the 1960s, this company controlled about 400 000 ha of the 930 000 ha that were privately owned and the company always had a strong influence on the colonial administration. In the early 1950s, forest products constituted about three-quarters of the value of all exports, and the industry employed some 3000 workers out of a total labour force of about 20 000. Today, it employs less than 1000 people in a labour force of almost 50 000 people, and the value of lumber is only about 2 per cent of all exports.

In the 1950s the production of sugar and citrus on foreign-owned plantations quickly replaced forestry as the basis of the economy. The sugar industry, in particular, was a key element in the growth of the economy in the 1960s and 1970s. In 1964, a small factory in Corozal District that had been started in 1937 was bought and enlarged by Tate and Lyle, the British transnational giant. Known locally as the Belize Sugar Industries Ltd (BSI), this corporation opened a new factory at Tower Hill near Orange Walk Town in 1967. In 1972, after a long struggle between the corporation and the farmers and workers, BSI sold its plantations to Belizean farmers, while retaining its sugar factories.

By the early 1980s over 24 000 ha were in sugar cultivation and most of the 4000 farmers who grew cane were small producers, frequently with less than 2.5 ha, and often indebted for their trucks and tractors. When sugar prices were high, these farmers gave up subsistence farming to expand cane production, and so became dependent upon internationally determined prices and quotas. While their standard of living improved, their incomes were still limited by their delivery licences and often suffered from annual fluctuations.

The fall in the price of sugar since 1980 has resulted in a crisis in the sugar industry and in the lives of the thousands of Belizeans who have become so dependent on it. In 1981, sugar exports accounted for 63 per cent of total domestic exports, but the spot market price for sugar fell from US$0.30 per lb (66 cents per kg) in 1980 to US$0.07 per lb (16 cents per kg) in 1984. In 1985, BSI closed the Corozal factory and laid off 600 workers. In August 1985, Tate and Lyle signed an agreement that left it with only a 10 per cent shareholding, a management and marketing contract, and a licence to *import* between 5000 and 6000 tons of white sugar to satisfy the domestic market.[18]

While the sugar industry was in crisis, a promised expansion in the citrus industry appeared to offer an alternative base for the economy. The citrus industry, based chiefly on the production of orange and grapefruit concentrates in Stann Creek District, has, despite price fluctuations, become the second most valuable export crop of Belize, worth over 10 per cent of total domestic exports by value since 1982. The Cooperative Citrus Growers Association of Trinidad and Tobago with over 300 local farmers, most of whom farm under 1.5 ha, controls production, but the processor, Belize Foods Products, is a subsidiary of Nestlé, the Swiss transnational company. However, in 1985 a gigantic land sale seemed to put Belize on the brink of a massive expansion in citrus, under US control.

Between 1947 and 1982 the huge BEC estates changed hands several times and were reduced as some land was sold and some was passed to the government in lieu of taxes. BEC became part of the International Timber Company in the 1970s, by which time it had been reduced to about 353 000 ha. Bought by a US businessman in 1980, BEC was resold soon after to Barry M. Bowen, a wealthy Belizean who controlled an extensive commercial empire, including the Belize Brewing Co., several importing agencies, majority shares in the country's largest retail store, an aerial crop-dusting service, and the Coca Cola franchise. When Bowen was unable to service the loan he had taken from a Panamanian bank and the government ruled him liable for the debt in 1985, he put together an enormous land deal with Coca Cola.

In October 1985 it was announced that the BEC lands, consisting of 277 649 ha, would be divided and shared in a US$6 million deal by Bowen, Coca Cola, and two Texan millionaires, Paul Howell and Walter Mischer. The Belize government, whose strategy is to attract such foreign investment, was delighted with the plan, despite criticism that this deal, which amounted to the largest single foreign investment by a US company in a nation covered by the Caribbean Basin Initiative, smacked of neo-colonial plantation economics.[19]

The purchasers, contrary to the law, had not submitted a development plan to the government, and it soon became apparent that the grandiose scheme was in trouble. Coca Cola has announced that it will sell almost half of its shared 79 000 ha but will retain its 20 000 ha in sole ownership. Apparently the Overseas Private Investment Corporation, influenced by the Florida citrus growers' lobby, has not provided the political risk insurance that Coca Cola requires.[20] While Coca Cola's plans are stalled, Howell and Mischer are planning a 20 000 ha cattle ranch, and Bowen is contemplating a 280 ha cocoa plantation and a 200 ha ranch. The results of the 'land deal of the century', as it has been called, are substantially less than the initial euphoria led people to believe, but, while the original plans have been scaled down, the experience does indicate the degree to which the Belizean economy is moving away from its colonial dependence on Britain and is becoming increasingly linked to the US.

Since independence, and especially since the change of government in 1984,

> there has been a marked increase in the US presence: embassy officials, USAID and Peace Corps personnel seem to be everywhere – they are present in every ministry, in virtually every government program and in most private non-government organizations. An agreement between the government and USAID, signed on 28 February 1985, gives the US government wide sway over the Belize government's policies and programs including specifically its foreign trade regime, domestic price policy and practices, levels of public sector savings, agricultural policy, and the performance of two crucial government institutions.[21]

US trade with Belize has increased and the export-oriented economy is increasingly dependent on the US market. US corporations, many of them based in Texas, are rapidly dominating the leading sectors of growth in the Belize economy.[22] One consequence of this development is the marked orientation of the Belize business community towards the US. The Belizean élite is a typical 'comprador bourgeoisie', serving as the agents of foreign corporations upon which it is completely dependent. This economic dependency is reflected in the commercial élite's political and cultural orientation which is imitative of the values and lifestyle of the Chambers of Commerce of Houston and Miami. A strong Anglophile orientation persists in some sectors of Belizean society, but this is generally viewed as old fashioned and is ignored by the youth. Cultural and political orientation tends to follow the direction of trade.

The social pyramid of Belize remains broadly based, as the number of people who have risen from the peasant or working classes into the middle and élite ranks is still very small. The observation, made over a quarter of a century ago, that 'the potential ability of the population was scarcely tapped, as there was no real outlet for it',[23] remains essentially true, despite the expanding educational system and new employment opportunities for women. While 85–90 per cent of all children complete eight years of primary schooling, secondary schools remain a privilege for a minority and a mere 3.5 per cent of adults have professional or technical training. Those few who have educational and economic advantages are generally able to ensure that their children will, at the very least, maintain their social position so, in the absence of expanding economic opportunities, social mobility remains very limited. Without major economic developments that offer opportunities for Belizeans, as distinct from foreigners, it is unlikely that any really significant shifts will take place in the relations of class, race and ethnicity in the social structure.

Although the various racial and ethnic groups in Belize continue to be associated with certain economic activities, few economic issues are as racially or ethnically divisive as they are, say, in Guyana. This view is not contradicted by the fact that the colonial élite kept the various ethnic groups separated in economic organization as in other spheres, and it certainly promoted, among other racial and ethnic stereotypes, prejudicial ideas about the kinds of work for which different peoples were believed suited. Each group was thus encouraged to fear, despise and envy the other groups, to feel they were better or worse than others, and all were taught to look up to the white or light-skinned élite of landowners, merchants and colonial officials who controlled the society. But in this social pyramid there were few occasions for actual confrontation, so, although prejudices persist, there is no tradition of inter-racial violence in Belize. Cultural and racial differences constitute obstacles to the development of working-class unity in Belize as elsewhere, but the economic organization and work environment of Belize are also aspects of the *culture*, in the broadest sense, of all these ethnic groups. The obstacles and opportunities Belizeans face in the course of trying to develop their economy and improve their standard of living are part of an experience that can promote either unity or division, depending on the nature of the responses they make to these problems. Responses to the influx of Central Americans or to the increasing influence of the US could, for example, provoke greater rifts among the population or promote national unity. Much will depend upon the leadership of Belizean educators and politicians in the next decade.

LABOUR ORGANIZATION, POLITICAL PARTY FORMATION AND ELECTORAL POLITICS

The origins of party politics in Belize, as elsewhere in the West Indies, lie in the labour disturbances and the formation of trade unions in the 1930s and 1940s.[24] Labour agitation, beginning with demonstrations by Antonio Soberanis's Labourers' and Unemployed Association in 1934 and 1935, won several concessions on the industrial and political fronts. The legalization of trade unions and the removal of labour contracts from the jurisdiction of the criminal code ushered in a new era of industrial labour relations in the 1940s. Meanwhile, beginning with a return to the elective principle in the constitution of 1936, political and constitutional concessions were introduced piecemeal. The colonial administration, having passed laws in 1935 that gave police the power to ban processions, redefined sedition (Soberanis was detained under this law from November 1935 to February 1936), and gave the governor extra powers in an emergency such as a riot, felt confident enough to allow 5 of the 13 members of the Legislative Council to be elected, albeit on a highly restricted franchise. A combination of property or income and literacy qualifications confined the electorate to less than 2 per cent of the population. In 1945, for instance, 822 voters were registered in a population of over 63 000. The proportion of voters increased slightly in 1950, partly because the minimum age for women voters was reduced from 30 to 21 years and partly because the devaluation of the dollar effectively reduced the property and income qualifications. In any case, the governor retained reserve powers to ensure that the Colonial Office would have its way on major issues.

A nationalist party, the British Honduras Independent Labour Party, later called the People's Republican Party, was formed in 1940, and in the following year mass meetings were held throughout the colony, demanding adult suffrage and the right to elect the government. The nationalist leaders, Joseph Campbell, Gabriel Adderley and John Lahoodie, were imprisoned in 1941 and Soberanis, the labour leader, went to Panama in 1942 because he felt inhibited about expressing his nationalistic feelings during wartime conditions. The General Workers' Union (GWU), which originated in an organization started by Soberanis, expanded rapidly in the five years following its registration in 1943 to claim over 3000 members. Based in Belize Town, it had branches in the districts, even in remote mahogany and chicle camps, that helped to raise the political consciousness of the workers. The wretched conditions under which these people laboured and their families lived were translated, through protracted struggles with the Belize Estate and Produce Company and the colonial government, into a protest against colonialism itself.

Despite these significant developments, however, electoral politics was restricted by the narrow franchise in the 1940s, and the handful of proto-nationalists elected to the Legislative Council, whose goals included a 'Natives First' campaign, represented chiefly the urban merchants and professionals. The Belize Town Board (later City Council),[25] which was elected on a broader franchise, was an arena for some of these early nationalists but most candidates were from the educated middle classes. Most important among these were the alumni of St John's College, the élite Jesuit secondary school in Belize City, who, inspired by the papal encyclical, *Rerum Novarum*, formed a Christian Social Action Group (CSAG). When they ran as the 'Natives First Independent Group' in 1947 they won four seats and control of the City Council. They started a newspaper, the *Belize Billboard*, to present their critique of colonial policies and they participated in an 'Open Forum' of public meetings where they were joined by Soberanis after he returned to Belize in 1948. The Open Forum group sharply distinguished itself from the Legislative Councillors who expressed loyalty to the British Crown. Belize, far from slumbering as has been asserted,[26] was in a political ferment in the 1940s.

Among the chief issues that agitated Belizeans were universal suffrage and constitutional reform, the proposed West Indian Federation, import controls and immigration, the Guatemalan claim, and, not least, the widespread economic distress and unemployment that followed the return of almost 2000 labourers from abroad and the renewed depression in the mahogany and chicle industries. In October 1949, some 1166 people were registered as unemployed in Belize City and by March 1950, this had increased to 2415.[27] Though the CSAG was concerned about the plight of poor working people, they kept their distance from the more radical president of the GWU, Clifford Betson. Following a successful strike against the Belize Estate and Produce Company at the sawmill in Belize City, and other strikes at the Corozal sugar factory, and on the Belize waterfront in 1947, Betson called for the introduction of socialism in Belize in his New Year's message in 1948. The *Billboard* editors, Leigh Richardson and Philip Goldson, a former teacher and a former civil servant respectively, dissociated themselves from what they called this 'dangerous tendency'. Socialism, they claimed, was the enemy of 'individual progress and national unity'.[28] These middle-class members of the CSAG were anti-socialist as well as anti-colonial, and pro-free-enterprise capitalism as well as pro-American.

Among these early politicians was George Cadle Price, later to be the leader of the nationalist movement, of Belize's chief political party, and the country's first prime minister. Middle class by family background and education, Price first considered a career in the Catholic Church. After graduating from St John's College, he studied with the Jesuits in the United States in the 1930s. When he returned to Belize in 1942, instead of entering the priesthood he became secretary to Robert Turton, a white Creole chicle millionaire who was an elected member of the Legislative Council between 1936 and 1948. Price failed to get elected to the Belize Town Board in 1943, but was successful in 1947, along with other St John's alumni, John Smith, Herbert Fuller and Karl Wade. By 1949, 'all the principal actors in the nationalist drama that was about to unfold were in place',[29] and the devaluation of the British Honduras dollar on 31 December precipitated modern Belizean politics.

The several strands of Belizean politics came together in 1950 because the devaluation provided an opportunity for the various labour and nationalist forces to rally around a clear issue. First, devaluation was effected by the governor, using his reserve powers, in defiance of the Legislative Council and after repeated assurances by the British government, since the devaluation of sterling the previous September, that the Belize dollar would not be devalued. This action, then, exposed the limits of the existing representative system and the extent of the colonial government's power over Belize. Their inferior colonial status was an aggravating insult to the educated middle classes who wanted a more representative and responsible form of government. Second, the devaluation led to an immediate and easily calculable fall in the purchasing power of the people, while it protected the interests of big transnationals like the

Belize Estate and Produce Company, whose trade with the sterling area would be at a disadvantage without devaluation. The working people of Belize, subjected already to widespread unemployment and poverty, were the chief sufferers when devaluation resulted in a rise in the price of imported US goods, including food.[30] Devaluation, therefore, provided a clear issue to unite labour and the middle classes in nationalist opposition to the governor and the colonial administration. On the very night that devaluation was declared, the People's Committee was formed and the independence movement was born. Out of this event and this movement emerged Belizean party politics.[31]

Between 1950 and 1954, the People's United Party, formed upon the dissolution of the People's Committee on 29 September 1950, consolidated its organization, established its popular base, and articulated its primary demands. In this initial phase the strong support of the GWU, whose president, Clifford Betson, was one of the original members of the People's Committee, was crucial. Before the end of January 1950, the People's Committee and the GWU were holding joint public meetings, discussing issues ranging from devaluation to labour legislation, and from federation to constitutional reform. Without the support of the GWU, the only extant mass organization of the working people of Belize, the early success of the Committee, and subsequently of the PUP, would have been impossible.

Yet on 28 April 1950, the middle-class members of the CSAG took over the leadership of the union. Nicholas Pollard became president, John Smith vice-president, and Price and Goldson members of the Executive Council. Betson fought this takeover but, after seven years as a militant, pioneering union chief, he was given the dubious honorific title of 'Patriarch of the Union'. The provisional leaders of the PUP named in October 1950 were Smith as party leader, Richardson as chairman, Price as secretary, and Goldson as assistant secretary. Six months later, at the GWU's annual convention, the two organizations became virtually identical as Pollard was re-elected president, Price vice-president, and Goldson and Richardson became, respectively, assistant secretary and corresponding secretary. The political leaders took control of the union to use its strength, but the union movement declined in the 1950s as it became increasingly dependent upon the politicians. Rivalries and splits between the politicians resulted in a badly divided and weakened labour movement, with the result that constitutional rather than labour issues predominated in Belizean politics.

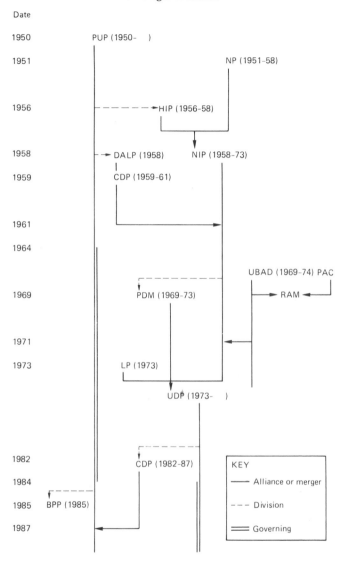

Figure 3.2 Party political genealogy of Belize, 1950–87. BPP, Belize Popular Party; CDP, Christian Democrats Party; DALP, Democratic Agricultural Labour Party; HIP, Honduran Independence Party; LP, Liberal Party; NIP, National Independence Party; NP, National Party; PAC, People's Action Committee; PDM, People's Development Movement; PUP, People's United Party; RAM, Revolitical Action Movement; UBAD, United Black Association for Development; UDP, United Democratic Party.

In November 1950, five of the PUP's six candidates were elected to the Belize City Council. During the subsequent months the PUP concentrated on agitating for constitutional reforms, including universal adult suffrage without a literacy test, an all-elected Legislative Council, an Executive Council chosen by the leader of the majority party in the legislature, the introduction of the ministerial system, and the abolition of the governor's reserve powers. In short, the demand was for the Westminster-style of representative and responsible government that was being introduced elsewhere in the West Indies. The colonial government, however, alarmed by the growing support for the PUP and its militant anti-colonial rhetoric, retaliated by attacking two of the party's chief public platforms. The governor dissolved the Belize City Council in July 1951 on the pretence that it had shown disloyalty by refusing to hang a picture of the King, and in October the publishers and owners of the *Billboard*, including Richardson and Goldson, were charged with sedition. When these two PUP leaders were convicted and sentenced to 12 months' imprisonment with hard labour and two more years on good behaviour, John Smith resigned from the leadership and membership of the PUP. The removal of three of the party's four chief leaders was a blow to the party, but it left George Price in a powerful position. A pragmatic and skilled politician, Price consolidated his position and has led the PUP ever since. In 1952, Price comfortably topped the polls in the Belize City Council elections, gaining almost twice as many votes as Smith, who stood as an independent. By the end of the year, with Price as the secretary and effective leader of the PUP and president of the GWU, these organizations were associated on a national level with the people's cause and were a force with which the colonial government had to reckon.

Universal adult suffrage was achieved a decade after Jamaica, and was linked in Belize, as elsewhere, to the establishment of an elected majority in the legislature. The period between early 1953 and April 1954 has been described as a 'prolonged election campaign' in which 'the colonial government openly took sides in favour of the "responsible" leaders of the so-called National Party against the PUP'.[32] The National Party (NP), led by Herbert Fuller, consisted of members of the old Legislative Council. It was characterized by a fanatical loyalty to the British monarchy and was supported largely by the Anglophile Creole élite. The PUP, they charged, practised racial and religious prejudice, was communist and pro-Guatemala. The PUP leadership was young and identified strongly with labour and Catholics, but it

O. Nigel Bolland

Table 3.5 Percentages of total votes for major parties in general elections, 1954–84

Party	1954	1957	1961	1965	1969	1974	1979	1984
People's United Party	66.3	59.1	63.4	57.8	57.6	51.3	51.8	43.3
National Party	22.9	12.5						
Honduran Independence Party		17.7						
National Independence Party			23.2	39.4	39.8ᵃ			
Christian Democratic Party		11.4						1.4
United Democratic Party						38.1	46.8	53.3

ᵃ Includes votes for People's Development Movement.
Source: Government Gazettes, Belize City.

was certainly not communist. The PUP received limited support from Guatemala in these early days, when the reformist Arbenz government was still in power, but clearly the leaders perceived Belize as belonging to neither Britain nor Guatemala. In fact, several of them were evidently pro-American, and the US flag and 'God Bless America' were often prominent at PUP rallies. Attempts by the governor and the NP to discredit the PUP on the issue of its contacts with Guatemala failed. When the voters went to the first poll based on universal adult suffrage on 28 April 1954, the issue was really colonialism: a vote for the PUP was a vote in favour of self-government. On that historic day 14 274 people, or almost 70 per cent of the electorate, voted. The PUP gained 66.3 per cent of the vote and eight of the nine elected seats in the new Legislative Assembly (Table 3.5). In Belize North, Price won 75 per cent of the vote against Smith, the former PUP leader, and in Belize South, Goldson won 53 per cent of the vote against Fuller, the NP leader.

For 30 years, from 1954 until 1984, the PUP won every general election and most local elections, against several opposition parties. The PUP, unlike the NP, had from its inception sought support from the majority of the people, from all racial and ethnic groups. Its leaders recognized very early that their only hope of challenging the colonial government lay in mobilizing working people throughout Belize, not relying, as did the NP, on the Anglophile professional and middle classes and the support of the colonial administration. Much of the PUP's activity initially took place in Belize City where a third of the population lived and there was a tradition of politics, and the GWU carried the message into the districts. The party had no clear economic philosophy and carefully dissociated itself from communism; perhaps because both Jagan's government in British Guiana and Arbenz's in Guatemala had recently been overthrown by Britain and the US, respectively, on the grounds that they were introducing communism. What economic goals it had were expressed in terms of 'distributive justice', to be achieved by 'cooperativism' and 'wise capitalism', the last concept being undefined.[33] This philosophy was faithful to that of the CSAG, from which the main PUP leaders emerged, and which itself had close ties with the Jesuit-sponsored credit union movement.

The principal goal of the PUP for 30 years was to bring about the constitutional changes necessary for independence and to achieve these through 'national unity'. The need to develop nationalist sentiment in a wide variety of classes and ethnic groups, in rural and urban Belize, led to the creation of a typical populist party, whose policies and strategies were defined by a leadership élite with little real participation from the membership. These characteristics have had three persistent, long-term consequences: (1) a tendency to factionalism, as fragile alliances between leaders with different goals and values, or simply with competing ambitions, fragment, re-form, and re-divide; (2) a strong emphasis on patronage and other particularistic connections, needed to win electoral support; and (3) the tendency for the leadership to become older and increasingly out of touch with the majority. In a small country like Belize, politics inevitably is highly personalized, and factional struggles within or between parties are often characterized by strong personal loyalties and attacks. Hence, issues are often obscured by both hero worship and mudslinging, conditions that are exacerbated by the fact that all the newspapers are vehicles for one or another political party or faction.

Personal vilification characterized the serious split in the PUP in 1956 and the general election the following year. When Pollard was expelled from the secretaryship of the GWU for alleged peculation, he and Price formed a new trade union, the Christian Democratic Union, and retained control of the PUP. Richardson and Goldson, while retaining control of the GWU, broke away from the PUP and formed the Honduran Independence Party (HIP). Though in 1957 the PUP's share of the vote fell to 59 per cent, Price's victory over his former political associates was impressive. Price himself obtained 70 per cent of the vote in his constituency, and all the opposition leaders

– Goldson and Richardson of the HIP and Fuller of the NP – were defeated. The PUP won all nine elected seats and Price assumed leadership in the Legislative Assembly. During the next year, however, further crises shook the colony.

While engaged in constitutional talks in London at the end of 1957, Price visited a Guatemalan minister to discuss the future of Belize. The British secretary of state denounced Price and broke off the negotiations. When Price was removed from the Executive Council on the grounds that his actions were inconsistent with his councillor's oath of loyalty to the Crown, a political crisis resulted. The governor, in a broadcast, accused Price of preparing to sell Belize to Guatemala. Two PUP assemblymen defected and, early in 1958, Pollard broke with Price and was expelled from the party. The two opposition parties amalgamated to form the National Independence Party (NIP) and, soon after, Pollard created the Christian Democratic Party (CDP). The attacks by the British government and governor on Price were designed to discredit him, but instead they made him the focus of events, and the attacks of his Belizean opponents gave the opposition the appearance of being largely negative. The anti-Price campaign, far from isolating and weakening him, left him in undisputed control of the PUP and able to concentrate his considerable skills on the anti-colonial issue. In November 1958 the PUP won 29 of 33 seats in seven municipal elections and Price became mayor of Belize City.

The colonial administration's preoccupation with Price backfired. By expelling him from the Executive Council they had not dislodged him from the centre of politics. The Legislative Assembly, with two official members, three nominated unofficial members, and two PUP defectors, was a largely unrepresentative body, while Price retained popular support. Nevertheless, at about this time, Price himself came to accept the British constitutional process of decolonization.

For the crucial constitutional conference in London in 1960, a prominent Belizean lawyer, Harrison Courtenay, brought the PUP and NIP together in a united front. The constitutional advances achieved through this conference ushered in a new phase in Belizean politics, one less volatile and more distinctly structured along two-party lines, with each party contending for the 18 elected seats in the legislature. In the 1960s, the PUP and George Price consolidated their power. The PUP's success in three consecutive general elections was overwhelming: it won all 18 seats in 1961, 16 in 1965, and 17 in 1969. With the collapse of the West Indies Federation, in which

Belize had never participated, and the British government's determination to hasten its withdrawal from the region, the PUP's political strength and Price's aspirations toward national independence had become respectable. The introduction of the ministerial system of government and Price's elevation to the status of first minister in 1961 and premier in 1964 helped consolidate the PUP's supremacy and simultaneously reduced the status of the opposition. The successive defeats of the NIP resulted in a split in 1969, when Dean Lindo formed the People's Development Movement (PDM). Price promptly called a general election, and the two opposition parties hastily entered an alliance. The effort was in vain, and Goldson, leader of the NIP, was the sole candidate to beat the PUP.

In the late 1960s a new generation appeared on the political scene: young people who could not remember Belize before the PUP, who saw Price and his ministers as an ageing establishment, and who were impatient for social change and independence. Young men like Evan Hyde, educated in the United States, and Said Musa and Assad Shoman, who became lawyers in Britain, were influenced by the political currents around black power and the mobilization against the Vietnam War. For these young idealists, radicalism meant something different from the conceptions of Price and his colleagues 20 years earlier, though both groups were inspired by social justice and both, ironically, were unfairly labelled racists and communists.

Whereas the PUP government pursued a policy of development that depended heavily on foreign investment, the younger generation argued that such policies would lead to increasing dependency and neo-colonialism in a region dominated by the United States. The young radicals were also dissatisfied with the organizaton of the PUP, whose élite leadership controlled policy tightly. Eschewing the PUP and its loyal opposition alike, Hyde, Musa, Shoman, and others started an extra-parliamentary opposition, using public meetings, demonstrations and mimeographed broadsheets to mobilize people in activities ranging from breakfast programmes for poor children to education about the consequences of cultural and economic imperialism. For a while in 1969, Hyde's United Black Association for Development (UBAD) and Shoman and Musa's People's Action Committee (PAC) combined in a united front. Although they succeeded in showing that discontent was considerable in Belize, and a latent force among the youth and poor, these young radicals failed to organize a social movement and their efforts soon diverged. Hyde stuck to journalism with his newspaper *Amandala* and became associated with the opposition parties in the 1970s, whereas Musa and Shoman joined the PUP where they constituted its radical wing.

In the 1970s, the PUP lost some of its popular support, though it continued to win the national elections. In part, this was a consequence of the more united opposition that existed since the NIP, the PDM, and the small Liberal Party merged to form the United Democratic Party (UDP) in September 1973. In the 1974 general election, the PUP's support dropped to 51.3 per cent, its lowest ever, while the new party received 38 per cent and won six of the 18 seats. The UDP received most of its support in the south, in Dangriga and Toledo District, but it also obtained 48.8 per cent of the vote in Belize City to the PUP's 50.2 per cent. While the PUP seemed able to co-opt some of its former critics and to remain a broadly based party under the consistent leadership of George Price, the UDP had several leaders in its first decade. Dean Lindo, the lawyer who replaced Philip Goldson in 1974, was himself replaced after he lost his seat to Said Musa in the general election of November 1979. The new leader, Dr Theodore Aranda, a Garifuna, was challenged by the more traditional middle-class Creole leaders of Belize City, who succeeded in replacing him in 1983 with Manuel Esquivel, a physics teacher and former mayor of Belize City who had been a leader of the Liberal Party. The disgruntled Aranda, representative of Dangriga, then formed a new Christian Democratic Party (CDP).

The PUP won the 1979 election with 51.8 per cent of the vote to the UDP's 46.8 per cent, but it was losing support, especially among young people. The UDP appeared new and dynamic in comparison with many of the old, lackluster leaders of the PUP. The PUP clearly had difficulty attracting new talent and its leadership was aging. Though Belize achieved independence on 21 September 1981, the economic crisis of the early 1980s eroded PUP support, even where it had been traditionally strong in the rural areas. Moreover, the continued presence of British military forces in Belize, made necessary by Guatemala's persistent claims, was a painful reminder of the new nation's dependence. (A Belize/Guatemala Joint Commission was established in May 1988, but, given the volatility of Guatemalan politics and the intransigence of its military, it is unlikely that Guatemala will formally recognize Belizean independence in the near future.)

Following a UDP landslide in the Belize City Council elections in December 1983, in which the UDP won all nine seats by a massive majority, Price shuffled his cabinet. Though the situation demanded major changes, Price prevaricated and continued to rely on his loyalists. The PUP was, in fact, deeply divided, and, once independence was achieved, there was little to hold the old populist coalition together. Louis Sylvestre, the long-standing chairman of the party, led the Anti-Communist Society and joined the UDP in attacking Shoman and Musa, his cabinet colleagues, as agents of Cuba and the Soviet Union. In return, he and his wealthy associates were accused of corruption and incompetence. When the PUP's 'left wing' challenged Sylvestre's chairmanship at a national convention in 1983, they lost in circumstances that resulted in many of the younger party militants becoming disillusioned.

According to the Independence Constitution, each division must have between 2000 and 3000 electors and the number of representatives was increased from 18 to 28. In the first election under this constitution, on 14 December 1984, 75 per cent of the electorate voted, giving 53.3 per cent of their votes to the UDP and 43.3 per cent to the PUP – a crushing defeat for the latter, which retained only six members in the House of Representatives. Most important for the PUP's future, perhaps, was the defeat of Price himself by 570 votes to 876. This was followed by some rapid changes in the PUP's leadership. On the right wing, Sylvestre and Frederick Hunter resigned and formed the Belize Popular Party in June 1985, while their associate, Elijio Briceno, served three years in a US jail for drug trafficking. On the left, Musa was elected party chairman in 1986, but Shoman left the PUP to engage in independent political education. In 1987, Aranda completed his disaffection from the UDP when he merged his small CDP with the PUP. The official leader of the opposition in the House and a deputy leader of the PUP since 1986 is Florencio Marin, the powerful head of the northern caucus, but Price remains the party leader.

Manuel Esquivel's stature as leader of the UDP has been enhanced since he became prime minister. The usual advantages of electoral success and access to the resources of patronage have helped Esquivel, and he dramatically asserted his authority as party leader in a cabinet shuffle in June 1986, after only 18 months in office. In doing so, 'he appeared to discipline those ministers who were attracting most public criticism and at the same time severely cut down the responsibility of Dean Lindo, the only person who might still be thinking of making a bid for the leadership'.[34] Soon after the PUP made significant gains in the seven Town Board elections on 16 March 1988, winning 49 per cent of the vote and 29 of the 49 seats,

Lindo stepped down from the chairmanship of the UDP. The two parties appear quite evenly matched on the eve of a general election in 1989, but the endemic faction-fighting in both parties makes the result highly unpredictable.

What has emerged in almost 40 years of party politics in Belize is a stable two-party democratic system based on the Westminster model. The peaceful change of government in 1984, after three decades of PUP dominance, shows that Belizeans are committed to democratic and orderly procedures. Yet it is also striking how few changes in power have been taken place in Belize. In part, this may be explicable by the dominance of the issue of decolonization: hence, the PUP and its leader, so closely identified with that issue, lost much of their appeal once independence was achieved. In part, also, it may be explained in terms of generations, with the 'younger' UDP appealing more successfully to a youthful electorate than the 'ageing' PUP. Yet another factor is surely the dynamics of the politics of patronage in a small, new nation in which the development of patronage relations is closely tied to the expanding role of the state. The 'spoils' of a new system of self-government – such as the placing of schools, clinics, roads and community centres, and the allocation of jobs and contracts – enables the party leaders, as ministers, to consolidate their position.

However, this is achieved at a cost in the long run because it tends to ossify the party leadership and because the politicians are always tempted to promise more than they can deliver. In a highly dependent economy, such as that of Belize, the politicians are limited in their means of patronage and this becomes an obstacle to any party's continuing rule. Moreover, the tendency of ministers to use their position to enrich themselves, though often expected of them, leads eventually to resentment, charges of corruption, and general political discontent. This is not to say that such elements are not present in larger or older political systems, but they seem especially pertinent in situations where self-government is being established and where the distance between the electorate and the elected is extremely short. The small scale of the society, and especially of the constituencies, enables voters to reach their representatives – and, often, ministers of government – directly. The result is a highly personalized, particularistic form of politics, characterized by issues of loyalty and by the phenomenon of frequent schisms in which political leaders try to keep their faithful followers together.

While such particularistic politics is often associated with racial and ethnic identification, this aspect has not come to dominate Belizean politics as it has elsewhere. Ethnic identity affects political allegiances in Belize, but it rarely seems to determine them and both the major parties continue to try to draw their support from the various ethnic groups. Certainly, in recent years, the rapid and total shift in party control of the Belize City Council from PUP to UDP, and the 180-degree turn of the Garifuna leader, Aranda, from the UDP to the PUP, cannot be explained simply in terms of ethnic politics. Though the possibility of a more ethnically based politics persists, especially with the salience of the 'aliens' issue and the proliferation of ethnic associations, questions of economic development and material welfare remain paramount.

In fact, with regard to three of the major questions confronting the new nation of Belize, the two political parties have more in common than not. First, as has been said, both parties accept the Westminster-style political system that Belize has inherited and, despite the history of schisms in Belizean politics, there appears to be little room for a third party. Second, both parties accept the need to try to draw support from all regions and ethnic groups and, in particular, curb the tendency for Belize City to dominate national politics. The latter has been a feature of Belizean politics for half a century, as a result of the concentration of population, and especially of the more educated and wealthier middle classes in Belize City and of the more liberal franchise there in the 1930s and 1940s. Today, 10 of the 28 representatives are elected from Belize City, and the leadership of both parties continues to be dominated by Belize City persons. Nevertheless, Esquivel has struck the same balance in his cabinet as Price had in his last cabinet, namely seven Belize City and four district persons.[35]

Third, both parties perceive that foreign capital investment, largely from the United States, is the prerequisite for economic growth and material well-being. Though elements in the PUP favoured curbs on the control and exploitation of the nation's resources by foreign capital, and were anxious about the increasing degree of US influence, Price's government adhered to an economic development strategy that was scarcely distinguishable from the overtly 'free enterprise' commitment of the UDP. Both parties have sought the support of the business community of Belize and the success with which the UDP won some of the merchants to their camp in 1984 contributed to its electoral victory. Since the PUP became alienated from the labour movement, and even contributed to the destruction of the most influential trade union in 1981, both parties

have effectively conspired to avoid the development of class consciousness in Belize. Whether or not people are coming to see the
two parties as being ideologically similar, it is probably true that 'the
two parties will continue their traditional existence as multi-class
parties with the effect of maintaining the status quo and offering the
people no real alternative path of development'.[36]

CONCLUSION

Around 1950, it appeared possible that the nationalist movement in
Belize would be based on the labour movement, uniting most racial
and ethnic groups in a radical populist party that placed labour issues
high on the agenda. When the middle-class leaders of the PUP took
over the GWU, however, they used it for their own political purposes. Party schisms led to divisions in the labour movement until the
latter was eventually rendered impotent. Instead of the nationalist
movement being based upon an increasing class consciousness, therefore, it resulted in a two-party system in which both parties were led
by the middle classes and eschewed the conscientization of the
working class. These leaders have adopted a political system in which
they have authority but little real power. The continuing division of
the society along the 'essentially irrelevant lines' of party allegiance
prohibits the emergence of a working-class movement and promotes
an illusion of choice and mass participation while maintaining the
status quo.[37]

POSTSCRIPT

In a general election on 4 September 1989, the PUP won by the
narrowest margin ever, taking 15 seats to the UDP's 13. These results
defy analysis in terms of simple ethnic politics, nor do they reveal any
sharp regional or rural/urban differences. While eight of the PUP
representatives were elected in the north and west, and seven of the
UDP representatives were elected in Belize District, six of them in
the city, the share of votes received by each party was close almost
everywhere (see Table 3.6). The biggest margins of victory were for
Dean Barrow of the UDP, the very capable former foreign minister,
who received 64 per cent of the vote in his Belize City constituency,
and Glenn Godfrey, the new PUP attorney general, who received

Table 3.6   Belize Election Results, 4 September 1989

District	PUP		UDP		Percentage of Registered voters who voted
	Percentage of votes	Candidates elected	Percentage of votes	Candidates elected	
Belize	49.9	5	48.3	7	61.8
Corozal	50.7	3	48.2	1	83.7
Orange Walk	48.5	2	50.1	2	85.4
Cayo	51.4	3	46.3	1	77.2
Stann Creek	51.2	1	47.1	1	71.3
Toledo	49.3	1	49.8	1	75.3
Total	50.1	15	48.3	13	72.5

Source: Official Election Results, in *The Belize Times* (10 September 1989). Percentages do not add up to 100 because of spoilt and rejected ballots, and rounding.

almost 65 per cent in Belize Rural South, a constituency that includes San Pedro Ambergris Caye. The difference in the parties' strength between Belize City and the districts was generally quite small, however, the UDP achieving 50.2 per cent to the PUP's 48.1 per cent in the city, while the PUP won 50.9 per cent to the UDP's 47.6 per cent in the districts.

The most striking difference between Belize City and the districts was in the voter turnout; just over 60 per cent of the registered voters in Belize City voted, compared to an average of over 78 per cent in the districts. This suggests a growing cynicism in the city where, despite a new drainage system and expanded construction activity, unemployment remains high. In the whole country, the percentage of registered voters who voted was down slightly, from 75 per cent in 1984 to 73 per cent in 1989, but this may be because more of the 82 556 electors (compared with 64 447 in 1984) could not vote because of emigration.

The most powerful members of the new PUP cabinet are also the most experienced: George Price, the prime minister, is also minister of finance, home affairs and defence; Florencio Marin, the deputy prime minister, is minister of industry and natural resources; and Said Musa is minister of foreign affairs, economic development and education. There is unlikely to be any major change in orientation or policy from the last PUP government.

108   *O. Nigel Bolland*

ACKNOWLEDGEMENT

I wish to thank Westview Press for permission to use material from my book, *Belize: A New Nation in Central America* (Boulder, 1986).

NOTES

1. Belize was known as British Honduras from the mid-nineteenth century until 1973 and, before that, as the Belize Settlement or the Settlement in the Bay of Honduras. To avoid confusion, Belize is used throughout this article to refer to the territory that has been an independent nation since 1981. For a recent historical and contemporary survey see my *Belize: A New Nation in Central America* (Boulder: Westview Press, 1986).
2. Sidney W. Mintz, 'The Caribbean as a Socio-cultural Area', *Journal of World History*, Vol. 9, No. 4 (1966), pp.912–37.
3. Said Musa, when he was the attorney general and minister of education and sports, wrote on the eve of independence, 'Our country Belize is strategically located to play a pivotal role between the countries of the Caribbean and the countries of Central America'; *The New Belize*, Vol. XI, No. 7 (July, 1981), p.9.
4. E.G. Squier, *The States of Central America* (New York: Harper and Brothers, 1858), p.588.
5. O. Nigel Bolland, 'The Labour Movement and the Genesis of Modern Politics in Belize', in Malcolm Cross and Gad Heuman (eds), *Labour in the Caribbean* (London: Macmillan, 1988).
6. In a paper presented at the First Annual Studies on Belize Conference, 25–26 May 1987, Harriot W. Topsey, the Commissioner of Archaeology, referred to 'an escalating ethnic war' in Belize: 'The Ethnic War in Belize', in *Belize: Ethnicity and Development* (Belize City: SPEAR, 1987), p.1.
7. See 'Race, Ethnicity and National Integration in Belize', in O. Nigel Bolland, *Colonialism and Resistance in Belize: Essays in Historical Sociology* (Kingston: Institute of Social and Economic Research, 1988).
8. See West Indian Census 1946, part E (Belize, 1948).
9. Belize 1980 Population Census, Bulletin 1 (Belmopan: Central Planning Unit, 1982).
10. The census refers to Creole as 'English', an indication that it is still not recognized as a distinct language.
11. M.G. Smith, *The Plural Society in the British West Indies* (Berkeley: University of California Press, 1965), p.310.
12. *Ibid.*, p.310.
13. M.G. Smith, *Culture, Race and Class in the Commonwealth Caribbean* (Mona, Kingston: University of the West Indies, 1984), p.35.
14. C.H. Grant, *The Making of Modern Belize: Politics, Society and British*

Colonialism in Central America (Cambridge: Cambridge University Press, 1976), p.8.
15. O. Nigel Bolland, 'African Continuities and Creole Culture in Belize Town in the Nineteenth Century', in Charles V. Carnegie (ed.), *Afro-Caribbean Villages in Historical Perspective* (Kingston: Afro-Caribbean Institute of Jamaica, 1987).
16. See Bolland, 'Race, Ethnicity', *op. cit.*
17. O. Nigel Bolland and Assad Shoman, *Land in Belize, 1765–1871* (Kingston: Institute of Social and Economic Research, 1977), pp.77–83, 102–109.
18. *Belize Briefing* (October 1985).
19. Trevor Petch, 'Dependency, Land and Oranges in Belize', *Third World Quarterly*, Vol. 8, No. 3 (1986), pp.1002–19. Attention has also been drawn to the fact that Malcolm Barnaby, who was US ambassador to Belize during the negotiations, was hired in 1986 as a consultant to Coca-Cola and the Howell–Mischer partnership.
20. *Belize Briefing* (October 1987).
21. Assad Shoman, *Party Politics in Belize, 1950–1986* (Belize: Cubola Productions, 1987), p.39.
22. Petch, *op. cit.*, p.1018.
23. D.A.G. Waddell, *British Honduras: A Historical and Contemporary Survey* (London: Oxford University Press, 1961), pp.77–8.
24. Bolland, 'The Labour Movement', *op. cit.*
25. Belize Town was redefined as Belize City in 1943.
26. Grant, *op. cit.*, p.61.
27. Bradley's report, 31 October 1949, CO 123/401/66985; Governor R.H. Garvey's report, 30 September 1950, CO 123/406/66985.
28. *Belize Billboard* (3 January 1948).
29. Shoman, *op. cit.*, p.21.
30. Reflecting the shift in Belize's chief trading partner, the Belize dollar has been tied to the US dollar since 1976 and is worth US$0.50.
31. Assad Shoman, 'The Birth of the Nationalist Movement in Belize, 1950–1954', *Journal of Belizean Affairs*, No. 2 (1973), pp.3–40.
32. *Ibid.*, p.22.
33. *Ibid.*, p.35, quoting article by Richardson and Goldson in Jamaica's *Daily Gleaner* (5 September 1952).
34. Shoman, *Party Politics*, *op. cit.*, p.82.
35. *Ibid.*, p.83.
36. *Ibid.*, p.59.
37. *Ibid.*, p.89.

4 Politics and Society in the South-Eastern Caribbean

Tony Thorndike

INTRODUCTION

What is noteworthy about the English-speaking islands of the south-eastern Caribbean is the extent of the popular consensus underlying the political culture of their small populations, the predictability of the responses of their peoples and governments to political events, whether internal or external, and, together with their historical partners elsewhere in the region, the distinctiveness of their political culture when compared with other regions of the Third World. They total ten in number, nine constituting the Commonwealth Leeward and Windward Islands, and Barbados, the largest in size and re-sources (Table 4.1). Seven are full members of the sub-regional group, the Organization of East Caribbean States (OECS) – Antigua and Barbuda, Dominica, Grenada, Montserrat, St Kitts–Nevis, St Lucia and St Vincent. All are independent except Montserrat, which shares British dependency status with the British Virgin Islands (BVI), the only associate member of the OECS, and little but prosperous Anguilla. They share a history and heritage, even though the French-based *patois* of Dominica and St Lucia is common to that of their French departmental neighbours, and have assimilated the political norms and values of the former colonial power – Britain – to a remarkable degree.

The character and content of the islands' political culture has been shaped by three major factors. The most important is the historical, followed by the economic, the consequence of economic dependency and varying degrees of economic underdevelopment, and finally the environmental, that of small size, limited resources and geo-political location. It is a political culture that is essentially inward-looking and insular, where the surrounding sea is a barrier rather than a highway. It is also conservative in tone and expression, and where there was

Table 4.1 Size, population and gross national product

	Size (km²)	Population (1986)	GNP ($million) (1986)
Anguilla	91	7 000	10
Antigua and Barbuda	440	80 300	180
Barbados	430	254 000	1339
British Virgin Islands	153	12 200	79
Dominica	751	83 000	111
Grenada	344	100 000	104
Montserrat	104	12 500	42
St Kitts–Nevis	269	46 000	77
St Lucia	616	130 000	194
St Vincent	388	110 000	98

Sources: Size and population: *The Latin America and Caribbean Review 1988* (Saffron Walden, Essex: World of Information Press); GNP: Caribbean Development Bank, *Annual Report 1987*.

once strong fidelity to the British Crown there has developed a growing identification with the United States, its values and interests. This shift was boosted by the US-led intervention in Grenada in October 1983 – in which most participated and all supported – and their consequent militarization by what is to them the colossus to the north. Noticeable by their absence are ethnic factors, such as those found in Trinidad, Guyana and Suriname with their large Indian populations, and racial tensions – at least, of the degree experienced in the United States Virgin Islands (USVI). Neither are class differences so pronounced as in, for instance, Jamaica, and so they command relatively little importance.

THE HISTORICAL LEGACY

All societies are products of their past and none more so than those of the south-eastern Caribbean. Virtually all their peoples are black and mulatto descendants of those displaced from their original African homelands by slavery and who experienced up to 300 years of colonial rule. Indigenous African cultures were all but lost in the brutal transportation process and in the slave markets and plantations that awaited the unwilling migrants. No wonder that their language and social organization became variants of English practice or that their political institutions became those of their British colonizers. With post-World War II constitutional decolonization came a firm belief in political pluralism institutionalized through parliamentary democracy, based firmly on the theory and practice of the Westminster model. This belief took root despite the very small European presence and the historical distortion of notions of democracy by white and largely uneducated sugar planters expressed in slavery and colonialism. Apart from the many North American and European tourists who arrive every year, the white presence is now small, ranging from 5 per cent of the population in Barbados to the meagre 0.2 per cent in St Kitts.[1]

As political modernization proceeded after the World War II, a phenomenon became apparent. The slave experience and prolonged colonialism had produced a deeply ingrained psychological dependency; political, social and legal assumptions derived from the European colonial experience were adopted virtually without question. George Beckford argued that this was the inevitable consequence of an hierarchical and authoritarian plantation system which bred inferiority.[2] But deference to – and a general distrust of – authority, was combined with a low level of political hopefulness amounting to cynicism. Yet paradoxically there was a widespread belief that a new government would change things for the better, as witnessed by the relatively high rate of government defeats through elections, often involving large swings in voter choice. Between 1966, when Barbados achieved independence, and mid-1988, there have been 49 general elections in the Leewards and Windwards and Barbados involving 21 changes of government (Table 4.2). The period also witnessed one armed insurrection and several attempted military *coups* which challenged the established political culture.

The armed insurrection was that mounted by the Marxist–Leninist New Jewel Movement (NJM) in Grenada on 19 March 1979 to initial popular acclaim, which led to the establishment of the People's Revolutionary Government (PRG). Under the PRG there were many positive achievements in health, welfare and education, but most of the gains were to be lost as the regime eventually collapsed in bitter argument over the direction of the revolution and the composition of the leadership, culminating with the killing of Maurice Bishop, the NJM leader and prime minister of the PRG, several ministers and some 60 civilians on 19 October 1983, by the People's Revolutionary Army (see Chapter 5). The deeply unloved Revolutionary Military Council was imposed, but it survived for only six days before US troops parachuted from the Grenadian sky on 25 October to

Table 4.2   Elections and government change, 1966–88

Anguilla[a]	**1971**, 1976, 1980, 1981, **1984**
Antigua and Barbuda	**1971**, **1976**, 1980, 1984
Barbados	1966, 1971, **1976**, 1981, **1986**
British Virgin Islands	**1967**, **1971**, 1976, **1979**, **1983**, **1987**
Dominica	1970, 1975, **1980**, 1985
Grenada[b]	**1967**, 1972, 1976, **1984**
Montserrat	**1970**, 1973, **1978**, 1984, 1988
St Kitts–Nevis[c]	1966, 1971, 1975, **1980**, 1984
St Lucia	1969, 1974, **1979**, **1982**, 1987, 1987
St Vincent	1967, **1972**, **1974**, 1979, **1984**

Dates in bold indicate general elections involving change of government.
[a] Anguilla separated from St Kitts–Nevis–Anguilla in 1969 but did not assume colonial status until 1980.
[b] No elections were held during the period of revolutionary government (1979–83).
[c] The 1966 election was as St Kitts–Nevis–Anguilla.

the obvious and clear relief of the beleaguered and traumatized people.[3]

Less dramatic were the series of crises in Dominica, arguably the poorest of the south-eastern Caribbean islands, between 1978 and 1981. They began with a number of repressive measures by the Dominica Labour Party government headed by Patrick John soon after independence, backed up by a newly established defence force. It was then revealed that John had contracted with mercenaries in 1979 to invade Barbados (and had in fact travelled to Barbados in disguise to await the invasion and a proclamation of himself as leader of both Dominica and Barbados), at the same time as conspiring with South African interests to lease up to a third of Dominica for ostensibly sinister purposes.[4] One by one his cabinet deserted him, and his fate was sealed when he ordered the defence force to attack protesting crowds outside the government building in the capital, Roseau.

John was replaced as prime minister, but almost immediately the worst hurricane in living memory struck. There were widespread allegations of corruption over the distribution of emergency aid, in general, and building materials, in particular. Compounding these allegations was evidence of proposals for yet another lease of a substantial part of the thickly forested island to a mysterious US corporation with alleged South African connections. The US government also expressed anger at the activities of a company operating in the United States engaged in selling Dominican passports at very high prices to rich refugees from world trouble spots, which were then used to obtain American visas. The resounding election victory of Eugenia Charles and her Dominica Freedom Party in 1980 was therefore welcomed by many inside and outside of the region, but the crisis did not end there. John was subsequently implicated in three armed attempts, involving mercenaries and elements of the defence force, to overthrow the government in 1981, the last involving fatalities.[5] John later received a long term of imprisonment, the defence-force leader was executed for murder, and the force as a whole was disbanded. Fortunately, the experience of these and other less dramatic crises in the region, served only to reinforce popular faith in political pluralism and parliamentary democracy.

POPULAR REPRESENTATION VERSUS PARTICIPATORY DEMOCRACY

The penchant for electoral change can be explained in part historically, at least at the working-class level: colonial government represented persistent repression long after slavery was abolished in 1834 and even after colonial welfare began to make an impact from 1945. Another reason is a genuine belief that politics *matter*. Electoral records confirm this, for none of the 49 elections shows a turnout of less than 53.6 per cent (Montserrat, 1966), while the highest was 95 per cent (Antigua, 1976). The average per island ranged from 61 per cent in Antigua and St Lucia to Grenada's 84 per cent. Most were at the upper end of this scale, as witness St Kitts–Nevis with 74 per cent, St Vincent with 75 per cent, and Dominica with 78 per cent, although there were often wide variations around these figures according to the particular circumstances surrounding each poll.[6]

Indeed, elections are critical to political legitimacy in the English-speaking Caribbean, a reality rashly denied by Grenada's PRG. To the NJM revolutionaries elections were merely between 'Tweedle-dum and Tweedledee parties' which used bribery to create 'rum and corned beef politics':

> [it] meant that you came to the people two weeks before an election having not at all come to them for the preceding five years. . . . You had what we call 'five seconds democracy' . . . you go into a polling booth and you vote, and for the five years you are ignored until two weeks before the next elections.[7]

Their solution was 'participatory democracy'. Bishop outlined the philosophy behind it in 1974, a full five years before he and the NJM came to power.

> Electoral politics represents one form of politics . . . another form you can call people's politics, whereby for example people can take the road, can take to street marches, advocate civil disobedience. . . . Our position . . . is that elections in the sense that we now know would be replaced. . . . We envisage a system which would have village assemblies and worker's assemblies. In other words, politics where you live and politics where you work.[8]

The participatory system that emerged in Grenada post-1979 was based on the seven parishes. Such was its initial appeal that it was expanded down to village level, each village zonal council reporting to the parish council, which channelled opinions to the national level via the NJM party branch. Occasionally, the councils sent delegates to join those from the mass organizations, such as the National Women's Movement, at a National Conference of Delegates called to debate a particular issue, normally the budget. A foreign supporter enthused, 'Parliament has moved out of town into the communities. . . . Political power has been taken out of the hands of a few privileged people and turned over to thousands of men, women and youth'.[9]

The reality was, however, quite different, for Leninist philosophy dictated strong party control. The fulcrum of power remained at all times with the Central Committee, and participatory democracy was far more useful as a medium to explain policy and to further political education through the study of Marxist literature in which Stalin's works played a prominent role. As for council resolutions, they were best described as generalized 'wish lists' of all that was desirable,[10] although they did not provide the leadership with an idea of local priorities and a limited indication of the popularity or otherwise of government policies. But criticism was limited due to the fear of preventive detention, the fate of over 200 deemed to be 'counter-revolutionaries' or 'anti-social trouble makers'. Not surprisingly, popular participation in the experiment waned considerably as time went on.

The NJM's participatory democracy did not live up to its promises, but there was, and remains, some substance in its criticism of the Westminster system. Although partisan politics in the south-eastern Caribbean is indulged in with undoubted enthusiasm, notwithstanding the prevailing cynicism about politics and politicians in general, the people do not enjoy democratic government, if by that is meant a correlation between votes cast and seats won, opportunities for popular participation in the decision-making process, and mechanisms permitting accountability of the elected to electors. The 'first-past-the-post' system has never been seriously questioned, although it has produced distortions and rarely reflects partisan preferences in the respective National Assemblies, often to a disturbing degree.[11] Rather, it has been effectively used to centralize power when there exists a splintered opposition, a tactic not unknown in Britain. Once elected, there is no provision for an Assembly member to be recalled, nor is there any bar on the length of office by the prime minister or premier in the case of the dependent territories. These were problems reformers in Grenada unsuccessfully tried to address in the aftermath of the collapse of the revolution.

There has not been a long process of political participation at the mass level which might help to explain the role that elections play in establishing political legitimacy. Although planter government and weak metropolitan influence was progressively replaced by Crown Colony rule and strong British control in the late nineteenth century, there was, thereafter, little opportunity for popular representation in British Caribbean administrations, generally, except for the very small but propertied middle-class sector, and even less for participation. The turning point was 1944 when universal franchise was granted to Jamaica, a concession that reached the south-eastern Caribbean in 1951. Thereafter participation in the political process was enthusiastic.

DEMOCRATIC SENTIMENTS AND PROCEDURES

The strong popular attachment to politics exists in spite of these paradoxes and problems because of deeply held beliefs in the premises and assumptions of the Westminster model. They evolved and developed as much outside the political system as within it, by participation in religious organizations, often of the revivalist and charismatic type, and, above all, in trade unions and the labour movement, generally. These bodies were pressure groups and friendly societies acting for and on behalf of their members. They had to be efficiently administered using established procedures, a task made easier by the efforts of the educational system which transmitted British values and produced at least functional literacy in English even for the common labourer.[12] The need for administration and a concern for legal niceties was reinforced by often restrictive legal practices: trade unions were not fully legalized until after 1940, following the recommendations of the Moyne Commission, established by the imperial government to investigate the causes of widespread labour disturbances in the British Caribbean between 1935 and 1939.

All this was in line with the credo of Crown Colony government, namely, administration based on legally backed rules and procedures, an influence that seeped down to the lowest levels of society. Middle-class professionals, labour leaders and priests ensured that the rights and duties of members and constitutions of community organizations were determined by and, for the most part, reflected what was considered right and proper. There was also the importance of government as employer to consider, from the provision of middle-class jobs in the secretariat to those of road repairers in the Public Works Department. To work was to absorb the mores and practices of government; the smaller the island the more pervasive the presence of government, and the less scope there was for private sector and subsistence farming as alternative avenues for employment.

It all added up to an ideology of proceduralist orthodoxy and conservatism. But it was not conservatism wedded to the status quo. On the contrary, if a government did not succeed in the quest for material and social improvement or if corruption exceeded what was generally tolerated, then it could expect defeat at the polls. Given this background, it is not surprising that the rules and conventions surrounding representative government as it evolved through successively liberal constitutions were embraced by the people at large. So much so, in fact, that the Westminster system was eventually regarded as an autochthonous form of government, its origins across the ocean being virtually forgotten. S.A. Smith's forecast that 'in developing countries, constitutional factors will seldom play a dominant role in the shaping of political history' and that authoritarianism and one-party regimes or military governments would become the norm[13] could not, and did not, apply to these islands, nor to their English-speaking neighbours elsewhere in the Caribbean, for constitutionalism *was* their political history.

This quest for orderliness was to an extent helped by the nature of the Westminster model itself, the vagueness of which permitted flexibility and variation. The model incorporates five assumptions, each less clear than the other. First is a cabinet, ensuring a strong executive but one also responsible to parliament. As this does not imply a system of checks and balances, it has permitted abuse by charismatic leaders in some of the islands, notably Sir Eric Gairy in pre-revolutionary Grenada. Second is the articulation of interest through competing parties; more particularly two parties in an adversorial framework with one as the loyal opposition. All except Antigua and Barbuda have opposition parties represented in parliament. That the Antiguan parliament does not – due to a highly fractured opposition – goes some way to explain a degree of popular unease that is not experienced in the other islands. Third is a non-partisan and corruption-free bureaucracy and military, although what constitutes 'partisan' and 'corruption' is, as in other societies, culturally and loosely determined. Fourth are freedoms of expression, press and assembly, backed up by the concept of the rule of law. In the context of the south-eastern Caribbean, this can be taken to mean that all citizens are subject to the law, all are to be made aware of their rights and duties and be given an opportunity to fulfil them and to have the guarantee of a fair trial. The rule of law also implicitly demands the primacy of constitutionalism and an independent judiciary over the power, especially discretionary power, exercised by the government of the day. Bound up with this is the fifth assumption, that gross inequality, at least in opportunity, is not conducive to the model's ideal working, though capitalism and the capitalist ethos is accepted with varying degrees of reservation.

In short, the whole rests upon vague and *ad hoc* but firmly liberal bourgeois presumptions and assumptions: no wonder the model has been and remains an easy target for authoritarians, whether of the left, right or the bureaucratic-military variety, as much in the south-eastern Caribbean as in other places where it has taken root. Unfortunately, and with the notable exception of the New Jewel Movement before it seized power in Grenada, critics of the Westminster model generally fail to spell out the shape and philosophy of their alternative political institutions and processes. It would be difficult to do so, given the extent of the legitimating importance of elections. The freedoms of expression, press and assembly are likewise cherished, and their denial, as during the revolutionary period in Grenada, would clearly create resentment.

POLITICAL PARTIES

Besides promoting civil rights, the Westminster system also encourages coalition of interests through political parties. This development was neither smooth nor consistent, but it did mean the demise of the independent candidate, once a common feature in the eastern Caribbean: 'as the instrument of party became more of an imperative in an age of self-government, the number of independent candidates declined (and) today the election of an independent . . . is virtually impossible.'[15] Only in the BVI's small nine-member chamber do they constitute a significant presence.

As in most other countries in the Commonwealth Caribbean, many of the new political parties sprang from the trade unions of the 1940s, using universal suffrage as their springboard. Charismatic leaders emerged able to appeal to the relatively unsophisticated masses, used to such leadership through their churches. Often using biblical texts, stressing deliverance, with which their audiences were all too familiar, such leaders included Vere Bird in Antigua, Robert Bradshaw in St Kitts, William Bramble in Montserrat, Ebenezer Joshua in St Vincent and Grantley Adams in Barbados. The unions put up their own candidates in the first general elections, after which they formed labour parties. Except in Barbados, the union leaders also headed their respective parties, and the two were to all intents and purposes indistinguishable.

These labour union-parties quickly assumed dominance as vehicles of working-class politicization and ensured the passage of a rash of pro-labour legislation. Confrontations with employers, especially the remnants of the plantocracy, became politically highly charged. But the union-parties did not see themselves as revolutionary. On the contrary, they regarded themselves as democratic-socialist, their ideology being 'labourism' or the improvement of labour within existing society. No socialist reorganization was envisaged: rather, strategies such as state capitalism and 'industrialisation by invitation' were promoted.[16] Anti-colonialism was limited to the promotion of self-government rather than independence, to ensure the proper representation of working-class interests as and when necessary. In terms of foreign orientation, they were without exception firmly in the Western camp, by conviction, without prompting from Britain.

There were some exceptions to this sequence of events. In Dominica, labour did not become an organized political force until the late 1950s, the Dominica Labour Party winning the 1961 election over the hitherto dominant Independents, though trade unionism began at the same time as in neighbouring islands. As for Grenada, both unionism and the Grenada United Labour Party emerged only in 1951, following the expulsion from Aruba of the activist Eric Gairy. He made up for the late start with his remarkable charisma and a firm determination to show what a 'poor black boy' could do. Only in the BVI did the old order prevail, partly because of the nearby US Virgin Islands and readily available job opportunities: indeed, the BVI were benignly described as 'the rural area for the more commercialised St Thomas'.[17] But that did not prevent a successful 'Freedom March' to Government House in 1949 to demand constitutional reform.

The electoral dominance of the union-parties lasted for some three decades and only one, the Antigua Labour Party (ALP) remained in power by 1988. One by one they became quasi-independent of the parent union, the last being the ALP in 1968, to broaden their electoral base: they commanded over 80 per cent of the vote in the 1950s, an average of 68 per cent in the 1960s and only 56 per cent in the 1970s.[18] New parties emerged, often as breakaways from the union-parties and seized power. They included the Democratic Labour Party (DLP) of Barbados, which won three successive terms (1961–76) and returned to power in 1986; the St Vincent Labour Party (SVLP), also with three terms from 1967 to 1984; the United Workers' Party of St Lucia, a five-time winner between 1964 and 1979 and again from 1982; the People's Action Movement of St Kitts–Nevis and the Dominica Freedom Party, both in power from 1980; and the Progressive Democratic Party (PDP) of Montserrat. With the exception of the DLP, these parties were generally more conservative than the union-parties. Two were themselves upstaged by third-generation parties, without a doubt right-of-centre. In Montserrat PDP rule lasted for two terms (1970–78), before it was swept aside by the People's Liberation Movement (PLM), a PDP breakaway. Significantly, John Osborne, the PLM leader, was a multi-millionaire, a far cry from the once exclusively working-class leadership. In St Vincent, the SVLP was comprehensively defeated by the New Democratic Party, which won state power in 1984. Only in Antigua has the original party successfully fought back: the ALP lost to the breakaway Progressive Labour Movement (PLM) in 1971, but was able to regain power by capitalizing upon deep public concern at the extent of corruption that was associated with PLM rule. The ALP had also become more conservative and a notably close ally of the United States.[19]

More radical parties, such as the Antigua Caribbean Liberation Movement (ACLM), the Workers' Party of Barbados, the Dominica Liberation Movement and the United People's Movement of St Vincent are, for the most part, tiny and have very limited electoral appeal. This is due not so much to the 'first-past-the-post' system that discriminates against third parties, as to the influence on them, to varying degrees, of Marxism–Leninism and black power philosophy. Marxism and black power had swept through the region in the late 1960s and gained a number of youthful adherents, but their philosophies did not accord with the essential conservatism of the island populations. The outstanding exception was the NJM. A Leninist cadre party since 1974, it was able to succeed only because of the excessive violence, intimidation and corruption of Gairy's rule. Dominating the People's Revolutionary Government, it proved to be authoritarian, particularly in the area of human rights, and its bloody denouement was hardly an advertisement for revolutionary socialism. Since then, only the ACLM appears to have any chance of success, following the dilution of its original black power orientation, but then only if an alliance can be forged with other opposition groups or a future breakaway from the omnipresent ALP.

ECONOMIC DEPENDENCY AND EXPECTATIONS

The political culture of the south-eastern Caribbean islands has also been shaped by the realities of their position in the international economy. History not only bequeathed the Westminster system; it also left small and very open economies in its wake, their production geared to metropolitan-sponsored and -protected external markets whether of sugar – their original rationale – bananas or cocoa, or tourism and offshore finance, services subject to considerable fluctuations and metropolitan legal whim, respectively. This high degree of structural dependency is reinforced by functional dependency, the reflection of goals and instruments of policy which in turn is heavily influenced by the values associated with the phenomenon of psychological dependency.

Most noticeable is the wilful neglect, in many of the islands, of food production. While the emphasis upon cash crops encouraged food imports during the slave era, subsequent demand spread beyond the monied classes, partly out of the disinclination after emancipation to work the land because of its association with servitude, but also because of a lack of political will. By the same token, economic demands have for long been high, the metropole being expected to succour and fulfil high materialist expectations associated with metropolitan life styles.

The geographic nearness of the United States is clearly an important factor in shaping material demands. The fist major impact of American consumerist values followed the arrival of high-spending United States troops, introduced to the south-eastern Caribbean through the 1940 Anglo-American destroyers-for-bases deal, to be followed by increasing numbers of North American tourists for whom the former US Air Force bases were the new international gateways to a tropical, albeit expensive, paradise. As the United States gradually replaced Britain as the dominant metropole, a process that climaxed with the US-led invasion of Grenada in 1983, it was expected to foot the region's bills. To many, nationalist sentiment seemed to stop short of island treasuries. 'The United States have adopted us and we are not going to allow them to let us go', declared a prominent Grenadian businessman in 1988, adding that 'we have to establish a mechanism of positive communication where we can sit with our adopted father and mother to get the necessary assistance'.[20] Returning Caribbean migrants with their tales of US material cornucopias were a further ingredient. Added to this, Westminster-style electoral politics positively encouraged competing politicians to promise improvements in standards of living.

As a result, the gulf between expectations and the abilities to realize them widened, and governments struggled to meet huge import bills. In 1986, the Leeward and Windward Islands had a combined trade deficit of US$396.8 million,[21] while that for Barbados alone amounted to US$316.5 million.[22] Although the small states of the south-eastern Caribbean were no different in this respect from their larger English-speaking neighbours, the New World's new states, the mismatch was all the greater, striking one observer as a 'wasteful and parasitic economic value system'.[23] In sum, the south-eastern Caribbean is in the Third World but mentally part of the first. A premier of Montserrat once bewailed, 'we live in a bicycle society with Cadillac tastes'.[24]

These very pressures made independence an attractive proposition. Whereas Barbados opted for sovereignty as an expression of nationhood, after it was clear that a planned federation of the south-eastern Caribbean islands would never materialize, the others agreed with Britain that they were too small to support independence, though what constituted 'viability' was never spelt out. All the remainder, except the BVI, were offered associated statehood status which, under the terms of the 1967 West Indies Act, limited British responsibilities to defence and foreign affairs. It was, in effect, a grant of internal autonomy, and one that could be changed in favour of independence only through a two-thirds majority vote in the local parliament and in a referendum. However, Britain granted itself the unilateral power to end the relationship. All accepted, bar Montserrat, which argued that by remaining a British dependency, Britain would be obliged to give economic support. So it proved, and although British aid to the six associated states continued, it was never considered enough. Worse, it became clear that all multilateral aid and most bilateral assistance was available only to fully independent states.

Grenada was the first to demand independence. Gairy insisted that 'independence will support Grenada, the people of Grenada do not have to support independence.'[24] He requested that Britain use its unilateral power of abrogation in Grenada's favour and found a sympathetic ear in London. The British government had wearied of the association experiment, as it retained responsibilities but was permitted virtually no legal power to fulfil them; at another level, London was held accountable to the world community for the behaviour of its associates over which it had little influence, let alone control.

In particular, it had been put into an impossible situation over the secession of Anguilla in 1969 from the tri-island associated state of St Kitts–Nevis–Anguilla. The Kittitian Premier Robert Bradshaw had demanded British assistance to quell the rebellion, although inter-island affairs within an administrative group were deemed to be an internal matter under the West Indies Act. Arguing that the rebels were supported by the Mafia and other undesirable elements – allegations that the rebels encouraged as they wanted the British to return – he was eventually successful. But once the British forces landed on Anguilla on 19 March 1969 not a trace of external involvement could be found. Rather, it was painfully clear that, almost to a person, the islanders wanted to return to colonial status. Aside from the deep antagonism against Bradshaw, the reason was ultimately economic: there was the promise of far more aid from Britain than ever might come from poor St Kitts. It was therefore decided by the

British government in May 1973, that independence would be conceded to *any* dependency on demand, subject to evidence of public support (normally through an election) and unresolved third-party territorial claims.[25]

Accordingly, independence came to Grenada in February 1974 but in an atmosphere of violence, intimidation and strikes. The opposition to independence stemmed not so much from those wanting to retain the imperial connection as from groups afraid that independence would bestow unacceptable prestige on the government – and more particularly on the future prime minister – from which the restraining hand of London would forever be removed. The Grenadian opposition campaigned for a referendum under the Act in order to discredit the government rather than to retain associate status, establishing a tactic successively followed in all the other five islands. All were unsuccessful, and the final British associate, St Kitts–Nevis, assumed full independence in September 1983.

SIZE AND LOCATION

There is occasionally a tendency to assume that small-island politics are but mini-versions of those of their bigger cousins. Equally there can be a too-enthusiastic determinism, ascribing too much of what are perceived as small-island behavioural patterns only to size. So far as the polities of the south-eastern Caribbean are concerned, smallness has helped shape their political processes and has circumscribed political and economic options. But the influence of history and to a lesser extent location have been more important influences in shaping political and social structures and the direction of economic development.

Small geographic size and limited population have had both a positive and negative impact on the islands' political cultures and processes. Their societies are compact and homogenous with, in each case, a strong sense of community and widespread and interlocking kinship networks. The people, relatively unsophisticated, *expect* ready access to government and high-profile leadership from their 'heroes'. Political meetings have the flavour of revivalist rallies and supporters respond accordingly. With the leadership close to the people, the small-island governments have tended to be malleable and more responsive to public opinion than those in the larger polities.

But, by the same token, the presence of government seeps into every nook and cranny, and the leadership is dominant. It cannot be otherwise, given the importance of government employment, which in the smaller units can encompass up to two-thirds of the total workforce. Patronage as a form of political control is a characteristic of relatively poor societies with limited employment possibilities and all the more so in small ones, especially when an election is in the offing. The appeal of ministerial office is considerable in what are often overloaded administrations: Antigua and Barbuda for example had 17 ministers and 23 civil servants at permanent secretary rank in 1987. Although not so prevalent as before, crossing the floor, encouraged by offers of office, is not unknown; in small legislatures this can be a source of profound instability.

The importance of government as employer, together with the revenue that it creates, are important factors in explaining the notorious insularism of the south-eastern Caribbean. Whereas there are, through migration and education, close family and other links with *emigré* centres in Britain, the United States and Canada, and an eagerness to promote trade and co-operate politically with these and other extra-regional centres, only lip service is paid to the cause of regional integration. To federate would mean killing the goose that lays the golden egg, and, although the smaller islands were more enthusiastic than their larger counterparts in supporting the ill-fated West Indies Federation (1958–62), they were markedly less keen to combine amongst themselves after the Federation's collapse and once their economies began to benefit from the 1960s tourist boom. Colonial policy also had a part to play, for territorial governors in the Caribbean colonies dealt directly with the British Colonial Office rather than through local or regional channels. The whole fabric of the colonial system not only tolerated insularism but actively promoted it.

The experience of the Caribbean Community (CARICOM) in promoting regional trade and production since its foundation in 1973 also shows the scars of insularism. Nevertheless, CARICOM has, from the early 1980s, become increasingly important as a medium for political co-operation. A similar development is to be seen in the OECS where political co-operation was boosted by the 1983 Grenada crisis. Continuing concern that social and economic pressures might prompt another 'communist takeover' in an OECS territory was the primary force behind the initiative launched in May 1987 by John Compton and James Mitchell, respectively prime ministers of St Lucia and St Vincent, to unify the OECS states. 'We will have to wage war on pettiness and monumental prejudices' warned Mitchell,[26] adding later that:

> we will be more important to the security of the United States and Canada if we have a single voice speaking for a larger strategic area. This will improve our negotiating position in seeking to access funds for development.[27]

Although largely unreported, there was also concern about the implications to the OECS countries of threatened change in the preferential trade arrangements of the European Community and the need for a common policy. But in a short time Antigua and the BVI expressed opposition to further integration; after all, they had their own defence understandings with the United States, and neither relied on commodity exports, being primarily tourist economies. Other islands expressed reservations, too, and the proposal lost political momentum. An unforeseen outcome, however, was a new-found cooperation amongst opposition parties which established the Standing Committee of Opposition Parties of the Eastern Caribbean States (SCOPE), primarily to oppose union on the terms proposed, and for the reasons stated, although discussions on opposition and electoral strategies featured on the agenda.

The effect of insularism is particularly to be seen at the élite level. Here, personal and political relationships are especially close, if not verging on the incestuous. While the respective populations are indeed small, ranging from 253 000 in Barbados to Anguilla's 7000 with the median at approximately 90 000, the élite segment, political and commercial, is tiny. There is great potential for strife: as a comparative study suggested, it is probable, in what are essentially goldfish bowl societies, that conflicts among groups will be transformed into personal conflicts between individuals. It is likely, too, that processes for resolving conflicts at group level will be less institutionalized than in larger political communities, and that group conflict will be infrequent but explosive and will tend to polarize the entire society.[28] Public servants cannot escape behind a cloak of anonymity that patently does not exist. Conflict tends to be resolved at premier or prime minister level, an acknowledgement of the role of personality and of high office in small-island politics. For those in disagreement the future is bleak.

The significance of personality and the potential for personalist domination by the political leader is uncomfortably high in the hot-house atmosphere of the small island. Given that the Westminster system is so embedded in the popular consciousness of the English-speaking Caribbean, the consequences can be deleterious. Although by no means a phenomenon only of small size, personalism is the bedfellow of charisma. In early days, charisma derived more from strength of character and personality than any other factor, as witness the appeal of the old union-party leadership of which Vere Bird is the sole survivor. Charisma of this nature was also to be seen in the murdered Maurice Bishop and former Barbadian Prime Minister Errol Barrow.

The leadership of the newer parties, however, tended to derive their charisma from prime ministerial office and its requisites. While on the surface there are single ministries dealing, as one political analyst has observed, 'with specified areas within which specialism is permitted and by means of which bureaucrats advance their careers', the reality is that 'many of the ministries will be empty vessels and that the real power of administrative decision will be found in the office of the Prime Minister'. Civil servants, or even ministers on occasion,

> are frequently unprepared to take risks or make decisions out of routine without reference to superiors. Administration is therefore politicised, often centralised, and subject to the narrow political vision of the small state politician. . . . Avoidance of decision making may thus in itself become routine, with the result that crisis, when it looms, will be that much larger and change, when it has to be accommodated, will appear that much more threatening than would otherwise be the case.[29]

While there is plenty of scope for opposition, as the lively and libellous press bears eloquent witness, it is generally of little effect. Opposition within government whether at ministerial or civil servant level cannot be tolerated and offenders can be literally forced out of the political system into exile, just as known supporters of a defeated administration can expect to be discriminated against by the incoming government.

Like the factor of size, the geo-political location of the islands has had both a positive and negative impact. The relative closeness of North America has promoted economic development, especially in tourism and other service industries, though at the cost of unrequitable expectations. The negative impact is to be seen primarily in the arena of foreign policy preferences, which both reflect and reinforce popular sentiments. Like their larger counterparts in the region, the south-eastern Caribbean islands were, from their colonization by rival European nations, pawns in international politics. By and large they remain so. The Caribbean Basin, the geo-political concept defined in terms of the United States's security interests, is a cockpit of international politics where the East–West struggle in international relations represented by the challenge of Cuba and Nicaragua and formerly by Grenada is crossed by the North–South dimension, the unequal relationship between the rich and poor economies of the world. As during the long period of colonialism, there is no doubt where political sympathies at both élite and popular levels lie. Only by support for 'Western' positions can the problem of underdevelopment be addressed: their history dictates an unquestioning willingness to follow the lead of the dominant power of the time and place, while their economic dependency, small size and vulnerability make it a necessity.

CONCLUSION

The political culture of the south-eastern Caribbean islands can be summed up as one characterized by mimicry. The history and extent of their economic and psychological dependency dictated a degree of servility and a concern to reflect in their institutions the values and assumptions of their mentors. Identification with the norms and practices of the Westminster system complimented by support for first British and latterly United States foreign policy, was the path both to identity and respectability. That imperative extended equally to revolutionary Grenada for which the model was Soviet-style socialism and a pro-Cuban and -Soviet foreign policy in the name of proletarian internationalism. In that sense the revolutionaries were true to expectations. But the model they mimicked was radically different and antithetical to anything known or experienced by the other English-speaking Caribbean peoples.

It should not be concluded, however, that mimicry is by definition dysfunctional. The Westminster model is as much concerned with civil liberties as elections, political pluralism and parliamentary democracy. These islands have an enviable record since the 1940s in human and political rights, particularly when set against those of other parts of the Third World. As for Grenada, the People's Revolutionary Government at least tried to realize the socialist conception of human rights – those of health, welfare and education.

The question must therefore be: where now? The Westminster

model on which the political culture of the south-eastern Caribbean ultimately rests cannot be static, and, given the constantly strengthening political and social influence of the United States on the islands, there may be changes in their structures and operation of government, even constitutions, as new sets of imported values come to challenge the old. Can, or indeed should, these islands turn their smallness into a virtue, by combining all that is best in the Westminster order of things with the potential social benefits suggested by the Grenadian experiment? In other words, will a political culture emerge which is distinctive to the English-speaking Caribbean peoples in general and to the societies of the small islands of the south-eastern Caribbean in particular? Independence is still a recent memory for some territories: a few tiny islands or groupings remain colonial dependencies. In such circumstances change will take time, but change there will be. Just as societies without the means of change wither on the vine so may political culture. But this will not be their fate, for despite their insularist attitudes, their history and location ensure constant exposure to new ideas from the world beyond their shores.

NOTES

1. H. Hoetink, '"Race" and Color in the Caribbean', in Sidney W. Mintz and Sally Price (eds), *Caribbean Contours* (Baltimore: The John Hopkins Press, 1985), p.73. There is, however, a definitional and perceptual problem given the prevalence of the mulatto population, especially in Barbados.
2. George L. Beckford, *Persistent Poverty: Underdevelopment in Plantation Economies in the Third World* (London: Oxford University Press, 1972), p.235.
3. For an account of these events see Tony Thorndike, *Grenada: Politics, Economics and Society* (London: Francis Pinter), pp.135–75.
4. *The Nation* (Barbados) (1 June 1979).
5. Tony Thorndike, 'Dominica', *Latin America and Caribbean 1984* (Saffron Walden, Essex: World of Information Press), p.205.
6. Election turnout statistics to 1979 taken from Patrick Emmanuel, *General Elections in the Eastern Caribbean: A Handbook* (Cave Hill, Barbados: Institute of Social and Economic Research, University of the West Indies, Occasional Papers No. 11, 1979). Thereafter taken from electoral officers' reports.
7. C. Searle, 'An Interview with Bernard Coard', *Race and Class*, Vol. XXI, No. 2 (Autumn 1979), p.175.

8. 'Interview with Maurice Bishop', *Caribbean Monthly Bulletin* (Puerto Rico), Vol. 8, No. 3 (March 1974), p.31.
9. *Is Freedom We Making* (Grenada: People's Revolutionary Government, 1981), p.30.
10. Jay Mandle, *Big Revolution, Small Country* (Lanham, Maryland: The North-South Publishing, 1985), pp.61–2.
11. Anthony Maingot, 'Citizenship and Parliamentary Politics', in Paul Sutton (ed.), *Dual Legacies in the Caribbean* (London: Frank Cass, 1986), pp.128–30.
12. Keithlyn B. Smith and Fernando C. Smith, *To Shoot Hard Labour: The Life and Times of Samuel Smith, Antiguan Workingman 1877–1982* (Scarborough, Ontario: Edan's Publishers, 1986), pp.54–55.
13. S.A. Smith, *The New Commonwealth and its Constitutions* (London: University of London Press), p.83.
14. Patrick Emmanuel, 'Elections and Parties in the Eastern Caribbean', *Caribbean Review*, Vol. X, No. 2 (Spring 1981), p.15.
15. Paget Henry, 'Decolonisation and the Authoritarian Context of Democracy in Antigua', in Paget Henry and Carl Stone (eds), *The Newer Caribbean* (Philadelphia: Institute for the Study of Human Issues, 1983), p.297.
16. Quoted in Norwell Harrigan, *The Development of the Political System in the British Virgin Islands: An Overview*. Unpublished paper delivered to the Caribbean Studies Conference, St Thomas, US Virgin Islands, 27–30 May 1981, p.13.
17. Emmanuel, *op. cit.*, p.15.
18. Tony Thorndike, 'Antigua and Barbuda', in Colin Clarke and Tony Payne (eds), *Politics, Security and Development in Small States* (London: Unwin Hyman, 1987), pp.109–110.
19. *Caribbean Insight* (London), Vol. 11, No. 12 (December 1988), p.14.
20. Eastern Caribbean Central Bank, *Report and Statement of Accounts for the Financial Year ended 31 March 1987*, (Basseterre: ECCB, 1987), p.15.
21. Caribbean Development Bank, *Annual Report 1987*, (Barbados, 1988), p.17.
22. Patrick Emmanuel, 'Independence and Viability: Elements of Analysis', in Vaughan A. Lewis, *Size, Self-Determination and International Relations: The Caribbean* (Mona, Jamaica: Institute of Social and Economic Research, University of the West Indies, 1976), p.9.
23. *The Workers Voice* (Antigua) (19 March 1978).
24. *Trinidad Guardian* (1 November 1972).
25. Tony Thorndike, 'Associated Statehood: Quo Vadis?', in *The Caribbean Yearbook of International Relations 1977* (Trinidad: Institute of International Relations, University of the West Indies, 1980), p.65.
26. *Caribbean Insight*, Vol. 10, No. 7 (July 1987), p.13.
27. *Caribbean Contact* (Barbados) (January 1988), p.9.
28. Robert A. Dahl and Edward R. Tufte, *Size and Democracy* (Stanford, California: Stanford University Press), pp.93–4.
29. Paul Sutton, 'Political Aspects', in Clarke and Payne (eds), *op. cit.*, p.19.

5 Grenada: Society and Politics in a Small State

Colin Clarke

A particularly striking political change in recent years has been the erosion of the criteria thought essential to self-government. After World War II Britain's Colonial Office considered it 'clearly imposs-ible in the modern world for the present separate [West Indian] communities, small and isolated as most of them are, to achieve and maintain full self-government on their own'.[1] For this reason many West Indians welcomed the federation established under British aegis in 1958; only such an association, they believed, could win them self-government. Even thirty years ago, few expected Jamaica and Trinidad to gain independence on their own, let alone tiny Grenada.

Not until 1960, when Premier Norman Manley was told that Jamaica could gain independence within the Commonwealth, did political leaders anywhere in the English-speaking Caribbean envis-age separate nationhood. As Bernard Coard put it, 'with Jamaica's lead Trinidad soon followed. It was not so much a case of Trinidad's "size" being seen as having increased, as Trinidad's perception that the world's concept of the size required of an independent nation had altered.'[2] By 1962 there were nine sovereign states with populations smaller than Trinidad's 825 000: now 39 countries have fewer than a million inhabitants.

Jamaica's 1961 referendum broke up the West Indies Federation: Jamaica and Trinidad became independent in 1962 and Guyana and Barbados in 1966. Thereafter no theoretical justification remained to deny self-government to any Caribbean territory. Most colonies evolved into associated states, each internally autonomous but de-pendent on Britain for overseas representation and defence.[3] Full independence then beckoned as a panacea. Egged on by the UN Decolonization Commission, colonial territories, however small or poor, found it desirable to throw off imperial bonds: each new national creation caused other small units to ask why not us? As a Grenadian minister of the early 1970s noted, territorial size was irrelevant on the attainment of nationhood; he echoed a UN resolu-tion in commenting that 'inadequacy of political, economical, social or educational preparedness should never serve as a pretext for delaying independence'.[4]

By 1983 all six of the Caribbean associated states created after the break up of the West Indies Federation were independent, with Grenada taking the lead in 1974. Island leaders anticipated that merely declaring independence would win them international aid; indeed Eric Gairy, who took Grenada out of colonialism and associated statehood, is alleged to have stated 'Grenada will not support Independence: Independence will support Grenada'.[5]

Why should islands like Grenada want independence on their own? Caribbean parochialism has been fostered by geographical isolation – especially insularity – and colonial dependence. Above all parochialism is based on suspicion, even fear, of neighbours as competitors, rivals or agents of sedition. In the 1950s and 1960s this was principally 'a fear on the part of the wealthiest islands of having to carry their weaker associates'.[6] This apprehension triggered both the collapse of the federation and the rump 'federation' of smaller units in 1966; even Trinidad's offer to take its small neighbours into unitary statehood was withdrawn once Grenada responded positively to it. So associated statehood and independence were seized upon by Grenada and the rest not as *the* solution to decolonization but only after federation had ceased to be possible and because political advancement promised more local control and better opportunities for development.

Even before associated statehood was devised, Arthur Lewis had spelled out the dangers of autonomy for miniscule West Indian states.

> In a small island of 50,000 to 100,000 people dominated by a single political party, it is very difficult to prevent political abuse. Everybody depends on the government for something, however small, so most are reluctant to offend it. The civil servants live in fear; the police avoid unpleasantness; the trade unions are tied to the party; the newspapers depend on government advertisements; and so on. In cases where they are also corrupt, and playing with public funds, the situation becomes intolerable.[7]

Lewis undoubtedly had Grenada in mind. In 1962 Grenada's constitution had been suspended by the British-appointed administrator who judged Chief Minister Gairy to have 'violated the principles of honest government'.[8]

Grenada, then, is an apt case of a small sovereign Caribbean state, though it must be added that its recent history makes it an extreme example. It was the first Caribbean island with fewer than 100 000 inhabitants to become independent, and since then it has experienced three contrasted regimes – Eric Gairy's dictatorship 1974–79, the People's Revolutionary Government (PRG) 1979–83 and the New National Party elected in late 1984 after more than a year's interim government. How has each regime managed the social, political and economic problems associated with Grenada's small size?

GAIRY'S GRENADA

When Gairy led Grenada into independence in 1974 it had a population of 95 000 on its 344 km^2; the natural increase was 0.7 per cent per annum, outmigration to the UK having drained off many thousands of Grenadians in the 1960s; and the GDP per capita was a mere US$200. Between a quarter and a third of all employees who worked on plantations – most were labourers; the majority of self-employed workers were peasants, though rural people moved between own-account and paid work. Sugar was grown largely for distilling into rum; cocoa, nutmegs and bananas accounted for 90 per cent of exports.[9] Grenada was singularly powerless to influence the terms of trade with its major partner, the UK, because of its size and the nature of its produce.

Despite its small size, Grenada was socially complex and expressed a Creole stratification of plural cultures. At the top of this social pyramid there was a small Europeanized élite of ranked whites and browns, separated by a sharp social and cultural divide from the black masses of slave origin.[10] Smith has termed Grenada a plural-stratified society, a principal feature of which is social domination by an élite cultural minority whose values conflict with those of the cultural majority. Yet Grenada's independence from Britain had been strongly opposed both by the brown business community in the capital, St George's, and by the radical New Jewel Movement (NJM), headed by Maurice Bishop.[11] For each group feared Gairy's capricious and malevolent treatment once the ties of associated statehood were severed and Grenada became responsible for defence and foreign affairs. In fact, Gairy's policy after independence did not change in any marked way: his intention remained to exploit and oppress at home and to conform to US and UK expectations in his foreign policy.

Small size of the state was not a great geo-political disadvantage to Gairy's Grenada. Gairy was more interested in voicing his concern about UFOs at the UN and in forming a link with Pinochet's Chile than in pursuing radicalism in his foreign policy. However bizarre, Gairy's international connections gave no concern to the US or UK.

True to his judgement that independence would support Grenada, Gairy accepted rather than confronted the status quo. Even before independence, his 1950s' labour militancy had given way to manipulation of 'the crowd'; to attempts to get himself accepted by the social élite; and to enticement of US investment via retirement homes and the St George's University Medical School. But after 1974 Gairy set out more ruthlessly than ever to feather his own nest economically. Pocketing much of the US$10 million golden handshake from the UK, he terrorized local businessmen with his 'mongoose gang' and thereby extracted a personal share from plantations, hotels and businesses.[12]

Government malpractice and mismanagement were so widespread in Grenada that per capita income dropped by 3 per cent per annum in real terms during the 1970s and by 1979 fifty per cent of the labour force was unemployed, and the health and educational systems were in disarray.[13] How then did Gairy survive? By fear, by rigging elections, by suborning the police and defence force, and by his personal style of leadership which since the early 1950s had bound the older generation of the rural masses to 'Uncle', and via him to the Grenada Mental and Manual Workers' Union and its affiliated Grenada United Labour Party (GULP).[14]

Years before, Arthur Lewis had envisioned this type of situation, arguing that 'the only safeguard . . . is federation. If the government in island C misbehaves, it will be criticized openly by the citizens of island E. The federal government must be responsible for law and order, and for redress of financial and other abuse.'[15] There is an argument against federation, however, and it is that local autonomy ensures against external tyranny; if there is a tyrant, at least it will be a problem of the inhabitants' own making whose resolution lies in their own hands. Grenadians staged an almost bloodless coup in 1979 to get rid of Gairy; they could hardly have overcome an equivalent oppressor under, for example, Trinidad's suzerainty.

THE PEOPLE'S REVOLUTIONARY GOVERNMENT

Smallness was an immediate problem for the PRG which ousted Gairy, largely because the inadequate forces loyal to Bishop left the regime open to Gairy-inspired mercenary attack. In trying to resolve that potential problem by aligning itself with Cuba, the PRG increased US and UK hostility. And even in the Caribbean the PRG isolated itself from its Commonwealth neighbours by withdrawing its offer to hold elections. In each of these international situations, smallness spelled geo-political vulnerability.[16]

Small size was more crucial for the PRG than for Gairy because, while Gairy had been content to leave Grenada unchanged, the revolution had an active policy on almost every social and economic front, based on the non-capitalist path to development and ultimately the Marxist transition to socialism.[17]

Admittedly, contracts with Geest, the banana traders, were met, and tourists – 30 000–40 000 per annum, mostly from the US and the Caribbean – were encouraged, but dependency *was* diversified by seeking new markets for cocoa, nutmeg and mace in Eastern Europe.[18] Coard, the minister of finance, imposed strict fiscal control over a fairly successful mixed economy, with the peasant sector and the import houses remaining in private hands and accounting for about 80 per cent, while state enterprise was largely confined to areas where Gairy had made illegal acquisitions (20 per cent). By the early 1980s the GDP was growing at 3 per cent per annum, the national income per person was in the middle range for the Windward and Leeward Islands, and unemployment was below 20 per cent.[19]

Central to the PRG's development strategy was the construction of a new international airport at Point Salines, south of St George's and close to the island's finest beach at Grand Anse. This airport, a replacement for the obsolete installation at Pearls on the opposite coast, was an essential link in a programme of diversification by tourism, a strategy which was hardly revolutionary and merely endorsed the conclusion of the Tripartite Commission of US, UK and Canadian businessmen which visited the Caribbean in 1968. What was innovative about the PRG's 'new tourism' was its small scale, socially unobtrusive nature, and the impact it was intended to have on the rural economy by stimulating demand for peasant produce.

The airport became a symbol of the PRG's resolve to remove an impediment to rapid economic development, and Coard argued in Brussels that it was to Grenada what railroads had been to the USA.

But the US viewed the airport as a military base that Grenada could and would offer to its Cuban and Soviet allies. Despite enormous help from Cuba in men and materials and smaller loans from the European Community, Libya and Iraq, the cost of construction so escalated that it began to distort government expenditure in the year prior to the PRG's collapse.[20] Although it was shown that the Point Salines runway was shorter than those in several adjacent islands, and Plessey, the British sub-contractor, confirmed that the installation was not for military use, the US persisted in treating the development as a provocation.

In addition to the issue of the airport, the grounds for continuous US pressure on the PRG were its Marxism, its unconstitutional takeover, press censorship, lack of elections, holding of detainees, and pro-Cuban and -Soviet foreign policy. The pressure on tiny Grenada took many forms. The US mounted their military exercise 'Amber and the Amberines' (read Grenada and the Grenadines) off Puerto Rico in 1981; explicitly omitted Grenada from the 'benefits' of the Caribbean Basin Initiative in 1982; distanced Bishop when he attempted a rapprochement in June 1983; and finally invaded Grenada in October 1983 during turmoil following the assassination of Bishop.[21]

If the PRG was swept away because it was such a small, ideologically high-profile and geo-politically vulnerable target in the heart of America's backyard (and one must remember that the collapse of the PRG conveniently coincided with US need to compensate quickly for its humiliation in the Lebanon), what part did small size play in the social and political policies of the PRG and in the tensions that pitted revolutionary against revolutionary in the prelude to invasion?

Jacobs and Jacobs concluded that Grenada's social structure, in contradistinction to Smith's plural formulation, consisted of a landed and comprador bourgeoisie and peasant and proletarian masses:[22] the PRG argued that it was not ripe for socialism. A vanguard party – despite its in-built bourgeois tendencies – had to take power and hold it in trust for the masses while they were educated for socialism. Grenadian folk reaction to the PRG was quite otherwise. Delighted that the repressive Gairy had been ousted, the folk devoted themselves to the magnetic personality of Maurice Bishop, much as their parents had previously to Gairy.

The very smallness of Grenada was well-suited to the innovations in government which the PRG favoured. Representative democracy, modelled on Whitehall, was rejected for ideological reasons and because of Gairy's gerrymandering in favour of participatory democracy.[23] Well-documented attempts were made in the early 1980s to stimulate parish-pump politics by discussing the national budget at community level, though subsequent assessments have emphasized that ideas spread from the top down.[24]

Social projects in which the small size of Grenada played a positive role involved education, where a mass literacy campaign was success-fully carried out in 1980–81 and an innovative in-service teacher-training scheme was started up in 1980; and health, where mobile teams covered the rural areas, concentrating on preventive medicine, especially health education, nutrition and family planning.[25]

Notwithstanding the smallness of Grenada, the PRG's desire to change everything at once was beyond its capacity. Admittedly, the senior ranks of the civil service were strengthened by high-calibre appointments of Caribbean radicals, and an enormous amount of specialist work was carried out by sympathizers with the revolution from overseas. But the mass organizations, the militia, National Women's Organization, National Students' Council, National Youth Organization, Productive Farmers' Union and the Young Pioneers, through which the masses were to be led to socialism, were, on the government's own admission, inert, and the Central Committee of the NJM lacked the will and energy to put them on a sound footing.[26]

Those involved in PRG decision-making were pitifully few. When the PRG collapsed in 1983, the New Jewel Movement had only 350 members, less than 1 per cent of the Grenadian population, and only 72 were full party members.[27] Even more disadvantageous than the small size of the NJM was the isolation of its Central Committee from the masses, ideologically, though not socially and geographically. While its pro-Coard faction condemned Bishop for his 'right oppor-tunism' and weak leadership and prescribed 'a Leninist level of organization and discipline', together with joint leadership by Bishop and Coard, it never seems to have appreciated the importance of Bishop's popular appeal. Moreover, the Central Committee was so obsessed with these ideological considerations that it neglected numerous economic problems that required urgent attention – a liquidity crisis, declining agricultural output, and overspending on the airport to ensure its completion by March 1984, the fifth anniver-sary of the revolution.[28]

At the personal level too, smallness failed to provide the expected social cement. Although Bishop and Coard had been to secondary school together, lived next door to one another in St George's, and had been colleagues in the NJM for a decade, their association did not prevent Coard's unpublicized resignation from the Central Committee in 1982, rivalry over the leadership, the death of Bishop, or the collapse of the PRG.[29] But in such a small society rivalry between two such dominant figures must have been difficult to contain.

POST-INVASION GRENADA

Widespread revulsion in Grenada at the assassination of Bishop and his closest associates ensured a welcome for the invasion forces. Popular support for liberation, coupled to the smallness of Grenada, enabled the US to take almost complete control of the state – economically, strategically and politically – and to install an interim government headed by the Grenadian Nicholas Braithwaite. Within a month of the landings, the White House had appointed a task force of advisers to report on medium- and long-term strategies for restoring the economy, and by Christmas 1983 US$15 million had been spent on road resurfacing in the damaged sections between St George's and the international airport. So total was the rupture between Grenada and the Soviet bloc, that during 1984–85 two-thirds of the entire Grenadian budget was provided by Western sources, the greater part by the US alone.[30]

US economic priorities have not differed greatly from those of the PRG, however. Export agriculture has remained the backbone of the economy, and has been the largest employer, though tourism has been the sector with the greatest potential, employing 2000 persons directly and indirectly and contributing 40 per cent of the GNP. A major problem for the US and the interim administration it installed was to switch the direction of trade for certain commodities while stabilizing export levels: in 1984 a US firm was persuaded to buy more than 450 000 kg of nutmegs, thereby replacing a deal with the USSR.[31]

While expelling non-Grenadian activists and denigrating the socialist philosophy of the PRG, the US had to continue to fund a range of social projects initiated by the PRG in the fields of education, health, water supply, electricity provision and road construction. Nevertheless, there was a good deal of disruption in the nationalized industries and in education, from which foreign volunteers were expelled.

A major priority for the US was the opening of Point Salines

Airport, which it had previously dismissed as a military installation. US$21 million was earmarked to complete the project in 1984, and the runway was formally inaugurated in October of that year, to commemorate the first anniversary of the invasion. Private US funds were harnessed to government subventions, and substantial sums were invested in five new hotels which were to provide 600–700 additional beds in 1987 and thus underpin the viability of the airport and the economy generally.

Commonwealth objection to the incorporation of Grenada into the US orbit – a view not shared by the majority of Caribbean Commonwealth States – was expressed in a short-lived attempt to replace the Caribbean Peacekeeping Force (essentially US troops) with a Commonwealth detachment. Gradual military withdrawal of the US in 1984–85 coupled to British training of the Grenada police, stabilized the situation without weakening US control, and this control was most obvious in the manoeuvrings surrounding Grenada's return to democracy.

Central to US policy was the imprisonment – and political neutering – of the left-wing faction of the PRG which was in opposition to Bishop. The perpetual prevarications associated with the murder trial and subsequent appeal against conviction of the 18 defendants, suggest that their semi-permanent removal from the political scene has been the objective of the US, the interim administration and the Grenadian government, elected on a newly compiled roll in December 1984.

The US, fearing that Gairy's GULP would take advantage of the dismemberment of the New Jewel Movement and win the poll, proceeded during 1984 to engineer an alliance between the main opposition groups – Blaize's Grenada National Party, Brizan's National Democratic Party and Alexis's Grenada Democratic Movement. This amalgam, known as the New National Party, headed by veteran politician, Herbert Blaize, a premier during colonial days, polled 59 per cent of the vote and won 14 out of the 15 seats, while GULP (with Gairy on the sidelines) polled 36 per cent of the vote and took one seat. The Maurice Bishop Patriotic Movement – reviled by left and right – achieved only 5 per cent of the vote and all its candidates lost their deposits. Almost 85 per cent of Grenadians registered to vote did so.

After Blaize formed the government, the US presence, though increasingly concealed, remained all-pervasive. In addition to the areas of politics, ideology and political economy, it was to be found in the training of government officials, penetration of the trade unions, expansion of the St George's University Medical School, and in the island-wide emphasis on capitalist endeavour.

With the NNP in office, the small Grenadian economy developed steadily, though it lacked the generous funding hoped for from the US. From 1985 to 1988, the annual growth rate of the GDP was consistently above 5 per cent, largely because of the performance of the tourist, manufacturing and construction sectors.[32] However, the US, having provided aid to the tune of US$74 million between October 1983 and January 1986 – an expenditure per capita greater than for any other country except Israel – cut back so sharply in the latter year that Grenada had to take emergency measures to reduce its budget by nearly US$4 million, and contemplate 1500 redundancies in its civil service.[33] The economic growth rate was quite high, even by PRG standards, but agriculture remained almost static, and unemployment returned to levels previously achieved under Gairy – 30 per cent in 1986 rising to 40 per cent in 1987.[34]

Grenada's debt has been a growing problem. An IMF report in January 1986 showed Grenada's external debt was US$62 million or 44 per cent of the current GDP; and debt service had risen from 3.75 per cent of exported goods and services in 1981 to 16.5 per cent – in part reflecting the overseas borrowing of the PRG in its abortive attempt to complete the airport.[35] By 1987, the debt had risen still further to an estimated US$81 million, though by early 1989 Prime Minister Blaize was able to claim that current expenditure would, in the following year, be financed in full by domestic revenue – for the first time in a decade.[36]

Gairy was kept out of power by the creation of the NNP, yet that party's very coherence was in doubt from the start, for it seemed little more than a revamped GNP. After 1985, the NNP drifted increasingly towards autocratic and personalistic leadership – a recurring theme in Grenada's history – under Herbert Blaize, who despite a variety of debilitating illnesses, continually managed to upstage his two rivals in the NNP, Brizan and Alexis. Their disgruntlement with Blaize eventually dissipated their own mutual hostility, and they came to resent not only his persistent promotion within the cabinet of his cronies from the GNP, but his domineering and inconsistent government. Their objection to civil service sackings in 1987 was the ostensible reason for their resignation from the cabinet and their formation of a new party, the New Democratic Congress (NDC).[37] Blaize, having fought a terrier-like action against Brizan and Alexis, has more recently been at odds with Mitchell, who in January 1989 ousted him from the party leadership. Blaize reacted by promoting his close GNP associate, Ben Jones, to be his deputy prime minister and dismissing Mitchell from the cabinet.[38]

The outcome of these fissiparous tendencies, so common in the politics of the Lesser Antilles, was that Blaize's parliamentary support has been whittled away from 14 seats out of 15 to five or six. Unable to stand up to a no-confidence vote in the legislature, Blaize prorogued parliament in mid-1989 until a general election could be called at the end of the year. The NNP is divided into two factions headed by Blaize and Mitchell, and Gairy's GULP and the Maurice Bishop Patriotic Movement stand in the wings, but it is likely that Brizan and Alexis's NDC, headed by Nicholas Braithwaite – the United States' appointee to the headship of the 1983–84 interim administration – will win the next election and operate a modified economic policy (perhaps with more generous US support).[39]

Under Blaize, the tiny country has been turned systematically into the antithesis of the PRG's Grenada: indeed, it has become, as the US has willed, a 'free-enterprise' state. This was the keynote of the 1986 budget, which abolished personal income tax and re-emphasized capitalism. But value-added tax was introduced at 20 per cent, and this aspect has been disliked by the business community, traditionally Blaize supporters.[40] The NNP's anti-socialism has extended to the banning of 86 'subversive' publications, including the works of Marx, Lenin, Fidel Castro and Malcolm X – legislation which has received widespread condemnation both in Grenada and internationally.[41]

CONCLUSION

Theoretically, the significance of small size is difficult to specify, though the advantages and disadvantages can be characterized generally as balanced between having strong social bonds and lacking economic viability. Yet the simple pattern of plusses and minuses, in reality, may be disrupted by many factors – for example, social complexity, ideological differences, personal rivalry, the quality of economic management.

The PRG was mindful of the economic constraints imposed by small size, but committed itself to the construction of an international airport, which strained its finances to breaking point, and whose positive potential stimulus to the economy remained to the end in doubt. Moreover, the PRG, rejecting a pluralist model in preference to a Marxist class framework of analysis, allowed its ideological preoccupations to isolate it from the very masses whose cultural characteristics it denied but whose cause it claimed to represent.[42] Yet the very smallness of the society did enable 3000–4000 people (out of 15 000 gathered in Central St George's) to congregate swiftly, on 19 October 1983, not to support the revolution, but to free their hero, Bishop, from house arrest, thereby setting in motion the denouement of assassination, internal collapse and foreign invasion.[43]

The PRG also neglected the geo-political implications of small size coupled to ideological differences: it was deceiving rhetoric for Bishop to declare 'we are not in anybody's backyard'.[44] Grenada shows that small states pre-détente had to conform to the ideology of the superpowers in whose sphere of influence they were located: or at least they had to keep a low profile if they did not. Grenada's anti-American stance, its location in the Caribbean close to the USA, its military weakness – the People's Revolutionary Army had only 1800 soldiers – and the unwillingness of Cuba and the USSR to protect it, spelled disaster.

By contrast with the PRG, the New National Party elected in 1984 has been a creature of the US. Like Gairy's regime in the past, it has not created a geo-political ripple in the Caribbean. On the other hand, it has been unable to confront and could only embrace Grenada's problems of dependence and social inequality, rooted as they are in smallness.

ACKNOWLEDGEMENTS

I am grateful to Anthony Payne for allowing me to draw on materials from our research visit to Grenada and other territories in the south-east Caribbean in 1983, funded by the Nuffield Foundation; to David Lowenthal for permission to re-use parts of our joint article 'Island Orphans: Barbuda and the Rest' published in the *Journal of Commonwealth and Comparative Politics*, Vol. 18 (1980), pp.294–307; and to Allen and Unwin for letting me revise and re-print this chapter, which originally appeared in Colin Clarke and Tony Payne, *Stability, Security and Development in Small States* (London: Allen and Unwin, 1987), pp.83–95.

NOTES

1. UK Goot Report, *Report on Closer Association of the British West Indian Colonies* (London: HMSO, 1947).
2. Bernard Coard, 'The Meaning of Political Independence in the Commonwealth Caribbean', in *Independence for Grenada – a Myth or Reality?* (St Augustine, Trinidad: Institute of International Relations, 1974), pp.69–78, quotation on p.70.
3. C.G. Clarke, 'Insularity and Identity in the Caribbean', *Geography*, Vol. 61 (1976), pp.8–16.
4. R. Jacobs, 'The Move Toward Grenadian Independence', in *Independence for Grenada – Myth or Reality?* (St Augustine, Trinidad: Institute of International Relations, 1974), pp.21–33, quotation on p.30.
5. V. Lewis, 'Commentary', in *Independence for Grenada – Myth or Reality?* (St Augustine, Trinidad: Institute of International Relations, 1974), pp.53–5, quotation on p.54.
6. S.S. Ramphal, 'Federation in the West Indies', *Caribbean Quarterly*, Vol. 6 (1960), pp.21–9.
7. Sir Arthur Lewis, *The Agony of the Eight* (Barbados: Advocate Commercial Printery, 1965), p.16.
8. A.W. Singham, 'Legislative-executive Relations in Smaller Territories', in Burton Benedict (ed.), *Problems of Smaller Territories* (London: The Athlone Press, 1967), pp.134–48, quotation on p.144.
9. G. Brizan, *Grenada: Island of Conflict* (London: Zed Books, 1984). See also David E. Lewis, *Reform and Revolution in Grenada, 1950 to 1981* (Habana, Ediciones Casa de Las Americas, 1984).
10. M.G. Smith, *Stratification in Grenada* (Berkeley and Los Angeles: University of California Press, 1965).
11. EPICA Task Force, *Grenada: the Peaceful Revolution* (Washington: EPICA Task Force, 1982).
12. H. O'Shaughnessy, *Grenada: Revolution, Invasion and Aftermath* (London: Sphere Books, 1984); T. Thorndike, *Grenada: Politics, Economics and Society* (London: Frances Pinter, 1985).
13. F. Ambursley, 'Grenada: the New Jewel Revolution', in F. Ambursley and R. Cohen (eds), *Crisis in the Caribbean* (London: Heinemann, 1983), especially pp.193–200.
14. A.W. Singham, *The Hero and the Crowd in a Colonial Polity* (New Haven and London: Yale University Press, 1968), p. 144; A. Payne, P. Sutton and T. Thorndike, *Grenada: Revolution and Invasion* (London and Sydney: Croom Helm, 1984).
15. Lewis, *op. cit.*, pp.16–17.
16. J.R. Mandle, *Big Revolution, Small Country: the Rise and Fall of the Grenada Revolution* (Lanham, Maryland: North-South Publishing, 1985).
17. R.E. Gonsalves, *The Non-capitalist Path of Development: Africa and the Caribbean* (London: Caribbean Publishers, 1981); G. Sandford and R. Vigilante, *Grenada: the Untold Story* (New York and London: Madison Books, 1984).
18. Mandle, *op. cit.*, pp.22–42.

19. Ambursley, *op. cit.*, pp.206–42.
20. Thorndike, *op. cit.*, pp.126–7.
21. C. Searle, *Grenada: the Struggle against Destabilization* (London: Writers and Readers Publishing Cooperative, no date).
22. W.R. Jacobs and Ian Jacobs, *Grenada: el Camino hacia la Revolución* (Mexico: Editorial Katun, 1983), pp.25–6.
23. M. Hodge and C. Searle, *'Is Freedom We Making': the New Democracy in Grenada* (Grenada: Government Information Service, no date).
24. Mandle, *op. cit.*, pp.53–6; Thorndike, *op. cit.*, p.186.
25. Thorndike, *op. cit.*, pp.108–13.
26. State Department and Department of Defense, *Grenada Documents: an Overview and Selection* (Washington: State Department and Department of Defense, 1984), document 112.
27. Thorndike, *op. cit.*, p.79.
28. *Ibid.*, pp.118–30.
29. Fidel Castro, *A Pyrrhic Military Victory and a Profound Moral Defeat* (La Habana: Editorial Política, 1983); and Fidel Castro, *La Invasión a Grenada* (Mexico DF: Editorial Katum, 1983).
30. *Caribbean Insight*, No. 11 (1984).
31. *Caribbean Insight*, No. 2 (1984).
32. *Ibid.*, No. 5 (1989).
33. *Keesing's Record of World Events*, Vol. 32 (1986), p.34220.
34. *Ibid.*, Vol. 35 (1989), p.36690.
35. *Ibid.*, Vol. 32 (1986), p.34420.
36. *Caribbean Insight*, No. 5 (1989).
37. *Keesing's Record of World Events*, Vol. 34 (1988), pp.35889–90.
38. *Ibid.*, Vol. 35 (1989), p.36690.
39. *Ibid.*, Vol. 35 (1989), p.36690; *Caribbean Insight*, No. 8 (1989).
40. *Keesing's Record of World Events*, Vol. 33 (1987), p.34941–2.
41. *Caribbean Insight* No. 5 (1989).
42. M.G. Smith, *Culture, Race and Class in the Commonwealth Caribbean* (Mona, Jamaica: Department of Extra-Mural Studies, University of the West Indies, 1984).
43. For a mature reflection on Bishop's Grenada see Gordon K. Lewis, *Grenada: the Jewel Despoiled* (Baltimore and London: The Johns Hopkins University Press, 1987).
44. M. Bishop, *Selected Speeches 1979–81* (La Habana: Casa de Las Americas, no date).

6 Between Authoritarianism and Crisis-Prone Democracy: The Dominican Republic After Trujillo

Rosario Espinal

In the last three decades, the Dominican Republic has experienced major socio-economic and political transformations. It changed from a predominantly rural society where both economic and political power were monopolized by a dictator (Trujillo, 1931–61), to one with a more diversified class structure and a political system that has incorporated important democratic elements. Although welcomed, some of these changes were unexpected, in particular, the democratic transition in 1978. This transition took many by surprise not only because Latin America had been plagued by violence and authoritarianism since the early 1960s, but also because, based on academic predictions, the Dominican Republic was 'least likely' to democratize for several good reasons: (a) its monocultural economy and dependence on the external market; (b) its small size and geographical vulnerability; (c) its low level of industrialization when compared to other Latin American economies; (d) its high levels of unemployment, underemployment and labour force exploitation; and (e) its authoritarian political history.[1] With this background in mind, it is my purpose here to provide an account of the process of economic and political modernization underway in the Dominican Republic since the early 1960s, its impact on the class structure and the political institutions and ideals that have shaped Dominican society in the recent past, and the current dilemmas faced by a society that has been partially democratized in the midst of a severe economic crisis.

145

THE SEARCH FOR DEMOCRACY IN THE EARLY 1960s

The early 1960s represent a very important period in Dominican history. After three decades of dictatorial rule, the fall of Trujillo led to the reorganization of politics and society: authoritarian institutions such as Trujillo's Dominican Party and his secret police disintegrated while new social and political organizations emerged helping to modify the balance of power in favour of those previously excluded. It is beyond the scope of this chapter to analyse the numerous and complex political events that characterized the convoluted 'transitional period' stretching from mid-1961 to mid-1966.[2] Thus, the discussion that follows focuses on the significance of this period for the formation of social classes as political actors. My main objective is to show how the increasing mobilization of social actors and the fragility of political institutions like political parties and state agencies contributed to generate a 'crisis situation' that led to the 1965 civil war and the subsequent US military intervention.

Unlike the 1920s and 1930s when Trujillo came to power, by the early 1960s the economic and social structures of the Dominican Republic were complex. Instead of a mass of peasants mobilized by *caudillos* linked to a landed oligarchy, there was an expanded urban population that had increased from 16.6 per cent of the national total in 1920 to 30.5 per cent in 1960.[3] Instead of a small working class concentrated in the sugar sector, industrial workers had more than tripled between 1930 and 1960 as a result of the incipient import-substitution industrialization initiated by Trujillo in the 1940s.[4] Yet, despite these changes, few social and political organizations could emerge under Trujillo's harsh rule. This explains why, after Trujillo's assassination in 1961, political parties, unions, business and professional associations were formed and assumed centrality in Dominican politics.

Political organizations were the first to be formed. The most important ones were: the National Civic Front (UCN) led by members of the Dominican oligarchy opposed to Trujillo, the leftist 14th of June Movement and the reformist Dominican Revolutionary Party (PRD). In an effort to secure popular support, political parties proceeded immediately to organize trade unions. The first labour federation to be formed in 1961 was the United Labour Front for Independent Unions (FOUPSA), which was initially backed by all the newly activated political parties. FOUPSA soon played an important role in organizing shopfloor workers. This was reflected in a substantial increase in the number of officially registered unions as well as in the corporate gains made by workers, mostly concerning pay raises and the right to organize.[5] Also, with unions in the forefront, political parties were in a stronger position to wage a war against the remnants of the Trujillo dictatorship, which they did. Consequently, the incipient labour movement soon found itself engaged in a dual struggle for both economic and political reforms. This was part of generalized efforts to secure basic socio-economic and political rights that had been denied to society at large during the dictatorship. Thus, national strikes held in 1961 and 1962 helped not only to secure higher wages for the working population, but also to force Trujillo's top associate Balaguer into exile, thereby facilitating the organization of free elections.

While effective in ending the dictatorship, the early politicization of the labour movement had negative implications for the movement at the outset. Particularly negative was the splintering of unions that derived from ideological and political rivalries among political leaders and organizations. Soon after being formed, conservative dissenters divided FOUPSA to form Free-FOUPSA with the help of the US labour attaché, who, along with other US Embassy officers, had a high profile in Dominican politics at the time.[6] Simultaneously, the Christian-democrats formed the Autonomous Confederation of Christian Unions (CASC), while the Marxist left backed the Central Confederation of Organized Workers (CESITRADO) and a smaller confederation named La Union. Thus, by 1963, there were five labour confederations claiming to represent workers.[7] These labour splits, no doubt, weakened the labour movement and prevented unified action; yet labour militancy in the early 1960s was destabilizing enough in the eyes of a small, weak and intransigent business class facing the task of reorganizing the state after the breakdown of the dictatorship.

By 1963, a major outcome of labour mobilization was higher wages for the working population. The average annual real wage of industrial workers rose from 495 pesos in 1960 to 863 in 1962 to 1004 in 1964.[8] Yet the government soon reacted, curtailing labour activism in both the public and private sectors at the request of business. Already by 1962, both the newly formed Industrialists' Association of the Dominican Republic (AIRD) and the Employers' Confederation of the Dominican Republic (CPRD) had voiced opposition to workers' demands and complained about the extent of labour militancy. In a letter sent to the Council of State (the provisional government) on 17 May 1962, the CPRD stated the following:

> As a result of the sudden transition from an oppressive tyranny to an atmosphere of liberty which we currently enjoy, workers have gone too far in raising demands and going on strike without following the established legal procedures. This has a negative impact on business and the economy at large; it also brings worries and chaos to the nation.[9]

Similarly, in a press communiqué issued on 19 May 1962 the AIRD noted:

> The Industrialists' Association of the Dominican Republic . . . has observed with concern the increase in illegal strikes, which constitutes a serious problem for the normal development of economic activities necessary for the recovery.[10]

Subsequently, the Council of State enacted laws banning sympathy strikes, strikes that had a 'political motivation', and strikes in the public sector.[11] These regulations helped to contain labour activism as required by business, but were a setback for the incipient labour movement. More importantly, they helped to set the tone for the repression that followed.

After the coup of 1963 that ousted the recently elected Juan Bosch from power, other regulations were instituted by the Labour Ministry in an effort to further control labour activities. Resolution 8/64 required unions to report monthly to the Labour Ministry any changes in their structure, composition or by-laws. Resolution 15/64 specified the number of unions required to form a labour federation and the number of federations required to form a confederation.[12] Regarding these resolutions, it is worth noting that their main purpose was not to promote a state-controlled labour movement as had previously happened in Argentina or Brazil under populist regimes, but to slow down organizational activities and discriminate against those labour organizations disliked by business and government. This explains why the Dominican labour movement continued to be highly fragmented in spite of regulations that seemed likely to foster a more unified state-corporatist labour system.[13] On the other hand, as the *de facto* government installed in 1963 turned more repressive, unions and opposition parties came closely together to fight for the re-installation of democratic institutions and procedures. It is important to indicate that even though repressive measures instituted in 1963–64 helped to contain labour and political militancy, they were not sufficient to stabilize the government. Opposition to the *de facto* government, headed by Donald Reid Cabral, continued, leading to the short-lived and ill-fated civil war of April 1965.

A major factor contributing to the political instability of the early 1960s was the power vacuum resulting from the decomposition of governing institutions and the growing power of civil society. Not only was the ruling élite in disarray (namely, Trujillo's relatives and close collaborators), but basic institutions of political control like the Dominican Party and the secret police had disintegrated. Consequently, at the heart of the political crisis in the early 1960s was a state whose capacity to use the means of coercion had diminished while it lacked the institutional mechanisms to channel growing demands for economic redistribution and political participation.

Another factor preventing major restructuring of state institutions and power relations was the lack of a powerful revolutionary movement – Trujillo had been assassinated by a handful of opponents, not overthrown in the context of a popular insurrection. This meant that the capitalist state in its highly authoritarian form had been damaged after the fall of Trujillo, but its capitalist content was never threatened, as such, unlike the experience of Cuba in 1959 or Nicaragua in 1979. Even during the short-lived civil war of 1965, the main purpose of the struggle was to re-institute the constitutional government of Juan Bosch ousted in 1963. Moreover, to prevent any major turnaround, the United States was ready to intervene militarily in the wake of a popular insurrection. This was the United States' last resort after several years of increasing involvement in the internal affairs of the Dominican Republic in an effort to shape the political regime to be instituted after the fall of Trujillo. It is worth noting here that if it was true that the United States was instrumental in ending the Trujillo dictatorship, its main purpose was not to promote democracy, but to prevent another revolutionary crisis similar to that of Cuba. Hence, its willingness to proceed quickly with a military intervention, when confronted with a popular insurrection that had essentially a democratic objective.

The failure of internal powerholders – business, the army, the Church – to produce a stable government in the early 1960s was the result of two main factors, one domestic and one international. On the domestic side, a political class with governing experience was lacking: the traditional oligarchy, which had been to some extent marginalized by Trujillo, did not have the skills to compromise and make concessions and felt threatened by the level of social unrest that followed the breakdown of the dictatorship. In addition, there was an unfavourable international situation that only helped to aggravate internal deficiencies: as indicated above, the Dominican Republic became the focus of attention as the place to prevent another Cuba in the Caribbean. Consequently, with business, the army, the Church and the United States on guard, it became difficult for newly formed popular organizations and reformist-populist parties like the PRD to introduce democratic reforms and retain power regardless of their own mistakes.

Failure to stabilize a democratic government in the early 1960s facilitated the return to authoritarianism in the mid-1960s. In addition to the fear felt by the Dominican élite of popular uprising, the US played no doubt an important role in helping to rearrange the balance of power in favour of Joaquín Balaguer, a former Trujillo associate. Balaguer won the post-intervention elections held in June 1966. These were 'demonstration elections' that had as their main purpose the legitimization of Balaguer's advent to power in the midst of national and international opposition to US military intervention.[14] Once in power, Balaguer led an important process of conservative modernization that by the mid-1970s had altered the social and political make-up of the Dominican Republic.

MODERNIZATION AND AUTHORITARIANISM UNDER BALAGUER

With state institutions weakened and social actors threatened, Balaguer inaugurated his 12-year-long presidency (1966–78) in July 1966. The prevailing situation nourished his personality-based leadership style. Shortly after taking office, Balaguer announced his national reconstruction programme, which he labelled *Revolución sin Sangre* (revolution without blood) in opposition to the violent revolt of April 1965. To understand the essence of Balaguer's programme and its impact on Dominican society, it is important to examine the content of this 'revolution' along two lines – its modernizing and its authoritarian characteristics.

Balaguer's economic programme consisted in containing labour demands and promoting capital investment. The first law issued after

Balaguer's inauguration as president was the Wage Austerity Law (1966), which froze the monthly minimum wage of all salaried employees in industrial, commercial, mining and service enterprises at 60 pesos. The Austerity Law banned any collective negotiations over wages or fringe benefits unless voluntarily agreed upon by all parties involved. Simultaneously, Balaguer waged a war against organized labour which took various forms. The most obvious was labour repression. Labour leaders were deported, imprisoned and assassinated and union headquarters and factories were frequently occupied by the national guard in the wake of labour actions. The government also backed splinter actions within the labour movement. Active in this was the pro-government National Confederation of Free Workers (CONATRAL), which encouraged the division of the *Sindicato Unido* of Central Romana, the largest and most active union in the country. Also instrumental to splinter politics were the existing labour laws which stipulated that all that is needed to form a union is the decision to do so of 20 workers sharing the same occupation or workplace. An indication of the detrimental impact of anti-labour policies implemented in the late 1960s and early 1970s was the drop in the number of newly registered unions: while the annual average of newly certified unions was 47.8 in 1961–65, it was 25.2 in 1966–77.

As labour organizations were dismantled and labour demands repressed, those with capital were encouraged to invest. The centrepiece of the new developmentalist model was import-substitution industrialization. In 1968, the government passed Law 299 of Industrial Development providing industrialists with tax benefits and privileged access to foreign exchange. From 1968 to 1977, the government approved a total of 552 requests from industrial firms to receive the tax benefits granted by Law 299; of these 552 requests, 63 per cent corresponded to new import-substitution enterprises. Export industries, located in duty-free zones, also began to expand by the mid-1970s, employing largely female labour. Certainly, the presence of foreign capital in this process of economic expansion was significant. Overall, foreign investment rose from US\$2.5 million in 1969 to US\$215.0 million in 1978.[16] Yet local capitalists participated as well, either in joint ventures or by expanding their own medium-sized firms. This was soon reflected in the formation of many business associations – a total of 129 business associations were officially certified between 1966 and 1980[17] – and the increasing presence of business leaders in all aspects of Dominican life. Other laws approved in 1966–71 were designed to promote the expansion of the banking system, mining and tourism.

Partnership between business and the Balaguer government was manifest at the outset. 1967 was declared the 'Year of Development'. To help in the promotion of development programmes, Balaguer appointed a commission of 'private citizens' (mostly businessmen) and government officials to work closely with him in the formulation of public policies. This commission was later enlarged and transformed into a permanent national planning board attached to the presidency. The National Commission for Development (CND), as it was called, became the most important forum where national policies were discussed by business and government. The CND was particularly active in formulating the government platform during Balaguer's first re-election in 1970. Yet, by the mid-1970s, the CND had ceased to be an effective mechanism for corporate participation. By then, the economic situation had deteriorated, hitting hard industrialists who had benefited from Balaguer's grand design for modernization based on import-substitution. Concomitantly, the business class had expanded and diversified, and it was more capable of articulating group demands.

With higher oil prices, lower sugar prices, and an inflationary process underway, Balaguer's model of wage austerity and investment promotion found its limits by 1976. Various business factions began to clash with the government, while the CND, with its personalistic and clientelistic overtones, became ineffective in regulating business–government relations.[18] In 1976, subtle criticisms to the government were raised by top business leaders known to back Balaguer. They asked to be more fully incorporated into the decision-making process, claiming that they had the necessary experience and knowledge to be equal partners with the government. They requested regular meetings with President Balaguer to discuss national problems and strategies to confront them. Several meetings were held throughout 1976 which helped to channel the growing desire for participation within the business community; yet the personalistic and clientelistic nature of the Balaguer regime made a significant change in business–government relations unlikely.

By the late 1970s, the cornerstone of the *Balaguerista* governing coalition had broken down. For one, the bourgeoisie had multiple factions with multiple interests. Moreover, business factions that benefited from Balaguer's exemption policies – in particular those linked to import-substitution industrialization – were among the first to suffer the negative effects of the economic crisis manifested in soaring inflation and unfavourable exchange rates. Thus, in an attempt to keep his economic model of wage austerity and investment incentives alive, Balaguer persecuted in the mid-1970s small- and medium-sized merchants accused of speculating. This was politically detrimental to the regime because these business strata went on to support the opposition, in particular, the Dominican Revolutionary Party (PRD). On another front, the political opposition began to reorganize in 1976. The PRD overcame its internal crisis typified by the debate over an allegiance to democracy or to a 'dictatorship with popular support' as proposed by Juan Bosch. In 1973, Bosch left the PRD to form his own Dominican Liberation Party (PLD), proclaiming a more nationalistic and anti-imperialistic stance. In 1976, the PRD publically stated its commitment to liberal democracy and its firm decision to fight for free elections as the means to attain power. The PRD also distanced itself from the Marxist left and joined the Socialist International to secure social-democratic support internationally. This association proved beneficial to the PRD when elections were held in 1978. Prominent socialist leaders from Europe and Latin America visited the Dominican Republic, expressed public support for the PRD and the electoral process, and most importantly, put pressure on the United States to guarantee the holding of free elections. Although the changes experienced by the PRD in the mid- and late 1970s can be interpreted as a de-radicalization of the party, if examined carefully, they basically reflected a reassertion of the PRD's original mission, namely, the establishment of a liberal democracy.

At the heart of the crisis of the Balaguer regime was the social differentiation produced by the process of economic modernization, in particular, the growth of the middle class and the diversification of business. Unhappy with Balaguer's personalistic leadership style, these groups proved helpful in boosting the PRD in the late 1970s. With middle- and working-class support, the PRD formed a winning coalition to defeat Balaguer in the 1978 elections – in the city of Santo Domingo alone, the largest urban centre in the country, the PRD received 63 per cent of the votes cast. However, Balaguer continued to benefit from the rural vote, receiving 54.1 per cent of the votes in municipalities where less than 30 per cent of the population was urban and only 28.8 per cent in municipalities where more than 70 per cent of the population was urban.[19]

Various factors contributed to the democratic transition in 1978.

Quite important was the maintenance of civilian institutions of government. That is, in spite of Balaguer's personalistic leadership style and his control of Congress, the legislature always continued operating; elections were also held every four years despite well-known frauds in 1970 and 1974. Second, because repression under Balaguer was selective and targeted against organized labour and the radical left, most of society, including the emerging business and middle classes had grown accustomed to the protection of some basic civil liberties and felt less threatened in backing a transition to competitive politics. This is illustrated by the fact that even though business benefited tremendously from Balaguer's modernizing policies, prominent business and Church leaders were the first to express public support for the electoral process in the wake of an attempted coup set up by a pro-Balaguer faction on election day. Given the veto power of business, this action was crucial in facilitating the transfer of power (to appreciate its importance one must remember that the opposition of business to PRD rule had facilitated the coup of 1963, which then frustrated the democratic process).

Third, it is noteworthy that unlike the sudden collapse of the Trujillo dictatorship, the relatively smooth transition of 1978 contributed to secure the PRD victory. That is, the 1978 elections did not imply a major political restructuring in the balance of power among political actors; it consisted essentially in a change of government to one more committed, in principle, to social justice and political participation. Fourth, helping also to make the transition less traumatic was the relatively non-threatening position of the popular classes: unions had been weakened under Balaguer and the Dominican peasantry had traditionally been non-threatening to power-holders.

Finally, favourable to the transition was President Carter's human rights policy and the support provided by the Socialist International to the PRD. These two international factors, but particularly President Carter's stance on human rights, have frequently been referred to as the reason why the transition took place in the Dominican Republic. Yet, without undermining their significance, I contend that without the important socio-economic and political changes experienced by Dominican society in the 1960s and 1970s the transition to democratic rule would have been unlikely in spite of international support for it. Here the experience of Central America is illustrative, where last-minute international commitment to democracy has proven ineffective in bringing it about given the adverse internal conditions.

By 1978, the PRD had assumed centrality in Dominican politics. It won the 1978 national elections after succeeding in forcing Balaguer to guarantee a fair electoral process. The coup attempt on the part of a pro-Balaguer faction to prevent the PRD from taking office failed for the most part. Undemocratic compromises were made to grant Balaguer's Reformist Party a majority in the Senate, but the PRD assumed control of the Executive and the Chamber of Deputies. Thus, after 15 years of struggle to install a democratic government, the PRD once more had the chance to rule. But because the experience and memories of the 1960s were still vivid, the unsettling question was whether or not the PRD would remain in power and implement its progressive platform in favour of large disadvantaged majorities with the blessing of business, the army, and the United States.

COMPETITIVE POLITICS AND ECONOMIC CRISIS IN THE 1980s

The inauguration of the PRD government represented a turning point in Dominican politics. After 15 years of frustrated democratic attempts, the PRD gained power, promising to promote social justice and political participation. There were those with hopes, expectations and confidence that the PRD would govern to fulfil democratic aspirations of large sectors of society. Others, sceptical of democratic reforms, were fearful and threatened by the uncertainties inherent in the process, because, if nothing else, at least symbolically, the PRD victory meant the possibility of voicing long-suppressed demands. This, by itself, shook the foundations of authoritarian rule which had defined the parameters of political life in the Dominican Republic throughout most of this century. Specifically, the transition reopened 'organizational spaces',[20] once the most repressive elements of the authoritarian regime ceased; it also allowed for the emergence of organizational activities that could not have flourished otherwise. Thus, three main topics, to which the rest of the chapter is devoted, deserve attention here. They are, the reorganization of business, the reorganization of labour, and the transformations in the party system and within-party structures.

The increasing economic difficulties, together with the advent of the PRD to power, were crucial factors that contributed to the political activism and reorganization of the Dominican business class. Conflicts emerged not only between business and government and business and labour, but also among business factions as they fought for a larger share of the shrinking pie. One of the major conflicts was over the incentive system provided by Law 299. Overall, medium-sized industrialists felt excluded from the system of state resource allocation. Consequently, they fought for more accessibility to the tax benefits granted by Law 299 and a fairer representation of all industrial factions in the Industrial Development Directorate (DDI), the corporatist board in charge of approving requests for tax exemptions. The most heated public debate took place in January 1980, when the Association of Merchants and Industrialists of Santiago (ACIS) issued a press communiqué criticizing the content and form of implementation of Law 299.[21] One criticism was that the law had produced uneven industrial results, for it did not provide incentives for industrial development to occur outside the capital city of Santo Domingo. Another was that members of the DDI board – who had enormous power in deciding who would receive tax benefits – had not fairly represented the business community. Consequently, the ACIS proposed the decentralization of the industrialization process by channelling resources to the interior. They also proposed the democratization of the DDI's board which had been monopolized by the traditional Santo Domingo business élite which was in control of the oldest peak business associations. Conflicts among business factions over Law 299 reached its height in 1980–81; yet, thereafter, the issue ceased to be as controversial once changes in economic policy, due to the growing external debt, favoured the export sector over import-substitution industrialization.[22]

In an effort to consolidate leadership within the business community, the National Council of Businessmen (CNHE) – the peak business association – engaged in an aggressive campaign after 1976 to affiliate newly formed business associations. As a result, the CNHE enlarged its membership from four associations in 1974 to 11 in 1978 to 42 in 1982.[23] These attempts at business unification were encouraged by three factors: (a) the need to articulate a more coherent business position *vis-à-vis* the government and labour (under Balaguer, business interests had remained largely dis-aggregated, in part due to the limited organization of business and in part to Balaguer's personalistic style); (b) the uncertainties generated by the transition itself and the victory of the PRD, a party whose radical reputation was well-known, but whose actual governing behaviour was unknown; and (c) the influence that a pro-Balaguer business faction came to exert over the CNHE's board of directors in the wake of the transition (being out of power, pro-Balaguer business groups sought to exert influence over the government from the CNHE).

While conflicts among business factions proceeded during the first PRD administration (1978–82), government–business relations also deteriorated. With a pro-Balaguer faction in control of the CNHE executive board, the CNHE became an arena for voicing criticism of, and opposition to, the government. The most controversial issues were the short-lived price control policy enforced by the Guzmán administration and forcefully opposed by business, and the 'technocratization' of policy-making.[24] First, top government appointees in major economic ministries, such as agriculture, industry and finance, were alien to traditional business élites. Second, they confronted the serious problem of either allowing higher inflation and further devaluations or imposing price controls disliked by business. As a newly established government with significant democratic promises to meet, the Guzmán administration opted at first for the latter, thus risking business support.

By early 1980, the Guzmán administration was facing a vociferous business opposition (aggravated by the politicization of the CNHE), coupled to increasing labour unrest and intra-party rivalries, all of which reduced the capacity of the government to respond effectively to the economic difficulties and the challenges posed by the various social groups.

Like business, labour began to regroup once the PRD came to power. This was immediately manifest in an increase in the number of officially registered unions. Workers voiced long-suppressed demands that reflected many of the inherited social disparities which were awaiting solution. Complicating the scenario was the economic downturn that made redistribution a more difficult problem to deal with. Strikes proliferated, particularly among sugar workers and drivers. The decrease in the price of sugar and the increase in oil prices were at the heart of the problems. Drivers' strikes gained considerable attention, given their ability to disrupt traffic and paralyse the economy. These labour actions frequently turned into street violence, resulting in casualties that called into question the democratic character of the newly established government.

In the sugar industry, strikes, stoppages, threats of strikes and demonstrations were frequent between 1979 and 1985. Every year, at the beginning of the harvest, labour actions were organized to demand annual bonus payments as stipulated by Law 80 of 1974.[25] Between 1979 and 1982, workers received at least a half of the bonuses requested (usually the equivalent of a two-week or monthly wage). However, beginning in 1983, the struggle of sugar workers became more problematic as the crisis in the industry deepened. With the persistent decline in sugar prices and the reduction of the US sugar quota, the Dominican government, owner of two-thirds of the sugar mills, faced more problems in meeting workers' demands. Repressive measures to contain labour demands worsened, while workers themselves soon confronted another, yet more dramatic problem: that of keeping their jobs once the government began closing sugar mills following drastic reductions in US sugar quotas in 1985 and 1986.

During the second PRD administration under Salvador Jorge Blanco (1982–86), two important changes occurred. The first was a shift in the attitude of business towards the government. After fierce attacks by CNHE top executives against the Guzmán administration, an important sector of the business community became dissatisfied with the leadership of the pro-Balaguer faction which had dominated the CNHE executive board since 1979. In December 1982, the CNHE elected a new board, this time headed by Hugh Brache, a less vociferous businessman, who expressed at the outset his commitment to working with the government towards solution of the severe problems affecting the Dominican economy. The change in leadership was important, mainly because it contributed to reduce government–business tension which in previous years had produced an atmosphere of political conspiracy. Besides the change of leadership, another factor that contributed to softening the position of business was the government's rejection of the Keynesian approach originally favoured by Guzmán. By 1982, it was evident that the government favoured fiscal and wage austerity, as suggested by the International Monetary Fund (IMF) – the free-floating of the dollar remained a controversial issue for medium-sized industrialists who depended on a subsidized dollar to import raw materials and technology, but was ultimately accepted as a matter of necessity.

A more serious issue related to the implementation of austerity measures was the worsening of the standards of living of the lower and middle classes. Official negotiations with the IMF began late in 1982, leading to the implementation of adjustment policies by mid-1983. They included the usual items: fiscal austerity, restrictions of credit by the Central Bank to the public sector, a value-added tax on consumer items, and the free-floating of the US dollar (this meant ending par value and preferential exchange in place since the 1940s). As a result, popular responses began to be articulated in new ways; the most challenging one being the food-riots that started in April 1984.[26] Afterwards, Dominican society began to witness a major change in the form of popular struggle. Unlike the early years of the transition (1978–82), when social organizations such as unions and business associations occupied centre stage in Dominican politics, popular protests became expressions of mass, not of class, movements. That is, so-called popular organizations (neighbourhood, communal, religiously inspired organizations) assumed leadership over traditional working-class groups.

Making the task of governing more difficult was the fact that, from the start, the PRD became an arena of intra-party rivalry with various factions fighting to control party and state resources. Evidence of intra-party rivalry was already clear in the 1977 party convention to elect the presidential candidate. Two main factions were in confrontation: that of Antonio Guzmán, a moderate politician who won the party nomination, and that of Salvador Jorge Blanco, a liberal lawyer, who gained the support of the party's left wing. Under the Guzmán administration, Jorge Blanco's strongholds were Congress and the PRD – he was both Senator and party president. José F. Peña Gómez, the popular party secretary-general, remained as the party ideologue. Opposing Guzmán, Jorge Blanco played an important role as a supporter of democratic reforms; he pushed through the Amnesty Law of 1978 and campaigned in favour of banning presidential re-election. Moreover, as the Guzmán administration lost support among PRD followers and the public at large (mostly as a result of unpopular economic measures and the increasing corruption detected in higher spheres of government), Jorge Blanco was looked upon as the true democratic alternative – Jorge Blanco's victory in the 1982 national elections showed how intra-party rivalry, usually detrimental to party life, had at least one short-term positive result, that of allowing the PRD to retain power for four more years.

Guzmán's suicide in July 1982, shortly before handing over power to Jorge Blanco, reshaped the balance of power within the PRD. Jacobo Majluta, who had lost the party nomination to Jorge Blanco, inherited Guzmán's faction. Yet this time the roles were inverted.

Jorge Blanco controlled the executive branch of government while Majluta assumed leadership in Congress as president of the Senate. As in the previous PRD administration, intra-party tensions were transposed to government institutions. Once more the PRD was ruling with a highly fragmented party élite that had also divided the rank-and-file. Very quickly, PRD performance in government was worsened by the irresistible temptation to depend on clientelism and corruption to secure support. But despite its effectiveness in the past to promote political support, clientelism proved this time to be detrimental to the government. In the midst of an economic crisis which deprived both people and the government of abundant resources and imported goods, Jorge Blanco's unofficial, but widely known, policy of granting tax-exemptions to sympathizers to import expensive (and normally heavily taxed) products such as automobiles and exotic food, became offensive to large sectors of society.

Leadership fragmentation within the PRD culminated in three tragic events for the party. First, the 1985 party convention to elect the presidential candidate for 1986 was a fiasco. The convention ended in violence when a group of armed men assaulted the convention centre where the ballots were being counted (Jorge Blanco's faction was blamed for this since it appeared that Jacobo Majluta was ahead in the race). Second, Peña Gómez's poor performance in the party convention helped to further discredit his leadership. Third, the PRD was defeated in the 1986 elections.

As a result of the violent attack in the convention centre, the counting of the ballots was suspended. Subsequently, with the voting results unknown, the PRD experienced a paralysis, while a sense of crisis deepened in the country. The impasse was temporarily overcome in January 1986 when top party leaders agreed, without completing the counting of the ballots, to grant Jacobo Majluta the presidential nomination, while Jorge Blanco's faction retained major congressional posts. Peña Gómez, who was Majluta's opponent in the convention with Jorge Blanco's endorsement, decided to stay out of the deal in an attempt to preserve some of his damaged reputation. This undemocratic solution was unsatisfactory to many, and contributed to the PRD defeat in the 1986 presidential elections. Moreover, the events surrounding the convention were most unfortunate in that they helped to undermine the democratic reforms concerning candidate selection which had been introduced in the early 1980s.

Peña Gómez's poor performance in the convention can be linked to various factors. It is true that his race and Haitian origins have always worked against his aspiration to become president, but this time, he also suffered from the general decline of the PRD, his close association with Jorge Blanco, and his poor performance as mayor of Santo Domingo. Majluta, on the other hand, was a candidate of dubious honesty and efficiency. Because the agreement among top PRD leaders to nominate Majluta as presidential candidate was only a temporary solution to the crisis of leadership, the PRD lacked the strength and will to promote him effectively. To make matters worse, by 1986, the Jorge Blanco administration was extremely unpopular and discredited as a result of the austerity measures being implemented[27] and rampant corruption in the higher spheres of government. The opposition, in contrast, was united in its call for honesty and efficiency. Standing on these issues were both Balaguer's Reformist Party (re-named the Social Christian Reformist Party) and Bosch's Dominican Liberation Party. They ran a campaign against corruption, receiving together almost 60 per cent of the votes cast in the 1986 elections, 40.5 and 18.4 per cent respectively.

The victory of Joaquin Balaguer in the 1986 national elections can be accounted for by three factors: first, Balaguer had consistently received the vote of about one-third of the electorate, in good part due to rural support; second, Balaguer was able to gather the backing of a segment of the urban middle- and lower-income groups, unhappy with the decline in the standard of living and the sense of political chaos emanating from a divided and corrupt PRD (here the nostalgia for 'order' and 'progress' played an important role); and third, the PRD lost the support of the most progressive elements within middle- and lower-income groups, which favoured Bosch's Dominican Liberation Party (PLD). For instance, while the PRD lost 18.2 per cent in electoral support between 1978 and 1986, the PLD improved its share of the electorate by 17.3 per cent. Balaguer, meanwhile, showed remarkable consistency in his share of the vote, receiving 42.2 per cent in 1978, 36.6 per cent in 1982 and 40.5 per cent in 1986.

CONCLUSION

As documented in this chapter, the Dominican Republic has experienced major socio-economic and political changes in the last 25 years. Many were linked to the economic expansion and modernization resulting from the import-substitution industrialization programme instituted in the late 1960s. Yet this model of development began to confront serious limitations in the late 1970s when the oil crisis and the collapse of the sugar industry destabilized the Dominican economy. A legacy of the process of economic expansion was a more urbanized society, a better organized business class and a larger middle class. These changes in social structure, coupled with the maintenance of civilian institutions of government and the preservation of a political party system, even in the midst of authoritarian rule under Balaguer, contributed to the democratic transition in 1978. The defeat of Balaguer in the 1978 elections (the first truly competitive elections held since 1962) and the emergence of the PRD as a ruling party fostered, no doubt, democratic hopes. Yet, after eight years in power, the PRD had little to show in terms of democratic reforms. Free and competitive elections have been held and basic human rights have been, by and large, protected. Yet the PRD missed the opportunity while in office to foster the consolidation of the party system and the institutionalization of democratic politics. Instead, the PRD was plagued by factionalism and clientelism, which ultimately weakened the party's social bases of support and led to its electoral defeat in 1986. Aggravating the situation was the deterioration of the economy, as expressed in soaring inflation, persistent devaluations, and an overall decline in the standards of living which made democratic governability highly vulnerable to economic decay.

In concluding, I would argue that the failure of the PRD to promote democratic reforms poses serious problems for the consolidation of democracy in the Dominican Republic. It represents not only a setback for the PRD as a democratic party, but also for the very legitimacy of democracy as a viable system. That the PRD was the largest, best organized and most democratic party in the country must be stressed to understand both the democratic transition and the dilemmas ahead. In the midst of adverse structural conditions for democracy to flourish in the late 1970s, the existence of a somewhat consolidated party system and the strength of a democratic PRD were crucial in facilitating the transition to competitive politics. But if the strength of the PRD contributed to the 1978 transition, its fragmentation and decay have more recently contributed to generate a vacuum of power that could bring back more authoritarianism. In 1986 this vacuum of power was filled with the return of Balaguer. Yet, despite Balaguer's political skills and capacity to adapt to new circumstances, his personalistic leadership style constrains his ability to face major socio-economic and political problems dogging the country in the late 1980s. Even if his personalism in the conduct of politics may give people a sense of security and order they lacked under the PRD, it does not help to address the complex problems confronted by a highly urbanized and better organized society in the midst of one of the most severe economic crises of this century.

A major problem affecting the country, which is difficult to address through traditional personalistic and clientelistic methods, is the proliferation of protest movements promoted by lower-income groups over unmet grievances aggravated by the current economic crisis. Strikes of sugar and mining workers, drivers, medical doctors and teachers have been common, as well as the proliferation of mass protests in the form of riots. Overall, this situation produces a democracy that is always at stake, always in crisis, awaiting for a resolution that fails to emerge.

Balaguer's victory in the 1986 elections reflects the paradoxes of contemporary Dominican politics. An old-timer politician and master of conservative modernization was elected president in competitive free elections (the third in a row to take place since 1978). By itself, this represents an important gain in a country with a long-standing history of fraudulent elections. Yet, Balaguer's victory represented also the affirmation of a vertical authority that emphasizes economic growth over redistribution, order over democracy. Balaguer's rule this time, however, will be somewhat ephemeral when compared to his influence on Dominican politics in the past. His age no doubt imposes limits. But also, his developmentalist model faces major constraints at a time of economic liberalization and anti-statism.

With Balaguer in his eighties and the PRD fragmented and discredited, it is easy to predict that major political restructuring will take place in the 1990s. In shaping the future, the devastating economic crisis is no doubt a decisive factor, at least in setting the framework within which political choices will be made. Yet political leaders are not exempt from responsibility.[28] They set the agenda for national projects to emerge, highlighting what is possible or impossible, desirable or undesirable. With Balaguer at the end of his political career and the PRD in disarray, it is in finding a new kind of democratic leadership that the Dominican Republic faces the greatest challenge in the 1990s.

ACKNOWLEDGEMENTS

The main arguments presented in this paper were originally developed in my PhD dissertation. I would like to thank my professors, Robert Boguslaw, Pedro Cavalcanti, Silvia Pedraza-Bailey, John Zipp, and Barry Ames for their help and encouragement. Thanks are also due to Guillermo O'Donnell, Terry Karl and Laurence Whitehead who read my dissertation upon completion and provided invaluable commentary. I also want to thank Colin Clarke for his editorial help and his hospitality during my stay at the Latin American Centre in Oxford.

NOTES

1. See F.H. Cardoso and E. Faletto, *Dependency and Development in Latin America* (Los Angeles: University of California Press, 1979) and G. O'Donnell, 'Introduction', in G. O'Donnell, P. Schmitter and L. Whitehead (eds), *Transitions from Authoritarian Rule: Latin America* (Baltimore: Johns Hopkins University Press, 1986).
2. Three major works are: P. Gleijeses, *The Dominican Crisis* (Baltimore: Johns Hopkins University Press, 1978); A. Lowenthal, *The Dominican Intervention* (Cambridge: Harvard University Press, 1972); and J. Moreno, *Barrios in Arms: Revolution in Santo Domingo* (Pittsburgh: University of Pittsburgh Press, 1970).
3. Oficina Nacional de Estadísticas, *República Dominicana en Cifras* (Santo Domingo, 1980).
4. See for a discussion of this process of industrialization, R. Espinal, 'Classes, Power, and Political Change in the Dominican Republic', PhD dissertation (St Louis: Washington University, 1985).
5. A more detailed account of this can be found in R. Espinal, 'Labor, Politics, and Industrialization in the Dominican Republic', *Economic and Industrial Democracy: An International Journal*, Vol. 8, No. 2 (1987), pp.183–212.
6. H. Wiarda, 'The Development of the Labor Movement in the Dominican Republic', *Inter-American Economic Affairs*, Vol. 1, No. 1 (1966), pp.41–63.
7. Espinal, 'Labor, Politics, and Industrialization', *op. cit.*, pp.183–212.
8. The official exchange rate was then one dollar to one Dominican peso.
9. Confederación Patronal de la República Dominicana, *Revista Patronal* (April–May 1962).
10. Asociación de Industrias de la República Dominicana, *Revista Patronal* (April–May 1962).
11. *Labor Code of the Dominican Republic* (Santo Domingo, 1982).

12. *Ibid.*
13. See for definitions of state corporatism the following: G. O'Donnell, 'Corporatism and the Question of the State', in J. Malloy (ed.), *Authoritarianism and Corporatism in Latin America* (Pittsburgh: Pittsburgh University Press, 1977); and P. Schmitter, 'Still a Century of Corporatism?' in P. Schmitter and G. Lehmbruch (eds), *Trends Toward Corporatist Intermediation* (Beverly Hills: Sage, 1979).
14. See for an account of the 1966 elections, E. Herman and F. Broadhead, *Demonstration Elections: U.S. Staged Elections in the Dominican Republic, Vietnam, and El Salvador* (Boston: South End Press, 1984).
15. Espinal, 'Labor, Politics, and Industrialization', *op. cit.*, pp.183–212.
16. Banco Central de la República Dominicana, *Boletín Mensual* (Santo Domingo, various issues).
17. More data can be found in R. Espinal, 'An Interpretation of the Democratic Transition in the Dominican Republic', in G. Di Palma and L. Whitehead (eds), *The Central American Impasse* (New York: St Martin's Press, 1986).
18. Balaguer appointed personally all CND members.
19. R. Espinal, *Autoritarismo y Democracia en la Política Dominicana* (San José: CAPEL, 1987).
20. S. Valenzuela, 'Labor Movements in Transitions to Democracy: A Framework for Analysis', paper presented at the Conference 'Labor Movements in Transitions to Democracy', Kellogg Institute, University of Notre Dame (1988).
21. *Listín Diario* (16 January 1980).
22. The burden of the external debt hampered the process of import-substitution industrialization, which was heavily dependent on the external market for raw materials and technology.
23. CNHE internal documents.
24. L.A. Ginebra, *Discursos* (Santo Domingo: CNHE, 1983).
25. See for an extensive discussion of this R. Plant, *Sugar and Modern Slavery: A Tale of Two Countries* (London: Zed Books, 1987).
26. References to this problem are also made by M. Murphy, 'The International Monetary Fund and contemporary Crisis in the Dominican Republic', in R. Tardanico (ed.), *Crises in the Caribbean Basin* (Newbury Park: Sage, 1987).
27. See for some discussion of this, J. Hartlyn, 'A Democratic Shoot-Out in the D.R.: An Analysis of the 1986 Elections', *Caribbean Review*, Vol. XV, No. 3 (Winter 1987).
28. This issue is raised and discussed by J. Malloy, 'The Politics of Transition in Latin America', in J. Malloy and M. Seligson, *Authoritarians and Democrats: Regime Transition in Latin America* (Pittsburgh: Pittsburgh University Press, 1987).

7 Politics and Society in Venezuela

Diego Bautista Urbaneja

INTRODUCTION

The purpose of this chapter is to give some clues to the texture of the relationships between Venezuelan society and political life. The essay is divided into two parts. In the first I will trace the relationship between Venezuelan political institutions – namely, the government and the political parties – and some general aspects of Venezuelan society, such as race, religion, urbanization and political culture. In the second, I will write about the more identifiable social and political actors in the political process and about their interrelationships.

Some preliminary remarks are in order. Venezuela is a continental country, and a big one by Caribbean standards: its population is around 18 000 000 and its area 912 000 km^2. Venezuela has had a presidential representative democracy since 1958 when the dictator, Jimenez, was ousted. There have been six elections, one every five years. The last four have been won by the main opposition party.* Since 1973 the party system has been based on two big and very well-organized political parties, Acción Democrática and Copei, which between them obtain 85 per cent of the vote (Figure 7.1). The remaining 15 per cent is mostly a leftist vote, shared by five small parties of different socialist blends.[1] The electoral system provides proportional representation for minority parties, whatever their size. I am thus talking about an ongoing and stable, competitive democracy, and a very old one by Latin American standards. It is a fairly complex polity, with what one might call 'dull politics'. Venezuela's economy is capitalist, with a powerful public sector in the oil, energy and steel industries, and a mainly private sector in manufacturing, agriculture, services and finance. Prices, wages and interest rates are highly dependent on government decisions. The class division of this integrated society results from the economy: a working class, a

---

* This chapter was written shortly before the governing party, Acción Democrática, won the 1988 elections.

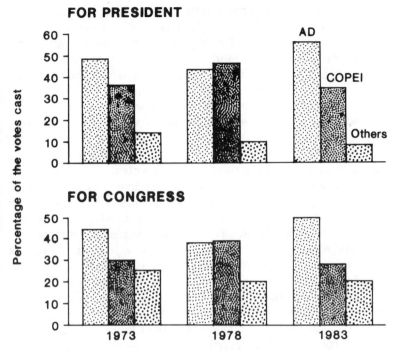

Figure 7.1 Venezuela's electoral results, 1973, 1978 and 1983

managerial class, every shade of middle class, and the array of marginal groups distinctive of Latin American capitalism. Portions of those groups are organized in trade unions, guilds, economic associations, often promoted – when not created – and controlled by the political parties.

GENERAL ASPECTS OF THE RELATIONSHIP BETWEEN VENEZUELAN POLITICS AND SOCIETY

Religion, Race, Gender and Politics

Venezuelan society is not characterized by racial, ethnic, linguistic or religious cleavages. This being so, its political institutions are not designed to deal with the issues that emerge from those sorts of social differences. Venezuelans are mostly Roman Catholic, but there is an unrestricted religious tolerance in the country. The predominance of the Catholic religion does not affect politics in a precise way. It provides a cultural frame in a very broad sense, which works as a general constraint to the more specific political institutions. One should not infringe the criteria that can be vaguely derived from the Catholic message about brotherhood, social justice and so on. But it is very easy not to infringe since they are so broad. This is all the more so as the religiosity of the Venezuelan people is in general very mild.

In the 1940s, as the current major political parties were being formed, the religious question played an important role.[2] The Comité de Organización Política Electoral Independente (Copei), a social Christian party, was strongly Catholic and a firm defender of private religious education, while Acción Democrática (AD) took a stance against religious education and supported the idea of an extensive, lay, state education. The educational question was at the time a salient one, and people with strong religious, Catholic, convictions leaned distinctively towards Copei. From 1958 onwards, the role played by the religious factor in determining political allegiance has diminished, as the differences between the parties *vis-à-vis* religious and public education have faded, and the Church has adopted an impartial role in politics. Nevertheless, it can be said that, in general, the stronger the religious conviction of a citizen, the more probable it is that he is a 'copeyano'. Moreover, the leadership of Copei is in a high proportion recruited among former students of the main Catholic schools, run by the Jesuit and the Lasallian orders.

Venezuela has a minority of blacks' and a minority of whites: approximately 10 per cent each. The vast majority is placed somewhere between these two poles, although many of them are considered – and consider themselves – white. This situation gives place to a complex and subtle pattern of racial discrimination which goes all the way through the descending degrees of 'whiteness', so that in moments of occasional anger you can hear brown people talking about, or to, slightly darker-brown people in a disrespectful way. This pattern of racial discrimination is not shared by all potential discriminators. I cannot give quantitative data, but an important part of Venezuela's population is quite liberal in racial relations. In any case, this kind of racial discrimination, which is practised at the personal level on an occasional basis and in a mostly covert way, does not rise to the political level. Neither the state nor the political parties have organs or sections dealing with specifically racial questions. Nor are racial conflicts issues in the political arena. Some relevant considerations can be added here. Until about 15 years ago the proportion of whites among the voters of Copei was larger than the proportion of whites among the voters of AD. This disparity has diminished (as have other kinds of disparity in the clientele of the two major Venezuelan political parties).

It is perhaps useful to make some comments about the racial composition of top political appointments in the government and in the parties. The vast majority of ministers, members of the governing bodies of political parties, parliamentarians, senior judges, and governors are white or light brown. That is so, even in leftist parties. This is the result of factors linking skin colour to socio-economic levels and access to education. A black or a dark mulatto running for a top-level appointment would find an informal, implicit, effective, yet ultimately surmountable obstacle of a specifically racial kind.

An Urban and Organization-dominated Political Culture

Venezuela is an urban country, and more than two-thirds of the population live in towns. Caracas has more than 4 million, Maracaibo one million, Barquisimeto, Valencia, Maracay more than half a million each. Every large city has its poverty belt, which in each case is extensive. They are composed of lower-class people, employed, unemployed or underemployed, lacking – or with very weak – sources of collective identification and normative patterns. These are good conditions for mass-media politics on the one hand, and, on the other, for the emergence of a charismatic leader of the populist sort. But Venezuelan politics is not mass-media politics. Not that the media do not play an important role in Venezuelan politics. Certainly they do, in the sense that the mass media give shape to events and play a powerful role in the social construction of reality; Venezuela has a powerful 'media complex', and there is much talk about the dominance of the media in Venezuelan political life.[3] But, as I said, I do not agree with this widely shared opinion.

When I say that Venezuelan politics is not a mass-media politics, I am referring to the fact that the main element in political competition is party organization.[4] The media exposure of the political leaders takes place in the context of a political system that has two very big political parties and several smaller ones. It is in this organizational context that media exposure acquires importance. Mass-media competition is an escalating competition between the two big organizations that are struggling for a thin and decisive slice of the electorate. But the big chunks have been shared already by the party organizations. Organization assures access to the media. If you don't have a good party organization, show-politics is of no value, and a good party organization can make a star of you, no matter how boring you really are.

With respect to charisma, Venezuelan democracy has had one or at most two charismatic leaders in 30 years. But even Carlos Andrés Pérez, the more obvious candidate for that term, would not dare to go into an election without the backing of AD's party organization. Here again, the organizational nature of Venezuelan politics frames and provides the setting for the eventual charismatic developments in political leadership.

The urban character of Venezuelan society has another powerful influence on politics. The accelerated rate of urbanization has brought a sharply increasing demand for services provided by government. More importantly, to the grasping of the texture of Venezuelan politics, it has imposed on the parties a heavy organizational and clientelistic task, in order to penetrate the organized and not organized, the economically integrated and the marginal sectors of the population. With reference to the poverty belts, for example, the major parties have to spread their organization to every *barrio* and sustain a constant proselytizing activity, mostly based on their capacity to deliver services, goods, credible promises and collective identification to this demanding urban, marginal, unorganized population.[5] If the party is the government, its capacity to deliver is obviously enhanced.[6]

I discern no clear dominant attitudes of a cultural character permeating political life. I would not say, for example, that we have an authoritarian tradition or culture, or a democratic one, for that matter. I think that at least in the Venezuelan case, these are very changeable domains. In this century, Venezuela has had several types of political regime. A long and very harsh dictatorship; a briefer and milder dictatorship; extremely mild dictatorships, if dictatorships at all; somewhat radical democracy; moderate representative democracy. Each type of regime has required – and obtained to some degree – a different political attitude on the part of the population. Of the six presidents we have had since 1958, two of them have had a distinctive unauthoritarian style of leadership, and two or three a clearly authoritarian one, and I think that in Venezuelan political life and in Venezuelan political institutions you find authoritarian and non-authoritarian styles of leadership dispersed in an unpatterned way. I revert again to the importance of political organizations. They provide the cohesion and the leadership, and it depends very much on the internal organizational processes whether the actual political leaders resulting therefrom will be authoritarian or non-authoritarian personalities, and whether they will have to draw upon the authoritarian or non-authoritarian aspects that coexist in the political attitudes of the Venezuelan people and inside every individual citizen.[7]

In Venezuelan political discourse it is commonly said that Venezuelans are used to being led by authoritarian figures. Although I find it unsupported by recent historical experience and today's behaviour, that widely shared view is important because it is the way Venezuelans perceive their own political values, and this self-perception is an important item in my description of politics and society.

For the last 15 years we have had a political situation marked by mutual tolerance, even amicableness, between political adversaries. That has been the result of the fairness of the political game and the reasonably good economic prospects for the majority of the population. However, the economy has been in crisis for some years and it is impossible to predict the consequences this will have on Venezuela's political culture.

An important aspect of Venezuela's 'amicable political culture' is the development of what I call a 'conversational system' in Venezuelan politics. By that I mean the constant social contact between the several élites of Venezuelan society: the entrepreneurial élite, the political élite – all are in touch all the time. The meeting ground consists of a series of social events – baptisms, burials, graduate parties, military promotions, birthday parties, cocktails, first communions, inaugurations of any kind – at which these élites see each other, get a direct version and feeling of one another's problems and views, promise and do favours, and soften tensions in a very personal way. This system inhibits the emergence of social ghettos, the existence of hostile and segregated cliques, and the development of potentially dangerous and hidden caste-like feelings in any element of the élite.[8]

The Missing Link Between State and Citizen

Venezuela has a major economic trait that permeates the character of the Venezuelan state and its relationship with the society. The Venezuelan state is the owner of the main source of external revenues – the oil. To a very important degree, the state does not depend on the taxes that people pay. The Venezuelan state does not take the money of the people and then redistribute it as it thinks proper. It distributes *its* money to the people and to *itself* – through social policies, public works, growth of the governmental bureaucracy, industrial policies.

As a consequence, the psychological link between the people, the society and the state is a very peculiar one.[9] The state considers that it does not depend on the people, but the other way round. The people lack – or possess in a rather weak degree – the tax-payer psychology in two ways. First, they do not feel that as tax-payers they have a right to a certain quantity and quality of governmental performance, and second, they do not feel that they have an obligation to pay their taxes. The psychological reality is deformed by a rhetoric which holds that the oil money is the money of the Venezuelan people, so that the state depends on the money of the people. This is too abstract a truth, if truth at all. Moreover, the rhetoric has to pay its due to reality. If it is true that the oil money is the people's money, the people have already paid their taxes, although nobody has actually paid them, except the state oil company. In my opinion this is a fundamental trait of Venezuelan society; one which permeates its workings in a deep, multiple, and not very definable but negative way.

In connection with this, the government party has a strong presence among all levels of state personnel. As a consequence, each election – lost by the incumbent party in the last four elections – is followed by a big turnover in state employees. That fact has inhibited the emergence of a professionalized civil service. Many bureaucrats owe their appointment to their party membership, not to merit. The Venezuelan citizen knows that, and the civil servant knows that the citizen knows, in a chain whose overall result is a further weakening of the sense of rights and duties in bureaucrat and citizen alike.[10]

Women, Youth and Politics

Women have had a substantial role to play in Venezuelan society. In large sectors of the population, men have defaulted in their supposed roles as provider of economic and moral sustenance for the family, and there has not been any welfare to support single mothers. Women have had to cope with a very heavy material and moral burden.

Women vote and have political affinities to the different parties in proportions roughly similar to those of men. Nevertheless, in the political establishment, the proportion of men in high state and party appointments is much larger than women. This is true, although to a diminishing degree, in all echelons of the government and the parties. Professionalized politics is mostly in men's hands. It is tempting to say that there is a bias similar to the one we found when we talked about the racial factor. It is also true, though, that women are getting increasing shares of high political responsibilities. Sub-cultures are important in this respect: there are state sectors in which there is a somewhat antifeminist organizational culture – the big state companies, for instance – whereas in other sectors certain appointments are often reserved for women, especially in domains related to the protection of consumer interests, education and health services.

Women are very active in the promotion of new social movements, which from the 1970s have acquired increasing relevance in Venezuelan social and political life. I have in mind the neighbourhood movement and the consumers' movement. It is not yet clear what kind of incidence these developments will have in Venezuelan politics. It is difficult to arrive at a valid generalization concerning the neighbourhood movement, as it is a very heterogeneous one. But everbody talks of it as eventual pillar of the future development of Venezuelan democracy towards a more participatory stage, probably having in mind the more articulate and mass-media-exposed neighbourhood associations, mostly middle-class ones.

People under 25 years form nearly 60 per cent of the population. It is difficult to identify the political consequences of this fact. On the demand side – what Venezuelan youth takes from Venezuelan politics – this means massive claims for educational and recreational services to be responded to by the state. These demands express themselves in a diffuse way – for example, through increasing delinquency – as youth does not constitute an organized pressure group. But, because the philosophy of the Venezuelan state includes the idea that the state has to cope with the educational needs of Venezuelan people, and because teachers' organizations are very powerful, there has been enormous public spending on education.[11]

On the supply side – what Venezuelan youth gives to Venezuelan politics – I find nothing specific. Despite much talk about widespread political scepticism among Venezuelan youth, it is not especially apathetic and continues to support the main political parties, though with less faith and a correspondingly greater utilitarianism than before. Also, through the parties, numerous new graduates benefiting from the massive educational schemes go to work in the bureaucracy to implement the reformist or the muddling-through policies of the major political parties or of the state itself.

Youth used to be the ideological sector in the political parties. In the 1970s, this inclination toward ideological discussion diminished, and we have seen the rather odd phenomenon of the youth sections of the political parties becoming the non-ideological ones. Some kind of ideological revival on the part of Venezuelan youth keen on politics is possible, but no signs of that are yet visible.

The Spanish philosopher, José Ortega y Gasset, has had a long and enduring influence on some aspects of Venezuelan political rhetoric and self-understanding which have to do with youth. Ortega's books were essential reading for Venezuelan would-be-politicians in the 1920s. He was a proponent of the notion of 'generation' as a key concept in understanding historical developments. This proposition was absorbed by the young leaders who were to found the big Venezuelan political parties. They saw themselves as a 'generation', and successive 'generations' of political leaders have been formed by this conception or have themselves taken it directly from Ortega's books, which continue to be commonly read. As a result, Venezuelan political leaders speak of themselves and think of themselves as belonging to some 'generation': 1928, '36, '45, '58, '68 (this one is mine). Perhaps there will be some talk about the generation of 1983, the symbolic date when the oil dream came to an end. The idea that successive political élites tend to see themselves as belonging to a generation is useful in the understanding of Venezuelan political dynamics.

SOME SPECIFIC ACTORS IN THE RELATIONSHIP BETWEEN VENEZUELAN POLITICS AND SOCIETY

In the second part of this chapter, I will focus on the more identifiable actors in the relationship between politics and society. Three groups of actors are important: the government, the political parties and the social organizations which have a social, economic or geographical base – trade unions, guilds, employers' associations, neighbourhood associations.

The Political Parties and the Government

The political parties are big and very well-organized machines. Acción Democrática is a social democrat party with about 1 500 000 members, and Copei is a Christian democrat party with about 1 000 000 members. They are built on the Leninist model of democratic centralism and a transmission-belt-like relationship with other social organizations, such as trade unions. The organizational networks penetrate every functional or regional division of the country and both parties have powerful international connections. They provide the people for, and orientations of, the government.[12]

From an ideological point of view the parties have the nominal differences associated with the social democrat and Christian democrat labels. But on a more practical level, both of them are supporters of the idea of a mixed economy, with a powerful public sector, a government-influenced and -protected market economy, and a private sector largely promoted by the state – a reformist and active state in the agrarian, educational, housing and health sectors. Their policies have produced the industrial sector and to that degree the middle class and the proletariat, whose mere existence as classes are thus very closely linked with the state and with the parties which have implemented those policies.

The state is flawed in its regular working by party penetration and the clientelistic practices of the parties, subjected as they are to pressing electoral imperatives. Nonetheless, these flaws should not be exaggerated. The ideological coincidence between the parties and the sheer financial power of the Venezuelan state have allowed the elaboration of a complex polity with a developmental and welfarist orientation which has maintained continuity over time. The same factors have allowed the emergence of a stable techno-bureaucracy at some levels and in some parts of the public administration: for example, in the middle levels of the steel and energy sectors. Even though party membership plays a key role, what is really obtained is an 'interrupted' techno-bureaucracy: if you have been an employee in the Agriculture Ministry for party reasons under an AD government and AD loses the elections, you are probably going to be removed and replaced by a 'copeyano'. But five years later, when AD next wins the elections, you are likely to be re-appointed to the Ministry of Agriculture, possibly in a higher position. The alternation in government of AD and Copei allows the clientelistic selection of beneficiaries to cancel or complement each other, depending on one's viewpoint.

Political Parties and Social Organizations

The political parties play a key role in the connection between government and some social organizations. The political parties fill the governmental machinery with policies and people, and at the same time control the trade unions and some professional associations. As a matter of historical fact, the political parties have promoted the creation of these organizations. The relations between the government and any social organization controlled by a political party are mediated by this party's interests. The interest of the party has a high priority in the criteria that direct the behaviour of the organization.[13]

There is a difference in the grip that the several parties hold on the various social organizations, and the degree to which different kinds of social organizations are controlled by the political parties. The trade union movement, for instance, is highly controlled by the political parties. AD has the lion's share here: it controls the national trades union confederation and several major sectoral and regional trade unions. The employers' associations, by contrast, are politically independent and it cannot be said that the parties control them, notwithstanding the fact that the various lists that compete in those associations' periodic elections often reflect political affinities. The professional associations, however, are usually controlled by the political parties.

The parties are the main channels of political access. They occupy the state and control civil society. The lower classes, whether organized or not, have access to the political process through the parties: as a party member, as a voter, as a member of a professional association or a trade union controlled by a political party. As they are subject to the electoral imperative, the parties play an important role in the formulation of policies with clear electoral consequences. In any case, the voice of the government party has a distinctive leverage in government decisions of almost every kind. Perhaps only highly technical decisions in the oil or energy sectors are free from party influence.

This being so, I would venture for a moment to apply the distinction between pressure politics and corporatist politics, fashionable in current political science, both to the relationship between the state and the social organizations and to the relations between the parties and the social organizations. When a political party controls a major social organization, this organization is incorporated, through its leaders, in the party's internal decision-making processes. Through this incorporation the social organization exerts influence on the government. This is especially so when the party is the government party, and has been notably the case with the peak trade union confederation and several of the major sectoral and regional trade unions, controlled by AD, when AD has been the government party. Recently, under an AD government, there have been attempts to include the peak trade union confederation on its own in an incipient neo-corporatist arrangement, together with the government and the employers' peak organization. But that attempt has failed. When Copei has been the government party, trade unions and professional associations controlled by AD behave as pressure groups on the government, keeping some of the corporatist-like influence through AD, as AD always maintains a strong presence in the parliament.

In the case of the employers' associations, as they are not controlled by any political party, they practise continuous pressure politics on government. A slight distinction can be made between the peak employers' association and the regional and sectoral employers' associations. In a formal sense, the relation of the regional and sectoral employers' associations to the government is of a pressure politics kind. The relation between the government and the peak employers' association is of a pressure politics kind as well, but as I said, some steps have been taken towards the establishment of a relation of a neo-corporatist kind. The employers' associations exert pressure politics on the political parties as well, often in a notorious and highly publicized way.

With respect to the political influence of Venezuelan entrepreneurs, I have to mention the so-called 'economics groups'. These are powerful private economic conglomerates with ramifications in the insurance, bank, real estate, industrial and commercial sectors. Some of them have a certain – and very difficult to determine – influence upon the behaviour of the government and the parties. Sometimes they are very well-connected with individual politicians; they give economic support to one or other party and obtain good-will in return.[14]

When making this distinction between corporatist and pressure-group politics, I have in mind the so-called 'macro' level. But in many decision-making arenas, the correponding business association and the professional organizations are formally incorporated in the corresponding state organ, giving rise to a net of neo-corporatist arrangements at the intermediate and micro levels.

I have mentioned the neighbourhood associations already. The political parties have sections to deal with neighbourhood issues and neighbourhood organizations. So far, the neighbourhood organizations have, in general, resisted the parties' attempts to control them. The neighbourhood movement has practised a pressure-group kind of politics on government and on political parties. An interplay of factors has led to this result. On the one hand, the neighbourhood organizations have not wanted to be co-opted by the parties, and thus they cannot participate in a corporatist way in the parties' policy information in urban matters. On the other hand, the state does not want to incorporate them on a corporatist basis in the governmental decision-making processes relating to urban conditions and developments.[15]

The neighbourhood organizations aspire to be a part of a formal corporatist arrangement at the state level, but they deprive themselves of the main instrument to achieve that aim, namely, 'a special relationship' with one of the main political parties. Nevertheless, some steps have been taken recently to incorporate the neighbourhood associations in the decision-making processes of government agencies responsible for urban matters.

Huge sectors of the population are not incorporated in any social organization. They are paid attention through the general policies of the state and through the reformist drive and the electoral interest and 'instinct' of the political parties. The latter, through their organizational networks, are very well aware of the needs and state of mind of the citizen who has no access to the political process through a corporatist or pressure-group connection, but only through the electoral process.

Political Parties and Political Culture

Political parties, besides their central role in the political process, play several parts in a more diffuse domain. I have already mentioned their role in an 'organization dominated' political life. Furthermore, the political parties are a source of collective and personal identity for large sectors of the Venezuelan population. They are the source of another trait of Venezuelan culture and society directly linked with politics, to wit, the strength of the 'electoral culture'.[16]

Venezuelan people have a very well-developed electoral culture;

the electoral phenomenon pervades daily life and conversation. We talk about elections – about elections to come, about the ones already passed, the national elections, the trade union elections, the guild elections. On the national level, every five years Venezuela is submerged in an electoral hurricane that is a mixture of a long carnival and a battle. Venezuelan elections are unique in duration; six months nominally – you can add eight months to get the minimum real duration; in expense – the last campaign (1983) cost $200 million, in my estimate; in turnout – 90 per cent of the citizens vote; and 'massiveness' – the big parties have electoral meetings of impressive size. I calculate that a standard meeting of a major political party in any one of the main towns exceeds 150 000 people, and there are several of these in an electoral campaign. The electoral process is a very effective mechanism for producing the feeling of political access, the reality of which is debatable, provided you can make that distinction between reality and feeling.

CONCLUSION

I have been discussing a relatively old political system, but I see its established ways threatened by change. Venezuelan politics suffer from intellectual exhaustion; from an excessive concentration of power in the hands of top party and state officials; from the excessive dominance of party organizations; and from the permanent presence of an electoral climate, shaped by the other three factors. Against that, and mainly outside the parties, you can see seeds of change – a lively, if marginal, intellectual debate; the emergence of new social movements; the appearance of regional forces clamouring for decentralization; the spread of a climate of opinion, fed by the lively debate, in which coexist, in an unstable way, the ideas of a more participatory politics, a more market-oriented economy, a stronger and more efficient state, a more stable civil service. These trends are compounded by governmental fiscal stress and the changes that the very sharp devaluation of the national currency has brought in the people's way of life. Perhaps a new sensibility is emerging, a new way of thinking, of doing things, brought about by the younger generations.[17]

In the near future there will probably be a loosening of the parties' grip on Venezuelan political life in favour of a more powerful and consequential public opinion – perhaps the future major actor in

Venezuelan political life. But apart from that, I cannot say at this moment whether all these new trends are going to have major formal and political consequences. Perhaps they will coexist with the organized political core, so that innovations assure a minimum of social and political change while the big political apparatuses provide a minimum of political cohesion. The game is on and it should be played in favour of one's preferred outcome.

POSTSCRIPT

In December 1988, Venezuela had its seventh set of democratic elections in the last 30 years. The Acción Democrática candidate, Carlos Andrés Pérez, won with 49 per cent of the vote against 40 per cent for Copei's Eduardo Fernández and 12 per cent for a small socialist party. The result conformed closely to poll predictions, although two novelties in Venezuelan politics were recorded. It was the first time that a Venezuelan president had been re-elected; and it was the first time since 1963 that the government party's candidate had been returned.

Other important changes in Venezuelan political life can be detected. Copei's candidate, Eduardo Fernández, obtained his nomination by inflicting a humiliating defeat on his contender, Rafael Caldera, Copei's founder and top politician. Fernández's victory marked the end of Caldera's hegemony in the party. Meanwhile, the majority of Acción Democrática supporters elected Pérez for their own reasons, not because he is their leader: in some senses he is a popular leader who happens to be in Acción Democrática. Indeed, the party is increasingly an effective electoral machine rather than a body capable of governing.

It was the intellectual exhaustion and lack of organizational powers of the two main parties, outside the electoral contest, that provided the context for the street riots that shattered Caracas and other Venezuelan cities in February and March 1989 – barely two months after the elections. Facing a severe economic crisis, the Pérez government announced an IMF-approved adjustment package that hit very hard the middle and lower classes. Bad timing and presentation of the measures added to their harshness. Within the space of four days, street violence and looting produced 300 casualties and material damage to the value of 5 billion bolivars, according to official estimates.

Nothing reliable is known about the riots or the rioters, but what is important, in the light of my analysis in the main body of this chapter, is the ignorance of the two major parties: they were unable to anticipate the disturbances, and were totally bypassed by them. Their sole reaction was to mouth clichés about the IMF, the rich and the poor, so out-of-touch were they with the actors.

Since early 1989, the trade unions, neighbourhood associations, business groups and various *ad hoc* organizations have come to the forefront of the debate about overseas debt, austerity and unemployment. The political parties that once towered over other organizations in power and significance are now having to share the socio-political arena with non-political agencies which are more intellectually alive and in touch with trends in social change. A major beneficiary of the parties' current weakness is the state itself. The incapacity of party politicians to cope with the economic crisis has permitted President Pérez to appoint independent ministers recruited on meritocratic criteria.

An unsettled period can be forecast for Venezuela, during which the society will seek out a new equilibrium. Accumulated social inequality, collective discontent and extensive corruption will have to be cleared away before Venezuela can regain its confidence as a stable democracy.

NOTES

1. H. Penniman (ed.), *Venezuela at the Polls: The National Elections of 1978* (Washington: American Enterprise Institute for Public Policy Research, 1980).
2. D. Levine, *Conflict and Change in Venezuela* (Princeton, New Jersey: Princeton University Press, 1973).
3. J. Martz and David Myers (eds), *Venezuela: The Democratic Experience* (New York: Praeger, 1977).
4. J.C. Rey, 'El Sistema de Partidos Venezolano', *Politeia*, Vol. I (1972).
5. J.C. Rey, H. Njaim, A. Stambouli, J. Brito, E. Vio and D.B. Urbaneja, *El Financiamiento de los Partidos Políticos y la Democracía en Venezuela* (Caracas, 1981).
6. J. Lombardi, *Venezuela: the Search for Order, the Dream of Progress* (Oxford and London: Oxford University Press, 1982).
7. M. Naim y Ramon Pinango (eds), *El Caso Venezuela: Una Ilusión de Armonía* (Caracas: Ediciones IESA, second edition 1985).
8. J.A. Gil Yepez, *El Reto de las Elites* (Madrid: Tecnos, 1978).

9. R. Valasquez, A. Calvani, A.R. Brewer-Carias, C.R.F. Silva, J. Liscano and M. Roche, *Venezuela Moderna: Medio Siglo de Historia* (Barcelona: Ariel, 1979).
10. *Venezuela 1979: Examen y Futuro* (Caracas: Editorial Ateneo, 1980).
11. M. Naim y Ramón Pinango (eds), *op. cit.*
12. *Ibid.*
13. *Ibid.*
14. E. Arroyo Talavera, *Elecciones y Negociaciones* (Caracas: Pomaire, 1988).
15. J.A. Silva Michelena (ed.), *Venezuela Hacia el 2000: Desafíos y Opciones* (Caracas: Editorial Nueva Sociedad, 1987).
16. Penniman (ed.), *op. cit.*
17. Silva Michelena (ed.), *op. cit.*

Part II
Independent Authoritarian Regimes

8 Society and Politics in Haiti: the Divorce between the State and the Nation

Christian A. Girault

Mais les nègres de ce pays ne sont pas conçus citoyens par ceux qui les gouvernent et les tuent.

Roger Dorsinville, *Ils ont tué le vieux blanc*, 1988

The birth of Haiti in the nineteenth century after a successful war of liberation waged mainly by ex-slaves, was followed by a rapid separation between the aims of the masses and the goals of the élite. The rural population was dispersed, but tried to gain access to the land. This access was denied by the various aristocracies which dominated the political scene during most of Haiti's independence period. In the end, a small and almost landless peasantry retained some use of the land. A strong hierarchical order emerged from an arrangement of social relations in which the urban élite, composed of various fragments – foreigners, a black and mulatto high class – exploited the rural producers, particularly through levies, marketing manoeuvres and usury.

The American occupation (1915–34) reinforced some of the most oppressive features of Haitian society without giving the benefit of economic prosperity. This led to the political crisis which erupted in 1946 and in 1956–57. The Duvalier regime, with its two phases under Papa Doc (1957–71) and Baby Doc (1971–86), attempted to solve the crisis through the use of violence and a rhetoric which made it akin to the fascist regimes of Mussolini and Franco. The argument of colour and of class – François Duvalier wanting to favour the black middle class – was used to crush all opponents. However, the Duvalier regime never enjoyed a wide popular support. Its duration is explained by various factors: pure luck, the weakness of the opposition, and the continuing benevolence of the United States (except for a brief period).

The fall of Jean-Claude Duvalier in February 1986 seems to have opened a new course for Haitian political life. After nearly 30 years of repression, political debate has surfaced again. But the very conditions of the departure of Duvalier, and the uneasy conditions of compromise between the various military junta and the civil masses, within an environment of economic bankruptcy, have cast a shadow of doubt on the democratic future of the country.

The dramatic sequence of events suffered by Haiti is second to none among the larger Latin-American republics (Cuba, Mexico, Chile) in terms of intensity and of complexity. But the small size of the country and its original culture, which has kept it isolated from the rest of the Caribbean, mean that its history and its socio-geographic features have been relatively ignored by the rest of the world. Thus the analysis of its political system poses a real intellectual challenge.

ORIGINALITY AND ISOLATION OF HAITI WITHIN THE CARIBBEAN

The Republic of Haiti includes several features which make it unique in the Americas. It was the first country to obtain its independence in Latin America and the Caribbean. It is also today the poorest country in this part of the world: Haiti displays extremely low levels of living. Setting these two facts side by side is very disturbing for the social scientist. Only careful analysis of two centuries of a convoluted history based on local sources can pave the way to an explanation of a political failure of this magnitude.[1] In the following section I present some evidence of long-lasting political mismanagement based on the concept of the authoritarian state.

Haiti is also a black nation in the sense that whites and mulattos comprise a very small percentage of the total population. This in itself is not unique – Jamaica is also predominantly black – but of the 15 or so black nations of the Caribbean, Haiti is by far the largest in size and population, with slightly over 6 million inhabitants (three times the population of the second in rank, Jamaica). From an African ethnic base, a truly Caribbean nation has emerged with its particular idiosyncracy manifested by the Creole (*kreyol*) language and the Vodun religion which are cultural adaptations of the highest significance. Here again, some elements of this Creole culture can be found in other islands of the Antilles (Guadeloupe, Dominica, Martinique, St Lucia) as well as in remote nations of the Indian Ocean (Seychelles, Réunion), but the deepness and authenticity of such original features establish, in Haiti, a novel creation in the Americas. Precisely because it is so different from the other nations, Haiti, although located right in the heart of the Caribbean, is very isolated from every other country.

It is surprising and fascinating to consider how in the Caribbean archipelago the elements of diversity tend to overshadow the trends towards unity, real but concealed. With Haiti the case is extreme: links with its closest neighbours, English-speaking Jamaica and Spanish-speaking Cuba are virtually non-existent, and its relations with the sister republic with which it shares the island, the Dominican Republic, are totally ambiguous. More than elsewhere, the divergence of orientations between the countries is striking, reducing to a minimum common expression of a Caribbean continuum. The explanation lies, of course, in the colonial (and neo-colonial) heritage as well as in the particular developments of nation-building in each country.[2]

Haiti has notably fewer resources than the Dominican Republic, but the main difference rests in the way these resources are tapped and used. Modernization and capitalistic infrastructures have had a much lesser impact on Haiti than on the Dominican Republic to the east. In fact, Haiti can still be presented as a nation of very poor peasants, whereas the surrounding countries exhibit a mix of agricultural, industrial and tourist activities and have been transformed by modernization in varying degrees.[3]

Three out of four Haitians still live in rural areas. They devote themselves to agriculture or activities strongly connected to agriculture – marketing of food staples, cattle raising, crafts. This agriculture produces a surplus which is dwindling as the population steadily increases. It is to be noted that rural–urban migration and out-migration have not reduced the pressure on the land as Haiti's rural densities are still increaing, although at a slower rate than previously. Yields are low, even though some argue that productivity is acceptable given the technology available. The end result is that petty agriculture is unable to feed the peasants themselves let alone the urban populace and Haiti has to rely heavily on food imports to prevent shortages which can evolve into major famines.[4]

The social and the spatial organization of the Haitian countryside is highly relevant to the problems of political life in the country. Although some of the peasants own the land they cultivate, most of them are smallholders without legal titles. Insecurity pervades social relations, because the peasantry, huge in numbers but dependent at various levels, is dominated by a select minority of large landowners (by Haitian standards), big middlemen, notaries and politicians, all categories which fall under the heading of *notables* (prominent men). The pattern of rural settlements reflects vividly this dependence. Peasant huts, small, fragile, unequipped and dispersed on the plots and along the paths and roads, contrast with the main foci of administrative, political and economic power called the *bourgs* (core villages). Here, a cluster of wood, cement or concrete houses, by no means luxurious, but affording basic comforts, provides the material support of a bourgeoisie, in the literal sense that historians of medieval Europe have used it.[5]

Seclusion is the second main feature of life in the rural provinces. Although the country is small in surface, circulation of goods and people is difficult, risky, costly and time-consuming because the relief is steep and the roads generally inadequate. Evaluated in time units, distances are exaggerated: 100 km can represent a five-hour trip by lorry or four-wheel-drive vehicle (often the only means of transportation usable). This difficulty of transit combines with a general deficiency of the media (press, radio, television) to account for the fact that in most of the rural areas news is scarce, transformed, deformed or censored. In the most remote areas (the districts close to the Dominican border, the adjacent islands, those parts of the mainland accessible only by boat) there are about 40 villages (out of a grand total of 150 in the country) which are real cul-de-sacs (end of the road villages) where entry of information and movement of goods and people are entirely controlled by gatekeepers commanded by the *notables* referred to above.[6]

In the urban districts, most of them built around a port town, the situation is different. Here the social hardships of acute unemployment, of economic deprivation and of low cultural level prevail. These problems are similar in nature to those experienced by the large metropolises of Latin America, but the extent of social marginality here makes them more akin to those of the capitals of Africa. This is particularly the case in Port-au-Prince, a city of around one million inhabitants (56 per cent of the total urban population of the country), the growth of which has been fuelled by a strong internal migration.[7]

In a peasant society subordinate to a large metropolis, the constraints of isolation (from the regional environment) and of internal seclusion of the vast majority put severe obstacles in the way of democratic life. The study of the political history of the country since its constitutional independence will confirm the stumbling block of dependence and will document the curse of authoritarian tradition.

THE AUTHORITARIAN TRADITION

Independence and the Establishment of a Dual Society

Haiti became independent in 1804 at the cost of probably more than 150 000 dead (out of a population of around half a million inhabitants). Starting with the first unrest of 1789 and the rebellion of slaves in 1791, the strife took on huge proportions. From a social upheaval it developed into a national liberation war against the best armies of the time: the Spaniards, the British and the French. At the end very little remained of the bases of prosperity that the French colony of Saint-Domingue had enjoyed. Thirteen years of merciless war had established only the principle that armed struggle would prevail.

Of course, the ideas of the French Revolution had influenced the process of liberation, but because of the ambiguous and later treacherous position of France on the abolition of slavery, the construction of a republic was not a goal shared by all. The establishment of a proper state apparatus came after all other solutions – colonization by another nation and autonomy – had been tried and found impossible. Only the military leaders saw the necessity of building a state to defend what had been obtained during the strife and also to stay in power and benefit from it. The vast majority of the former slaves thought that they had fought to attain their personal freedom and not to install new rulers. It is to be noted that, among these former slaves, half had been born in Africa or in other territories of the Caribbean, and that they spoke several languages – facts which did not make cohesion easy.

The leaders could not implement an economic system other than that of the plantation, since no other model was available for tropical societies. The plantation also had the advantage of providing a safe economic return and of facilitating social control through the bondage of gangs of workers. General Toussaint-L'Ouverture, King Christophe and President Boyer tried to maintain or resuscitate the estates and attach the workers to the plantations. To a large extent they failed. Many plantations were divided up into smaller estates.

Programmes of land distribution among the officers and soldiers took place, and some beneficiaries were established on state land. But, on the whole, social relations on and around the estates remained based on various forms of coercion.

The country was entirely militarized: administrative districts were placed under the jurisdiction of captains and commanding officers down to the smallest units which were run by non-commissioned officers. The financial and material necessity of defence (against the former colonial powers) and the project of annexation of the eastern part of the island (which would become the Dominican Republic) were taking a heavy toll. Peasant rebellions erupted from time to time, particularly in the southern peninsula where the producers had kept some autonomy *vis-à-vis* the feudal landlords. The ideology of these rebels was strongly egalitarian and libertarian. They rejected the taxes imposed on agricultural produce, and they advocated a social order free of the domination of the *notables* and the merchants.

During the second half of the nineteenth century the rural rebellions took on a different character. The bases for dissidence were the same: the resentment created by heavy taxes and large profit margins taken by the middlemen and the exporters. But these movements were much less autonomous than before. In fact, rural workers were enlisted in the armed bands destined to conquer power in Port-au-Prince to benefit *caudillos* who rotated rapidly as heads of state. It is symptomatic that these rebellions took place more frequently in the north of the country, where peasants and rural workers were incorporated within the framework of the neo-plantation.[8]

From the end of the nineteenth century until 1915, when the United States' occupation began, the political situation became quite chaotic. The constitution was permanently disregarded. The elections which took place had very little meaning. Opponents fled into exile because their lives were at risk, and from Saint-Thomas and Kingston they tried to foment rebellions that would reinstate them in power. Economically, the situation tended to worsen, as Haitian coffee and Haitian timber, the basic exports during the first century of independence, were the object of greater competition from new exporters. Financial crisis added to the chaos, as the clumsy and dishonest management of the internal and external debt gave leverage to imperial powers (notably Germany, France and the United States) to intervene overtly in Haitian politics.

Without any doubt a century of independent life had confirmed the nation in its existence. But the chasm that existed between a ruling élite, heavily militarized, and the rest of the nation made up of landless rural workers and peasants had never been abolished. On the contrary, contention between the two worlds (the *bourgs* and the cities on one side and the flat country and the hamlets on the other) strengthened the establishment of a dual society. The official society (*pays officiel*) spoke French, practised Catholicism, used law and codes and above all ruled, whereas the real country (*pays réel*) spoke only Creole, practised Vodun, used custom and tradition and had no access whatsoever to the polity.[9]

The US Occupation and the Persisting Political Crisis

Until 1915 the fate of the peasantry needed to be taken into consideration by the government, even if it was through coercion and manipulation. After the US intervention there were no more social forces in the provinces to resist the preponderance of the Port-au-Prince administration. The occupation, which lasted until 1934, modified, in an irreversible way, checks and balances of power in Haitian society, although the economic foundations of the country remained basically unaffected.

After the landing of the US Marines in July 1915, the Haitian army was dissolved and military resistance took some time to organize. From 1916 on, a guerrilla movement headed by C. Péralte, an officer of the dismissed army, harried the Marines, who deployed the sophisticated armament of the time (planes, machine-guns) to subdue the rebellion. It is to be noted that this movement had as its main territorial base the Central Plateau, a region where the peasantry is relatively well-off. Péralte was killed in 1919 and the movement was crushed two years later. The Americans created a *gendarmerie* (police corps) – the *Garde d'Haïti* – as in their view there was no need in such a country for a national army, which was costly and could create political problems. The model applied here was fairly analogous to the one adopted by the US in Cuba, the Dominican Republic and Nicaragua.

Although one of the reasons for the intervention was to favour the introduction of US capital and the advancement of US interests in the country, relatively little was achieved. The strengthening of the participation of Citybank of New York in the capital of the Haitian National Bank, the foundation of a few agro-industrial concerns, and the partial re-orientation of external trade towards the

United States, were the only tangible results of an occupation of 19 years, a disappointing confirmation of the unique character of Haitian society for the promoters of entrepreneurial development.[10]

Nevertheless, some technical developments of the Americans had a far-reaching impact. They systematically used public funds – totally controlled by their 'financial adviser' – to promote the modernization of equipment and infrastructure. Telegraph, telephone, new roads (often built under the *corvée* – forced labour – system), construction of public buildings and installation of a few schools and a few hospitals were powerful means of strategic command. The result was a centralization of economic forces: statistical data show, for example, that maritime transit tended to concentrate in Port-au-Prince and Cap-Haïtien, where custom duties were more easily collected. This modernization remained superficial, as the volume of investment and the progress of productivity were necessarily limited, but it gave strong orientations to the society.[11]

Under the Americans three presidents were 'elected' by select constituencies. The first two, Dartiguenave and Borno were mere puppets. The third one, Vincent, had more substance because of his intellectual and political skill. Inevitably, the occupation gave rise to an upsurge of nationalist sentiment, manifest particularly at the end of the 1920s. The arrival of commissions sent from the US to investigate allegations of human rights violations provided an opportunity seized by students and nationalist leaders to demostrate in Port-au-Prince. Apart from anti-imperialist opinions, in the same vein as those proferred in the Dominican Republic or Mexico at the time, a peculiar element began to surface – the colour question.

The colour question in Haiti has been long-standing. It stemmed from the fact that among the élite, be it economic, social or intellectual, the mulattos or browns have traditionally had a participation which is larger than the proportion they represent in the whole society. This fact had been recognized early on by historians and pamphleteers, but generally during the nineteenth century it did not give rise to a crystallization along political lines, for browns as well as blacks were able to co-opt members of the other shade of colour to their respective cabinets. Because the Americans carried out a racist policy during the occupation (often explained by the fact that many of the commanding officers came from the Old South), which consisted in hiring only light-skinned people for prestigious or better paid positions, the question became to a large degree political. Blacks at the end of the occupation felt deeply their exclusion from the (small) circle of power. This was even more evident under the presidency of Lescot (1940–46), a weak character manipulated by the Americans and bought off by the Dominican dictator Trujillo.

Nationalism became connected with a cultural revival of great significance. Several schools of thought emerged around certain intellectuals and literary journals. The leading figure of this renaissance was Jean Price-Mars, whose public lectures stimulated reflection on the nature of Haitian society. In *La Vocation de l'Elite* he criticized the schizophrenic attitude of the bourgeoisie which imitated the Western mores[12] and advocated a return to the authenticity of peasant society. He also advocated a study of Haiti's African legacy. His book *Ainsi Parla l'Oncle* (1928) was seminal for folk re-discovery and the recognition of the popular religion, Vodu.

Jacques Roumain blended militant nationalism (for which he was imprisoned), brilliant literary activity – both in poetry and prose – and serious ethnological research. His radical views opened the road to the founding of the Haitian Communist Party (1933). This party never became a mass organization, but maintained some influence, thanks to the quality of its intellectuals. Among the followers of Roumain, outstanding writers like J.S. Alexis and R. Depestre perpetuated this socially committed school until the 1960s and 1970s.

François Duvalier, a physician from Port-au-Prince, who gained acceptance for his work on sanitary programmes under the Americans, led ideology in another direction. In his argument, weakly supported by sociological studies written with the collaboration of L. Denis, he equated, in a simplistic way, the colour question to class struggle. For him the blacks were exploited by the browns and the salvation of Haiti would come about through the access to leadership of the black middle class, a particularly elusive category in Haitian society. Here is the basis of *noirisme* (black power or black superiority), a crude ideology, contemporary to the more refined *négritude* professed by the Martinican writer A. Césaire and the Senegalese L.S. Senghor.[13]

The luck of F. Duvalier – because it seems that a measure of chance is crucial to dictators and fascist leaders – was his appointment to the Ministry of Health and later Labour in the Estimé cabinet (1946–50). These positions provided an exposure to the public, gave him contact with local strong men in the provinces, and enabled him to take on a statesman-like stature. When Estimé was ousted by a coup staged by General Magloire (1950), Duvalier went into hiding, a fact which later allowed him to pretend to have been persecuted. At this stage the man had accumulated experience and personal knowledge of political and military figures. He became more and more secretive and shrewd; at the same time his rhetoric turned to demagogy.

In Haiti, as in other countries of the Caribbean occupied by the United States (Cuba, the Dominican Republic, Nicaragua), the occupation paved the way to dictatorships of long duration. But because the on-going crisis here was more serious than elsewhere, and because the colour question had been activated by ideologists along sectarian lines, the solution took on a specific character. The despotic regime did not originate in a national guard, but rather in a stratum of the population – particularly the urban middle class – few in number but aggressive and prone to vengeance. During the years 1956–57 a fascist solution was brewing. It foretold a long and tragic episode (in an already dramatic history).

DUVALIERISM: THE LIABILITY OF A FASCISTIC REGIME

The history of the Duvalier years, which represents the longest regime in Haitian history, remains to be written. Because of the grotesque and exotic features of this regime, the hard facts have been often missed. However, among superficial analyses, there exist a few carefully documented sources which deserve a mention. Diederich and Burt give a valuable insight into the darkest years of Papa Doc's rule.[14] The studies of G. Pierre-Charles, although written from exile, provide enlightening texts.[15] The articles of British journalist, G. Chamberlain, published in the *Guardian* and in *Caribbean Contact*, are extremely good pieces into which future historians will have to delve. Furthermore, a young Haitian social scientist, M.R. Trouillot, has produced an ambitious work of analysis and interpretation of Duvalierism which will stand up to future discussion.[16] The merit of these works is to expose, in a clear fashion, facts and episodes that the dictatorship and its supporters (external and internal) would have preferred to remain concealed, and that other authors have adulterated.

The accession of François Duvalier to the presidency is certainly one of the episodes which remains most blurred in this history. In 1956, a year of agitation and social explosion, F. Duvalier did not appear the most likely candidate to win the presidential election later postponed until 1957. Other contenders like Fignolé (populist),

Jumelle (technocrat), Déjoie (businessman and political figure from the south) probably had better support in terms of organization and finance, but they failed to recognize that Duvalier represented a special threat and they acted separately. Duvalier, with all the weaknesses of his organization, benefited from the division of his adversaries, and this was to be a permanent feature during his dictatorship. Also, Duvalier led a persevering campaign in the provinces, spending a good portion of his time in speeches and contacts with local bosses of the *bourgs*. He became a master in manipulating the two forces which give direction to Haitian politics: the army – the *Forces Armées*, successor to the constabulary installed during the occupation – and the United States. For example, he took advantage of the fact that the high command of the *Forces Armées* was largely discredited in 1957, after several interventions and a massacre perpetrated against the followers of Fignolé. A dissident officer, Kébreau, gave concrete help and protection to Duvalier during the last phase of the campaign. As for the United States, whose leaning was in favour of Déjoie, he managed to secure its neutrality.

The electoral returns of September 1957 have never been accepted by the opponents of Duvalier, but it seems that the black leader won by a short margin over Déjoie with good general support in the provinces (except for the south, which was committed to Déjoie). However, the tension that characterized the last weeks of the campaign had been such that Déjoie, Fignolé and Jumelle soon fled into exile. This was certainly not the inauguration of a democratic regime.

Violence and Rhetoric

The violence suffered by Haiti during the pre-electoral process of 1956–57 did not come to a halt after the election. On the contrary, it reached new climaxes at the end of the 1950s and the beginning of the 1960s. Duvalier's opponents denied his victory, and resorted to any means at their disposal to defeat him. But Duvalier's policy did not favour compromise and throve on the confrontation. Duvalier promoted a strategy of tension at a time when turmoil and rapid political transformation affected most of the countries of the Caribbean. In Cuba the Castro regime, installed in 1959, turned to Marxism after the victory of Playa Girón (1961). In the Dominican Republic, the assassination of R.L. Trujillo provided scope for democratic transformations which were abruptly stopped by several coups and a second United States' occupation (1965). Jamaica, after the brief episode of the Federation of the West Indies, seceded and gained full independence in 1962.

Several invasions of Haiti took place, originating in the Dominican Republic or Cuba. Their organization was generally haphazard and unprepared but, in retrospect, it is clear that Duvalier enjoyed pure luck, because his defence was not particularly well planned, either. At one stage, guerrilla bands reached Kenscoff, a village in the mountains no more than 25 km from Port-au-Prince. However, the reaction after the defeat or the retreat of the guerrillas was ruthless: the villages or hamlets which had been in touch with the guerrillas – called *camoquins*, a derogatory term for the communists – became scenes of carnage. The dictator took no more chance with the bourgeoisie than with the peasants. Members of the families of notorious opponents were arrested, jailed or even slaughtered *en masse*, as in the case of the inhabitants of the town of Jérémie, in the south. Terror reigned, and the exact number of people slain during this bloody first phase of the dictatorship is not exactly known; it may be of the order of 50 000.

On the internal front, Duvalier was faced with social forces which were far from being receptive to his ideas and methods. The *Forces Armées*, obviously, represented a special risk for him, although they had been temporarily neutralized. The positions of chief of staff and commanding officers were traditionally held by members of the mulatto élite who were considered, as such, foes. This is the reason why he created a militia in July 1959 for his protection: these were the *Volontaires de la Sécurité Nationale* (VSN), more widely known by the nickname of *tontons macoute* (bogeymen). This militia expanded from its Port-au-Prince base to include sections in every *bourg* and all the rural divisions of the country. In this manner a counter-force of some 50 000–60,000 men (and women), roughly equipped and normally unpaid, intimidated the whole society. (The corresponding number of military personnel was of the order of 6000–8000.)

In the case of the Catholic Church, Duvalier played safely, exposing the fact that the bishops were without exception *blancs* (whites or foreigners in Creole). He expelled the archbishop of Port-au-Prince, Poirier, a Frenchman, and broke up a few congregations deemed hostile to his power. After a phase of tension with the Holy See – Duvalier was excommunicated in 1964 – a new Concordate was signed in 1966 and he appointed to the archdiocese of Port-au-Prince, Ligondé, a black man and his kinsman, who was to keep silent on human rights violations until the very last years of the Duvalier regime. In the same way, trade unions and student organizations, active in the 1950s, were tamed. From 1961–62 onwards, the regime had nothing to fear from a few token associations infiltrated by spies and police.

In a few years all opposition had been crushed. The leaders had gone into exile; the few militants still in the country, of various communist affiliations, kept up an underground opposition, but further repression hit them severely in 1965 and 1969. In 1964 Duvalier changed the constitution and, through a plebiscite, proclaimed himself president-for-life. Meanwhile, the years 1964–71 epitomized the isolation of the regime. The facts that Haiti established strong diplomatic links with Liberia and received Emperor Haile Selassie with decorum, were small compensations, in keeping with the regime's 'black ideology'!

Duvalier's attitude towards the United States was (intentionally) Machiavellian. When the United States worried about the dictatorship and repatriated its military mission, Duvalier issued a speech in which he threatened to join the non-aligned countries (1962). But he knew that the United States would not allow a second Cuba. His blackmail served him well: the Colossus of the North, while keeping its distance from the atrocities of the regime, never tried to destabilize him. The United States would have been embarrassed to find a substitute for the dictator. This reciprocal *Realpolitik* was to bear fruit in the sense that the external security of the regime remained assured, as a recompense for services like the acquisition of the Haitian vote at crucial sessions of the Organization of American States and the ban of communists by law in Haiti. This policy left scope for better relations in the future.

Duvalierism, protected by its militia and isolated from external influences by terror and censorship, had time to develop its own political base. The basic idea was to promote the deserving black middle classes, rural as well as urban, by pitting blacks against browns. The speeches of Duvalier, compiled in his *Oeuvres essentielles (Fundamental Opus [sic])* are full of variations on the theme of race and class. Here one encounters the mediocrity of Duvalier's thought as well as the cunning of his political manoeuvres. Appealing to colour solidarity, the masses are called to support the aspiration of the most competent men to gain access to power. By doing so, they will contribute to the redemption of Haiti. As in any dictatorship, a cult of the leader is inaugurated. The system of propaganda reached levels of demagogy and ridicule when the discourses, the editorials

and even a Duvalierist catechism(!) were written by zealous court-
esans such as Blanchet, de Catalogne and Désinor.

The dictator became alternatively a brilliant intellectual of the
Third World, speaking for the poor and the bereaved, or Papa Doc,
the good doctor who acts as a father, who cares and cures. As a
matter of fact, Duvalier also let the people think that he was en-
dowed with supernatural powers. Well-versed in Vodun himself, he
worshipped at his own *hounfort* (temple) and consulted renowned
houngans (Vodun priests). He tried to encourage sentiments of sacred
awe which could be added to his already solid reputation for terror.
On the material and semiotic side, the diffusion of the emblems of the
regime became important in a country devoid of modern means of
communication and where illiteracy is so widespread. The effigy of
the leader had its place in every house, where it could serve as a proof
of good citizenship. The guinea fowl, the symbol of the *tontons
macoute*, was depicted with slogans on their barracks, and Duvalier
went so far as to change the national flag from blue and red (horizon-
tal stripes) to black and red (vertical stripes) to symbolize the radical
stance of his black revolution.[17]

**From Papa Doc to Baby Doc: Perpetuation and Fall of the Duvalier
Regime**

In spite of its manipulation of symbolism and its terrorism, it is
probable that the Haitian masses were never taken in by the slogans
of the regime, inasmuch that it is possible to evaluate their political
consciousness from scant evidence and few studies. The Duvalier
plebiscites – including the 1971 referendum by which the constitution
was amended to facilitate the transmission of power to his son,
Jean-Claude, thus transforming the regime into a dynastic republic –
were all won by 99 per cent returns of *yes* votes. But these results did
not deceive observers, because it was well-known that the electoral
register had never been properly compiled, and that the balloting
procedures had been rigged from the outset. Political rallies were
attended, but only because of the appeal of free liquor and, in some
cases, the distribution of cash. If these measures were not sufficient,
the physical pressure of the *tontons macoute*, the main organizers of
these events, compelled attendance.

The practice of power at a time of crisis – in this chapter the
economic difficulties of the dictatorship are only briefly referred to –
was, however, very different from the rhetoric. The attempts to

displace the bourgeoisie from its strongholds did not get very far. Even during the reign of Papa Doc one noted that, more often than admitted, a policy of compromise with mulattos and whites was followed. This tendency was to become much more important during Baby Doc's period in office. In the traditional import–export sector, strategic in an open and archaic economy like Haiti's, the mulatto and white establishment came to terms with Duvalier at the price of some concessions, such as the recognition of a few black entrepreneurs or opportunists close to the Duvalier clan, and the payment of political taxes to the regime. The same was true of the wholesale sector, where the Levantine businesses agreed to collaborate with Duvalier. The few transnational corporations (Reynolds Mining, Royal Bank of Canada) were not disturbed in their dealings. In the matter of economics, Duvalier's *noirisme* remained merely a threat and an admonition geared to secure a few seats at the corporate table and some points of business profit.[18]

The transition from Papa Doc to Baby Doc after the death of the former in April 1971 operated smoothly. The regime stood firm, although some potential instability was noted. Firstly, Baby Doc was a weak political figure compared to his father. His personal ability was in doubt: he did not obtain his *baccalauréat* and he never travelled abroad. Public-speaking problems and overweight hampered his physical presence. During the first years of his reign, the real power was in the hands of his mother, the First Lady, Simone Duvalier, widow of the dictator, who represented the hard line of repression. The dependency of Jean-Claude on his mother was reduced in the late 1970s, only to be replaced after his marriage in 1980 by the strong influence of his wife, Michèle Bennett and his father-in-law, Ernest Bennett, a coffee and cacao exporter from the *bourg* of Le Borgne. In fact, the analysis of the power structure under Baby Doc should not be done in terms of individuals but in terms of small groups who competed in the palace for positions, exactly like *camarillas* close to the monarchs in sixteenth-century Italy. These persons of varied background used the name of Duvalier, and the fragments of ideology attached to it, to perpetuate a system which favoured their interests. This structure explains the fact that Baby Doc could stay in power for 15 years, a term even longer than his father's. But beneath the apparent stability, future historians will note the frequent skirmishes in the corridors of the palace, the intrigues and the disgraces which drove the powerful of the day into house arrest and often exile. Cabinet shuffles and rotations at the

head of the feared agents of repression – the *macoutes*, the presidential guard, and a new élite army battalion, the *Léopards* – punctuated
political life. Some names of ministers, like Cambronne, Merceron,
Lafontant still stand for strong influence and outright corrupt
management.

Circumstances in the 1970s changed somewhat, and this accounted
for a notable variation in Duvalierism. From 1970 on, bilateral aid
originating with the United States and later with France, Canada,
Israel and Taiwan, as well as multilateral technical co-operation
programmes, undertook numerous *projets*. Non-governmental
organizations, often religious in nature, entered the country, establishing chapels, co-operatives and building schools, dispensaries and
wells. The extent of distress in Haiti was so large that it seemed that
there was scope for the display of all the generous and naïve sentiments of Western donors. On the other hand, assembly-line products, such as sports equipment, electronic components and apparel,
were established in export-processing factories in Port-au-Prince,
taking advantage of very low wages and abundant labour (mostly
female). Tourists, hitherto discouraged by bad press in the United
States and Canada, returned in significant numbers. The atmosphere
was more relaxed, even if it was by no means liberal. Jean-Claude
Duvalier proclaimed: 'My father accomplished the political revolution, I will achieve the economic revolution' – an evident gesture to
attract foreign investment. Political repression became less harsh;
prison or expulsion was preferred to killings. However, the young
president was unable to change the image of the dictatorship, since
his self-trumpeted ideology, Jean-Claudisme, for the reasons mentioned above, did not acquire sufficient substance.

At the turn of the 1980s the superficial modernization of the
country, only visible in the capital, and the very relative liberalization, came to a standstill. The economic indicators became very
depressed again. Years of drought and declining agricultural production pushed rural residents towards the cities, and some into the
risky journey to the United States as boat people. A minor agitation,
focusing on radio programmes and theatre performances, seemed a
threat to the regime, which responded by expelling dozens of
journalists and intellectuals in December 1980.

From this point onwards the fragility of the regime was exposed.
But no quick end to the crisis could be found. Growing contradictions
accumulated around the presidential palace. One was of an ideological nature. By marrying a mulatto woman in 1980, Jean-Claude

Duvalier not only established personal links with the previously vilified brown class, but was seen as betraying the racial ideology of his father. This weakened his support among the more convinced militants of the black cause. And because his wife was a woman of strong character and brought in her father and other members of her family, Duvalier Junior soon appeared as a puppet in the hands of this small group. The other contradiction was economic. A downturn in the economic sphere, marked by low prices for coffee, abrupt recession in the tourist sector, and slackening of the rate of expansion of assembly plants, created serious financial difficulties, which, in turn, led to interventions by the United States Agency for International Development and the International Monetary Fund. In the middle of this financial crisis, corruption reached huge proportions, while the fate of the poor was completely ignored by the government (except for charity programmes inaugurated by the First Lady).[19]

The contrast between absolute poverty and arrogant luxury became more patent than ever because the source of riches was based on corrupt dealings with fiscal revenues and aid money. The appointment of Marc Bazin, a Haitian official of the World Bank, to the Ministry of Finance, and his quick dismissal, because his commitment to sanitation of public funds was an inconvenience for many high-ranking persons, exposed the problem (1982). More and more journalists' essays and television reports showed to the outside world (particularly the United States, Canada and France) the scandalous nature of the long dictatorship with its dishonest and decayed façade. But the opposition was too weak to take up the challenge of displacing Duvalier by itself. Inside Haiti, a small Christian democrat party protested human-rights violations under the courageous leadership of Silvio Claude, himself imprisoned several times. Outside, the various groups and parties located in Montreal, New York, Mexico and Paris did not find a common ground, despite repeated attempts at unification. Above all, they were unable to mobilize men and women in large numbers and to raise money to support their movements.

What brought a new sense of social and political participation and eventually strengthened the opposition to Duvalier was the evolution of the Catholic hierarchy and the changed role of some Protestant churches. A radicalization of some elements of the Catholic Church was already evident in the 1970s. But the short visit of Pope John Paul II to Port-au-Prince in 1983 and his observation that some things must change, encouraged the more committed clerics to advance ideas of social justice. A statement in favour of human rights was issued by the Conference of Religious Organizations at the end of 1983. A literacy campaign called Mission Alpha was launched in 1985 and the Catholic radio station, Radio Soleil, became vocal in denouncing abuses. This message was kept general and non-political enough to accommodate the views of more conservative bishops and to avoid confrontation with the state apparatus. But it was evident that by 1984 positive action taken by the Church had the support of many people – particularly among the young generation – in urban areas and in some rural areas where local grassroots organizations had been able to loosen the rope that strangled the peasantry. Such was the political situation at the end of 1985 and during the first weeks of 1986, just before the departure of Baby Doc to exile in France (7 February 1986) in a United States Air Force plane.

THE AFTERMATH OF DICTATORSHIP: WHAT FUTURE FOR DEMOCRACY IN HAITI?

The years that followed Duvalier's downfall have been characterized by events taking place in close succession and their analysis is necessarily difficult. A *de facto* regime – the Conseil National de Gouvernement (CNG) – composed of military leaders and a few civilian figures gave way to an elected civilian president, L. Manigat, but only after an abortive electoral process punctuated by bloodshed in November 1987 and rigged elections in January 1988. This president himself was ousted by coup after only four months in power (June 1988). A second coup removed General Namphy, and Colonel P. Avril took the reins of power with the support of non-commissioned officers (September 1988). The constitution approved in 1987 by a large majority of voters, was suspended, and then partially put back into force in 1989. It seems that the balance of power is going to stay within the army, though this does not preclude further political instability. In April 1989 a coup fomented against Avril aborted; the *Léopards* and the Casernes Dessaline battalions were disbanded. The basic elements of the political crisis (weakness of the economy, corruption on a large scale, mainly through contraband and drug trafficking, criminal activities of paramilitary groups) are still present. But any serious analysis of these events should begin with a reminder of the circumstances in which Duvalier Junior left Haiti with his clique.

It was probable at the end of 1985 that some kind of revolution or at least a large popular movement was brewing in Haiti. Confrontation with the police had taken place in Gonaïves (third city in size in the country) and in Cap-Haïtien (the second city): popular opposition manifested itself more spontaneously in provincial towns left in complete neglect during the years of relative prosperity. The movement spread to Port-au-Prince at the beginning of January 1986 through a student strike, which closed all schools after the Christmas vacation. Political observers have noted that the capital was at all times more favourable (or rather less hostile) to the Duvaliers because of the higher concentration of the bourgeoisie, civil servants and direct and indirect beneficiaries of the regime. It was also solidly controlled by the *macoutes* network. However, a demonstration erupted in the city centre, closely followed by repression in the shantytowns. When Duvalier left, pushed by the mediation of the Jamaican prime minister and the American ambassador's intervention, his ultimate defences (the presidential guard and the *macoutes*) had not been defeated, and he himself appointed H. Namphy and the members of the CNG before his departure. Hence one is led to think that a 'revolution' had been frustrated or that a strong popular movement supported by mass demonstrations had not come to full maturation.[20]

This case is not unusual in the Third World, particularly in small countries where outside intervention at a crucial moment seems to be the order of the day for various reasons, among them the rapidity of news circulation, the availability of logistic support for intervention, and the noble justification of avoiding bloodbaths.

Coming back to the Haitian case, it can be said that the consequences of this unfinished revolution are manifold. The process of uprooting – *déchoukaj* in Creole – repressive institutions and individuals did not go very far. After the dissolution of the militia, the main commanders of the *tontons macoute* were left untried and most of them fled to a safe exile, while, locally, a few low-ranking *macoutes* were murdered in the streets by the populace and thus served as scapegoats. In spite of various weak attempts, not a dollar was recovered from the huge fortune deposited abroad by the Duvaliers and the Bennetts (estimated at a figure between US$400 million and US$600 million).[21] The true and impartial balance of 29 years of dictatorship set out in a definitive document – requested by presidential candidate M. Bazin, among others – has never been written: this would have had the virtue of allowing a fresh start, as the Nürenberg trials did for post-Nazi Germany.

For the opposition, the consequences have been equally serious. Devoid of popular legitimization, the opposition leaders coming back from exile generally did not grasp Haitian reality. Their parties were merely small apparatuses promoting the presidential candidate around whom they were structured. More often than ever before, they fell into petty quarrels and personal feuds. Moreover, three of the more prominent presidential candidates had been members of Duvalier cabinets: L. Manigat in the 1960s, H. de Ronceray in numerous cabinets over the years and M. Bazin briefly in 1982. Such is the strength, the pervasiveness (and the perversion) of a totalitarian regime – incriminating in its circle of corruption and repression all local political personnel and discrediting departing and non-conformist opponents as well.

With regard to a possible democratic future for Haiti, the question stays entirely open, and one is obliged to adopt the three main theses that illuminate the profound and brilliant study of Michel-Rolph Trouillot:

1. The Duvalier regime has not been the result of haphazard events. To understand it one has to go deep into the Haitian socio-historic process.
2. The Duvalierist state, born from a multifaceted crisis, has introduced a qualitative difference in the range of historic Haitian political structures.
3. This state can reproduce itself with a Duvalier or with somebody else as long as the very structural crisis on which Duvalierism superimposed itself as an ambiguous and criminal answer has not been solved.

CONCLUSION

The analysis of the relationship between society and politics in Haiti takes the analyst back to the point of departure: the uniqueness of Haiti in the Americas. Because of the historic conditions of nation-building in this small country, with its well-entrenched authoritarian tradition and the particular crisis upon which the fascist state imposed itself, the problem of establishing a democratic polity is immense.[22] The aggravating circumstances brought about by contemporary trends make the problem even more difficult: the economist points to the loss of competitivity, the dwindling resources, the flight of capital; the anthropologist observes some decomposition of family links, the corruption of the popular religion, Vodun, the difficulty of raising the national idiom, Creole, to an official position; the geographer notes the ever-increasing centralization on Port-au-Prince, the loss of some of the best human potential through emigration. All these elements call attention to an African syndrome made up of ecological crises, socio-economic vicious circles, and political dependence. Haiti would not be so anomalous in black Africa, and some analysts show that it fares relatively well compared with countries of the Sahel. So, while the future is far from being optimistic, all indications are that the Haitian nation with its robust (and attractive) idiosyncracy, will stand firm in the year 2000 and far beyond, even if the state cannot be reconciled with the nation in the short term.

ACKNOWLEDGEMENTS

I want to acknowledge the valuable comments of Giovanni Caprio and Aaron Segal on an early draft of this chapter and the editorial help of C. Clarke and A. Segal. I alone remain responsible for any errors about facts and their interpretation.

NOTES

1. B. Weinstein and A. Segal, *Haiti: Political Failures, Cultural Successes* (New York: Praeger, 1984).
2. C.A. Girault (ed.), *Atlas d'Haïti* (Talence, Gironde: CEGET-CNRS, 1985).
3. P. Moral, (*Le Paysan Haïtien. Etude sur la Vie Rurale en Haïti* (Paris: Maisonneuve et Larose, 1961).
4. A. Corten, *L'Etat Faible. Haïti et République Dominicaine* (Montreal: CIDIHCA, 1989).
5. C.A. Girault, *Le Commerce du Café en Haïti. Habitants, Spéculateurs et Exportateurs* (Paris: Centre National de la Recherche Scientifique, 1981).
6. R. Maguire, *Bottom-up Development in Haiti* (Rosslyn, Virginia: Inter-American Foundation, 1979).
7. M.S. Laguerre, *Urban life in the Caribbean. A Study of a Haitian Urban Community* (Cambridge, Massachusetts: Schenkman, 1982).
8. D. Nicholls, *From Dessalines to Duvalier. Race, Colour and National Independence in Haiti* (Cambridge: Cambridge University, 1979).

9. J. Montalvo-Despeignes, *Le Droit Informel Haïtien* (Paris: Presses Universitaires de France, 1976).

10. Giovanni Caprio notes that most of 'the (American) investments took place outside of agriculture'. In 1929 only US$8.7 million were invested in agriculture out of a grand total of US$35.2 million (G. Caprio, in C.A. Girault (ed.), *op. cit.*, plate 3).

11. H. Schmidt, *The United States Occupation of Haiti 1915–1934* (New Brunswick, New Jersey: Rutgers University Press, 1971).

12. J. Price-Mars, *La Vocation de l'Élite* (Port-au-Prince: Imprimerie Edmond Chenet, 1919).

13. R. Depestre, *Bonjour et Adieu la Négritude* (Paris: Gallimard, 1980).

14. B. Diederich and A. Burt, *Papa Doc: the Truth about Haiti To-day* (New York: McGraw-Hill, 1969).

15. G. Pierre-Charles, *Radiographie d'une Dictature. Haïti et Duvalier* (Montréal: Nouvelle Optique, 1973).

16. M.R. Trouillot, *Les Racines Historiques de l'Etat Duvaliérien* (Port-au-Prince: Deschamps, 1986) and its English adaptation: M.R. Trouillot, *Haiti: State Against Nation. The Origins and Legacy of Duvalierism* (New York: Monthly Review Press, in press).

17. On the fascistic nature of the Duvalier regime see C. Hector, 'Fascisme et sous-développement: le cas d'Haïti', *Nouvelle Optique*, Vol. 5 (1972), pp.39–72.

18. Nevertheless, Duvalier's gesticulations and economic mismanagement provoked recession, capital flight and exodus of professionals.

19. J. DeWind and D.H. Kinley III, *Aiding Migration: the Impact of International Development Assistance on Haiti* (Boulder, Colorado: Westview Press, 1988).

20. *Le Monde*, January–February 1986 (correspondence of D. Hautin-Guiraud).

21. Figures given by well-informed journalists, D. Hautin-Guiraud (*Le Monde*) and G. Chamberlain (*Guardian*).

22. For a constructive view of the Haitian future see the works of young Haitian scholars: A. Dupuy, *Haiti in the World Economy: Class, Race and Underdevelopment since 1700* (Boulder, Colorado: Westview Press, 1988); A. Dupuy, 'Peasant poverty in Haiti', *Latin American Research Review*, Vol. XXIV (1989), pp.259–271; F. Laraque, *Défi à la Pauvreté. Construire Haïti par Nous-Memes* (Montreal: Editions du CIDIHCA, 1987).

9 Politics and Society in Cuba

Roberto Espíndola

INTRODUCTION

In Cuba there is a peculiar arrangement of relations between society and politics which is distinct from those in the rest of Latin America and the Caribbean. This is not surprising as relations between society and politics, between the social and the political systems reflect the specific historical development and structural arrangements of a particular social formation. The question is really, how specific are those relations?

The specificity of the Cuban experience relates to the radical social change which captured the world's imagination in the 1950s and 1960s and which played a major role in the last two decades in making the Caribbean as a whole an area of superpower confrontations. Although all experiences of change have a very specific and individual character, often we can find some points of comparison between them, some patterns of regularity. There are, for instance, some points in common between the experiences of Arbenz in Guatemala, Jagan in Guyana and Allende in Chile, despite the many obvious differences shown by those cases of frustrated social change.

It should be argued, however, that the Cuban experience in these 31 years has been unique; it can hardly be compared with previous experiences or with any successful imitators. It is difficult, hence, to disagree with Miller and Whitehead when they argue that the Cuban Revolution could not have successfully developed somewhere else in Latin America.[1] The features of the Cuban case demonstrate, to some extent, that specificity.

THE UNFINISHED NATIONALIST REVOLUTION

Cuba's history in the last 100 years has been marked by the unfinished character of its nationalist revolution. In this last outpost of the Spanish Empire in the Americas, the nationalist insurrections

207

which began in 1823 were first suffocated by a strong Spanish military reaction and then aborted – when they looked like succeeding – by the US intervention in 1898. The US placed in power a tame government, controlled by US officials and unable to claim for itself the banners of the insurrection, thus preventing the liberal Creole class from taking the anti-colonial struggle to its logical conclusion.

Governments became identified with a repression backed – in the final instance – by Washington, while the opposition, conversely, appealed to the imagery of Martí and the *mambises*,[2] presenting itself finally as insurrectional. *Estar alzado*, to be up in arms against the current regime, was an image often used in the half century before Fidel Castro took to the mountains. Throughout the first half of this century opposition leaders frequently presented themselves as rebelling against governments identified explicitly with the US. That was the appeal Antonio Guiteras and Eduardo Chibás made in the midst of the 1933 insurrection.

Twenty years later, Castro and his followers also made good use of that insurrectional imagery during their rebellion against the Batista regime and throughout the ensuing guerrilla struggle. After they succeeded, recourse to nationalist banners increased as the conflict with the US intensified. Such an appeal was particularly instrumental in securing the support of the rural population and in appealing to the urban poor over the head of unions controlled by bureaucracies linked either to the Batista regime or to the Moscow-oriented Partido Socialista Popular.[3] It was an appeal to well-known nationalistic symbols and to memories which went back only two generations and stressed the role of groups which had been marginalized from active politics during this century.

INFLUENCE OF SOCIALIST IDEOLOGIES

Trade union organization in Cuba – in contrast with that of Europe where unions predated such ideologies – was born under strong influence from socialist and anarchist ideas which arrived in the island almost simultaneously with the railroads and the mechanization of sugar mills. Trade unions in Cuba – as was the case in Mexico and Chile – were from their early beginning heavily influenced by these ideologies,[4] whose revolutionary character helped explain the constant repression of the labour movement by the Spanish colonial authorities, and later on, by those of the Republic. The presence of these ideologies in a colonial society such as Cuba in the second half of the nineteenth century led to their playing a significant role in the nationalist rebellion against Spanish rule. It also led to an early confrontation of the newly-formed unions with the state: there was almost a cycle with a union being formed, launching a strike, being repressed and banned by the authorities and then re-emerging under a different name.[5]

This influence legitimized socialist ideas among the Cuban working class to a degree rarely found in other Latin American and Caribbean societies. It also explained the frequent attempts to form a socialist party closely associated with the unions.

A SUGAR-EXPORTING ECONOMY

Even now, sugar still accounts for 80 per cent of Cuba's exports. The economy has been diversified in the last 20 years and – besides nickel, coffee and tobacco – produces a wide range of non-traditional exports, but sugar remains the main source of export earnings – most of it tied to long-term agreements with COMECON.

This dependence on an agricultural commodity (sugar) and the absence of oil in the island, however, has meant that Cuba could not live as a strictly non-aligned state; it needed to find a secure market for the sugar which, after 1960, was no longer placed in the US market and it needed to find a supplier of oil.[6] 'Ah, if we could make our cars run on sugar', a high Cuban official said to me, 'how much freer we would be.'

The production of sugar, coffee and tobacco causes some radical problems for an industrializing state with a population becoming progressively more urbanized. The problem is particularly acute for the production of coffee – and to some extent of tobacco – which relies on isolated producers. The children of coffee-growing peasants are no longer prepared to go back to isolated areas of the countryside after finishing school; they prefer to stay in urban areas, close to schools, to modern hospitals and to a more diversified labour market.

Replacing human power with machines, particularly in the sugar sector, presents problems of its own. Although mechanized harvesters can replace hundreds of human canecutters, in practice they are cumbersome and heavy. Rains help the sugar cane to grow, but they also cause the mechanized harvesters to get bogged down in mud. Mechanized operations are facilitated by dry weather, but then the lack of water results in a low sugar yield.

CONFLICT WITH THE US

The paramount feature which has marked the Cuban experience since 1959 has been the conflict with the US. Despite differences in size and population, Cuba has been a geo-strategic obsession for the US since the former British colonies in North America became independent.[7] Early in the nineteenth century US leaders became concerned with the role Cuba could play by controlling the access to the Gulf of Mexico and to the Caribbean. Equally, and even more so, Cubans have lived in the shadow of this all-powerful neighbour which declined to annex the island but would seek constantly to control it. This mixture of proximity and apprehension was a main factor leading to the early break between the governments of Castro and Eisenhower. This occurred well before the revolutionary regime had taken any steps against US firms or interests in the island, and came to a head as early as April 1959 when the then Vice-President Richard Nixon met Fidel Castro in Washington and gave the first instruction to overthrow the new revolutionary regime in Havana.

Conflict between Havana and Washington, having gone through different stages, has constantly coloured the political development of post-1959 Cuban society. The appeal to nineteenth-century nationalist heroes and symbols may become part of the hagiography schoolchildren memorize and political leaders repeat (references to the spirit of the guerrilla struggle may have become rather abstract for the half of the population born after 1959), but the appeals to unite in the face of US hostilities remain as powerful as ever, constantly reinforced by SR71 spy planes overflying the island amid sonic booms and by hostile broadcasts from Florida. It is an enemy whose lights can be seen on a clear night by anyone looking towards Key West from Matanzas or Havana.

Islands close to the mainland shelf of North America, such as Cuba, the Bahamas and Bermuda have found that this proximity to the US involves constraints to their independence and development to a degree perhaps not experienced by the smallest continental states to the south of Mexico. As the hegemonic power in the hemisphere, the US tends to see and use nearby islands as means to project its sea power, as well as to control and protect its own coastline. Cuba is particularly affected by its situation, controlling the main accesses to the Gulf of Mexico.

This is based not in the perception by the US of an actual threat to its security but of a potential one. When US strategic planners pose the worst-case scenario of a direct conflict between the superpowers, they reason that more than 60 per cent of the oil supplies essential to the Western alliance would go through sea lanes open to attack from Cuba, although it is accepted that Cuba's navy does not pose a threat in any other instance. In fact, strategic planners expect the Cuban government to declare itself neutral in the preliminary stages of a world conflict. However, such declaration of neutrality would not be acceptable to the US, not only because of the potential threat to sea lanes but also because of the risk of having to deploy forces to protect its southern states from a possible attack.[8] Because of that, Cuba would have to be neutralized, a daunting proposition if we consider that in the early 1960s the US Department of Defense opposed a direct US invasion of the island on grounds that – even at that stage – it would have caused more than 45 000 US casualties.[9] Now, when Cuba can field over one million troops and more than half its population can be mobilized in defence tasks, the figure would be substantially higher. Hence, Cuba could be neutralized only by an aerial bombardment which would precipitate further Soviet reactions.

Besides the potential military threat, there are the constant hints of clandestine interventions to subvert the Cuban regime and well-documented attempts by the CIA to eliminate President Castro.[10] The frequency with which cases of CIA activity in Cuba become known, results less from clumsiness on the part of US officials, and responds more to the intention of keeping the Cuban government on its toes, forcing it not only to divert scarce resources to police activity, but also to keep a high level of police control over the population. If to these interventions are added the presence in the US of a militant and powerful exile community and Washington's almost permanent hostility towards the Castro regime, it is not surprising that the obsession is mirrored in the behaviour of the Cuban leadership. In fact, a recent Cuban defector recognized that there had been a sharp drop in attendance at voluntary militia training when President Jimmy Carter was in the White House and Wayne Smith represented US interests in Havana.[11]

Proximity to the US also means the impossibility of preventing the population from being tantalized by real or imaginary opportunities offered by the US economy. Tempting images are enhanced by the relative success enjoyed by Cuban exiles in the US, particularly if compared with other Hispanic groups. White exiles have found their professional qualifications ensure them access not only to a good income, but also to prestigious jobs at the state and federal level. Other exiles have met with success in business, enjoying the advantage of the market and financial support provided by the exile community. Such examples are more salient, hence better known, to those who stayed in the island; they are further supported by the behaviour of exiles who return as visitors and who often play up their successes. Even ordinary criminals see the US as a land of opportunities, as shown by the number of them who joined the genuine refugees during the 1980 Mariel exodus.

Although the Cuban authorities prevented visits by exiles and tried to hinder communications,[12] both because of security reasons and in order to prevent a demonstration effect which would boost economic and political demands, this is an impossible task in the light of the US proximity and the easy reception of US radio and television broadcasts. By 1979, the Havana government had decided that the population could not be isolated from contacts with US life style, particularly as visiting exiles began to provide a valuable source of foreign currency; official efforts focused instead on improving supplies of consumer goods.[13] Similarly, when the enhanced hostility brought about by the Reagan administration resulted in the 1984 launching of Radio Martí, this resulted in the end in an improvement in the broadcasts of local radios. Regardless of the possible pragmatism or dogmatism of decision-makers in Havana, proximity is clearly a factor which conditions policies and constrains the room for manoeuvre the government has in the deployment of scarce resources.

DEPENDENCE ON THE SOVIET UNION: GORBACHEV AND *PERESTROIKA*

In recent years changes in the Soviet Union and in Eastern Europe have modified the perception of Cuba's dependence on Moscow, bringing out into the open signs of stress and even disaffection. President Castro has declined to follow the example set by President Mikhail Gorbachev in terms of *perestroika* and *glasnost* policies, claiming that the process of 'rectification of past mistakes and negative tendencies'[14] made them unnecessary. The controversy between the two political leaderships has become quite public, with the Soviet and East European press publishing criticisms of Cuba's political system and economic management,[15] and Cuban officials replying not only with protests but also with open criticisms of the Soviet system. The latter, though, have not gone as far as to be published; this could be interpreted as a consequence of the greater degree of central political control exercised by Havana, but it also reflects a Cuban awareness of the realities of dependence.

Dependence on the Soviets for subsidies, oil supply, for modern weapons, industrial and nuclear technology and for a market for sugar exports has been a fact of life for the Cuban population. *El hermano mayor* as some Cuban officials refer to the Soviet Union, has been present in every sphere of life from consumer goods, to the magazines available at the newspaper kiosks, to the programmes on television and the products available at the local supermarkets. The science-fiction structure of the Soviet embassy, towering over Havana and bristling with antennae, is a constant reminder both of Moscow's presence and of a superpower's disregard for the architectural environment.

This dependence has been maintained now for nearly 30 years, ranging from the rough patch caused by Havana's attempts to remain neutral in the Sino-Soviet dispute in the 1960s to a period of considerable harmonization of foreign policies in the 1970s. The active role played by Cuba in Africa during the 1970s – autonomous though it probably was – did much for Moscow,[16] enhancing its friendship with Third World countries and providing the Soviet navy with the ports of call that its new strategic outlook required.

Despite the benefits Moscow has drawn from Cuba's role in Africa, it would be both simplistic and mistaken to interpret it as that of a Soviet proxy in the international arena. Cuba itself has drawn substantial benefits from its policies towards Africa and the rest of the Third World. Besides, there have been sufficient instances of dissent – even of conflict – over, say, Angola, Ethiopia and Zimbabwe to demonstrate a considerable degree of independence on the part of Cuba.[17]

That degree of autonomy should certainly not be ignored. Equally, the complete integration of the economy within COMECON would make it impossible to ignore Cuba's dependence on the Soviet link. Even if President Castro – or his eventual successor – wanted to shift allegiances away from Moscow and towards the West, they would not be able to find a market – let alone an expanding one – for their sugar such as the one provided by the Soviet Union and Eastern Europe. This dependence is now posing additional problems for the Cuban leadership as Soviet President Mikhail Gorbachev is cutting the costs and the wings of his Cuban ally by reducing the level of Soviet economic support.[18]

However, it is difficult to foresee any change in the near future as Cuba's level of integration into COMECON means that its sugar is essential to the Soviet and Eastern European economies, as well as offering markets, manufactured imports and technological support for which there is no alternative at present. Although Cuban officials claim that 'some changes' are taking place in the political system,[19] any liberalization similar to that of Eastern Europe is unlikely in the short term and for as long as Havana has the excuse of Washington's hostile policies.

INSULARITY AND INTERVENTIONISM

The Cuban experience has also been affected by geo-political constraints, most of which are, in fact, shared with other Caribbean islands, although perhaps to different degrees. Insularity poses serious problems for the independence of a country, making it difficult to receive support from neighbouring allies and depriving insurgent forces of a hinterland in which to hide. In the nineteenth century, this was a major factor in explaining the persistence of Spanish control over Cuba despite the poor level of political and military leadership shown by the Spaniards.

Precisely the same reasons have made islands a favourite means for large nations to project their power. Spain used Cuba to control its colonies; in a similar fashion the island was used by the US in the 60 years after Spain left. In the 1950s Cuba became a main US centre for the control of communist activities in the region.[20]

This is a central factor, too, for understanding the nature of a society characterized not by an isolationist insular character, but on the contrary, by one constantly attempting to use its insular situation to project its own power – and now by extension the Soviet one – over the region and beyond.

SOCIAL ACHIEVEMENTS

With a population of just over 10 million – almost 70 per cent of whom are white – this, the largest island in the Caribbean, does not present the problems of smallness or racial complexity which characterize neighbouring insular states. With a highly skilled labour force and demographic indicators closer to those of industrialized nations, Cuba does not suffer from manpower constraints: it is able to provide technical or military assistance to over 35 countries in the Third World.[21]

Cuba's industrial sector has developed fast, suffering not so much from the constraints of size as from those of a wasteful organization of the economy, added to the handicap posed by the US economic blockade. Despite those problems, industrial output has more than doubled since the early 1970s, enabling the economy both to provide for a wide range of consumer needs and to develop a considerable range of non-traditional exports. Nothing like the full benefit of the latter has yet been felt by the economy, mainly due to bottlenecks developed as a consequence of the growing external debt to Western governments and banks. Technical assistance and soft-loans from Sweden made it possible to produce good-quality paper primarily from the bagasse left after sugar is ground out of the cane. However, this has not resulted in the anticipated level of exports because of delivery problems: lack of hard currency makes it difficult to charter foreign freighters and an absence of credit prevents the expansion of the national merchant fleet. In 1987, lack of hard currency or credit to import spare parts led, for the first time, to a decline in industrial production.[22]

Despite these problems, the industrial sector has gone a long way towards meeting consumer demands (Tables 9.1 and 9.2). These efforts have had their limitations, as shown by the active blackmarket for imported consumer goods developed around the dollar-shops reserved for diplomats and foreign tourists. An even greater limitation has been the one imposed by the drop in the economy's ability to import essential industrial inputs, due to a lack of Western credit not unrelated to US pressure. Since 1986, this has prompted a halt in the expanding supply of consumer goods. Anxious not to disappoint consumers' expectations, the government managed until 1987 to maintain the same level of goods as in 1984, but 1988 brought about – for the first time since the 1960s – a drop in per capita supplies.[23]

Table 9.1 Supply of consumer goods 1974–87 (per capita)

	1974	1987
Clothes (m²)	24	69
Shoes (pairs)	3.04	4.49

Source: Instituto de Estudios de la Demanda Interna, Havana (1988).

Table 9.2 Supply of electric consumer goods 1974–84 (per 100 housing units)

	1974	1984
Refrigerators	29.9	64.9
Television sets	24.4	75.5
Radios	74.7	110.9
Irons	67.1	94.7
Sewing machines	48.2	55.4
Fans	22.0	70.9
Washing machines	1.7	43.8

Source: National Household Survey, Havana (1985).

The main and best-known achievements of the Cuban experience, however, have been in the areas of health, nutrition and education. Life expectancy, diet, proportion of the population at school compare well with figures for the industrialized countries; the same applies to accesss to medical doctors, despite the number of practitioners abroad as part of assistance programmes to other Third World countries. In these areas Cuba is certainly ahead of other countries in the region (Table 9.3). In fact, the population's age profile (Table 9.4) shows greater similarity to an industrialized country like Britain than to neighbouring Venezuela or the Dominican Republic.

The age profiles express not only the effects on life expectancy of improved health care, but also the consequences of population planning and birth control, even though the latter until recently was achieved with a greater reliance on abortion than on contraception. These changes are also reflected in a lower rate of population growth – at 10.2 per 1000, well below the world's average of 18 per 1000 (Table 9.5).

There are, however, other demographic indicators which point to some of the problems present in Cuban society. Both marriage and

Table 9.3 Social indicators 1980–85 (averages)

	Cuba	Venezuela	Dominican Republic
Life expectancy at birth (males)	72.6	65.0	60.0
(females)	76.0	70.0	64.0
Literacy (as a percentage of those aged 15+)	91.1	88.4	77.3
Caloric intake (daily, per capita)	2 948	2 664	2 330
Physicians (per 1 000 inhabitants)	2.6	1.3	0.4
Hospital beds (per 1 000 inhabitants)	5.5	3.0	1.6
Infant mortality rate (per 1 000 births)	13.6	26.1	67.0

Sources: Comité Estatal de Estadísticas, *Boletin Estadístico de Cuba* (January 1983–January–December 1986); Instituto de Estudios de la Demanda Interna, unpublished statistics (1988); Encyclopaedia Britanica, *Britannica Book of the Year* (1986–89).

Table 9.4 Age profiles of populations (%)

	Cuba	Venezuela	Dominican Republic	UK
Under 15	25.9	41.0	40.7	19.0
15–24	29.9	28.7	30.7	23.7
30–44	19.8	16.8	15.4	20.3
45–59	13.1	8.8	8.5	16.3
60 and over	11.3	4.8	4.7	20.7

Sources: As Table 9.3.

Table 9.5 Population growth (per 1 000 inhabitants)

Cuba	Venezuela	Dominican Republic	World
10.2	24.4	23.8	18.0

Sources: As Table 9.3

divorce, are more common than in Britain (Table 9.6). However, the explanation for the high rate of divorce relates only in part to the ease of legal procedures and to the existence of a state which, in lieu of parents, provides teenagers with free boarding schools, as well as with clothes and rations. The divorce rate also points to the stress for

Table 9.6   Annual Marriage and divorce (per 1000 inhabitants)

	Cuba	Venezuela	Dominican Republic	UK
Marriage	8.1	5.4	3.4	6.9
Divorce	3.1	0.3	1.2	2.8

Sources: As Table 9.3.

family life of a society permanently at arms, where those at work spend a good part of their spare time away from home at union or political meetings, militia drills, doing shifts at the 'physical defence committees' which provide security for workplaces at night, or doing voluntary work.

RACE AND GENDER

Gender and racial discrimination characterized Cuban society until the 1950s, to an extent similar to that found in most American societies at that time. The revolutionary process launched in 1959 publicly set itself as one of its tasks the eradication of such discrimination. After more than 30 years, it is undeniable that a great deal of progress has been made, but it is equally undeniable that discrimination still exists, particularly along gender lines.

The publicity the government has given to these issues has by itself had a significant influence in discouraging racist and sexist attitudes, or at least any public manifestation of discrimination. This process of socialization has been systematically reinforced by emphasizing leading roles played by blacks and women in the nineteenth century struggle for independence and in the guerrilla campaigns of the 1950s.[24]

This process has had considerable success in terms of eliminating racial discrimination; the extension of educational opportunities to the rural population and an incomes policy which has done away with the massive pre-1959 salary differentials have brought an end to discrimination against blacks in the labour market. At the same time, the educational processes have succeeded in creating an anti-racist culture. The success in creating equal opportunities for blacks is demonstrated in their relative absence from the ranks of Cubans in exile – most of whom are upper- or middle-class whites – and by the resentment of these changes shown by some white lower strata emigres.[25] However, this does not mean an end to the second class position of blacks, who remain under-represented in the top echelons of the government and state institutions, in the political leadership at the national level and in senior academic posts, though this does not appear to be the case in the armed and security forces.

No such success can be exhibited in the process of eliminating gender discrimination, despite the promulgation of the Maternity Code in 1973 and of an advanced Family Code in 1975, the equality accorded both genders in the 1976 Constitution, and practical steps such as the socialization of domestic tasks through work canteens, boarding schools and crêches. Women play now a more significant part in the labour force than before 1959, but they do not represent more than 38 per cent of the paid labour force. Efforts to encourage a greater participation of women in the political and trade union organizations have resulted in a few women joining the national leadership of the Communist Party and the Central de Trabajadores de Cuba (CTC), and in a disproportionate number of women taking grassroots responsibilities, but still very few have been elected by their fellow party or union members to intermediate positions of responsibility.

The difference in the success achieved by efforts to eliminate race-based discrimination and those to eliminate sexist barriers has been attributed to the fact that while racism exists and can be dealt with in the public sphere, sexism is a form of discrimination whose roots are in the private sphere, in the family.[26] Legal texts and government measures cannot by themselves eliminate discrimination rooted in family life. The defensive attitude often adopted by Cubans on this issue can be explained by the contradiction implied by the official rejection of gender-related discrimination and the equally official reluctance to interfere in the family.

THE NATURE OF CUBAN SOCIETY

The same process which has produced the social achievements mentioned above has also led to a society paradoxically characterized by a considerable level of popular participation in public life, coupled with an extreme difficulty for such participation to occur outside official channels. A social or political movement in Cuba today either becomes part of the state's ideological apparatus, or runs risks, such as that of being labelled as counter-revolutionary or being repressed as an illegal organization.

There are a number of features which explain this apparent paradox: Cuba's militarization; the high level of social control over private life; and the legitimacy enjoyed by the government – the latter expressed in a high level of support for President Castro and 'the revolution' in abstract, despite disagreements which may be voiced concerning specific policies or state officials.

These characteristics explain the presence of widespread but highly ritualized forms of political participation. The ritualism of political life is based on the image of Cuba as a society-at-arms. That image relates both to the attempt to see today's society as the logical extension over time of the 1950s guerilla struggle and to the perception of that society as being besieged by an omnipresent and powerful enemy. The former is a key element to preserving the legitimacy of the government and to socializing the young. Children are taught 'to be like Che (Guevara)'; young communists demonstrate their fervour and prowess by scaling the highest peak in the Sierra Maestra; accounts of the guerilla struggle are frequently published in the daily press – despite an official silence about the history of the 1940s and 1960s; and former guerillas are given what by now are the equivalent of gerontocratic honours.[27] The efforts required in daily life are couched in a nomenclature implying that everyone is now part of Fidel's guerilla column: best pupils, students reaching high averages, as well as workers exceeding their production quota are 'vanguards'; a harvest or an attempt to meet a production target is a 'campaign'; teams of workers are 'brigades'; even regular soldiers are officially known as 'fighters'.

But history is not enough for this effort to succeed. It is pointless to be a guerilla if the guerillas no longer have an enemy to fight. Then, a hostile Washington – particularly during a hawkish administration – becomes useful, providing a very real enemy the guerillas must defeat.

US hostilities towards Cuba certainly enhance the legitimacy of President Castro's regime, making dissent an act of betrayal which helps the nation's enemy. It also justifies a militarization of society, where every loyal Cuban has a job to do in the event of an invasion. At least once a year there is a nationwide military exercise, besides frequent local drills which mobilize the militias, sending schoolchildren into air-raid shelters, causing volunteers to dig trenches and placing the whole economy of a province on a war footing, with factories shifting their production and being moved into the country-side and a local leadership taking control, on the assumption that all contact with Havana has been cut off.

Daily life is equally affected by this sense of military alertness, with workers guarding their workplaces at night, neighbours taking turns to patrol the streets and Comités de Defensa de la Revolución (CDRs) keeping an eye on everyone and everything on their block. All this vigilance would be very difficult to maintain for any government unless there was a real threat. Hostile US policies, such as those of the Reagan Administration – launching clandestine operations, having the island frequently overflown by supersonic planes, organizing avy manoeuvres near Cuba's territorial waters and practising troop landings at the Guantánamo base – have played an important role in justifying such militarization.

Political and social life is, hence, greatly affected by this militarization, causing the stress and intolerance to be expected from any social group which perceives itself to be under serious threat. It also means that participation in official political activities, such as attending meetings of the local CDR, or the local Federación de Mujeres de Cuba (FMC), voting at elections for the People's Power assemblies, attending a meeting where the local People's Power delegate will report back, or going to a rally, become not acts of support for individual decision-makers or for a ruling political party, but acts of loyalty to the nation. Such participation, hence, becomes reinforced by strong social pressures at the grassroots level.

Equally, any form of political activity conducted outside these channels becomes not only hindered by the lack of structures and opportunities for such activity, but is also likely to give rise to harassment by neighbours and workmates. Although dissident groups, operating as human rights' groups, have been tolerated recently, anyone trying to go beyond that to form a political organization would, at best, be told that such activity is not legal and, hence, cannot take place; at worst, such an attempt could lead to arrest on charges of anti-state activity. Regardless of the official reaction, such an attempt would be likely to lead to hostilities or vigilantism at the local level. Dissident groups have had meetings and press conferences disbanded by local CDRs; activists find themselves followed by volunteers or visited by CDR officials if they arrive home with a guest.[28]

Anyone who disagrees with a specific policy or wants to denounce a malpractice must do it through the approved channels and by appealing to the accepted political symbols; for instance speaking at a workplace meeting to denounce an official as lacking in revolutionary vigilance, rather than organizing a petition accusing the official of corruption and asking for her/his removal. Anyone who tries to organize opposition to a specific policy, gets up a petition or tries to run a protest broadsheet is likely to be accused of counter-revolutionary activity. In fact, it would be easier to sabotage production by promoting extra hours of voluntary work in solidarity with Nicaragua than by organizing a strike.[29]

This social coherence, however, has been seriously shaken in recent years. The first important shock was the liberalization of the economy which began in 1980 and culminated in 1985 with plans to re-create a private sector. The second shock was the reversal of that liberalization announced in 1986 by President Castro.

After 1980 small farmers were encouraged to sell direct to consumers, in free 'peasant markets', the produce which exceeded the quotas they were required to sell to the state marketing authority. Craftsmen and artisans were allowed to sell their products in free street markets, builders, painters and plumbers could openly do private jobs. Householders renting their houses from the state Urban Reform Corporation were encouraged to buy their homes. President Castro even spoke of allowing private, and more efficient, restaurants to be opened.[30]

Suddenly, in December 1985, President Castro came to the conclusion that those steps were creating a new middle class, a class having access to incomes much in excess of the top salaries paid to state workers, and he began a painful process of denunciation and the reversal of the liberalizing process. This policy change led to the formation of the first organized dissent seen since the early 1960s. Stall holders, lorry owners, craftsmen deprived of their newly acquired source of income, became active members of groups of dissenters who printed leaflets thrown from the top of high buildings or from speeding cars.[31]

To confront this new opposition President Castro increased the size of the police force, but he also began a campaign of rectification, encouraging the denunciation of corruption among state bureaucrats. This process has led to a new openness in the press, the publishing of letters from consumers who complain about state officials, and the carrying out of modest forms of investigative journalism unknown in post-revolutionary Cuba.[32]

Such openness, that – to be fair – preceded Soviet *glasnost*, has its origins not only in President Castro's process of rectification, but also in several external factors. One of them has been the Radio Martí broadcasts from Florida, which the government decided not to jam. Now anyone can tune in to Radio Martí, forcing Cuban stations to try to present news bulletins as wide ranging, music as attractive and comedies as entertaining as, or more entertaining than, those of Radio Martí.

Foreign policy successes such as the restoration of diplomatic relations with most Latin American countries, the proposal by the Group of Eight for the OAS to re-admit Cuba, new trade links with Brazil and Argentina, the rejection of US-sponsored censures of Cuba at the UN Committee on Human Rights, and the election of Cuba to the UN Security Council, have provided additional incentives for the government to pursue a policy of openness at home. Unless it could be justified by an act of US hostility, any reduction of this openness would have costs for Havana's foreign relations.

SOCIAL AND POLITICAL MOVEMENTS

Although social and political movements played an essential role in the history of revolutionary Cuba, at present their scope in society is limited by the institutionalization of political life. Despite the formalization of the regime's political base in the 1960s, trade unions, the women's movement and the CDRs played a significant role as social movements during that period. The CDRs and trade unions not only channelled support for the revolutionary regime, they also provided an avenue for the political participation of members of the population outside the structures of the new Partido Comunista de Cuba (PCC). Within the revolutionary organizations a group of women presented demands for a reassessment of the situation of women in Cuban society, leading indirectly to the formation of the FMC, while ensuring that those demands were not used against the revolutionary leadership.[33]

Those movements became gradually institutionalized and by the 1970s they were, if not part of the state, at least part of its ideological apparatus. In a political and social system which defines itself as revolutionary, it is difficult for the authorities to accept the promotion of change outside established channels, a dilemma illustrated by the fact that policy changes take place only after President Castro has criticized existing policies and proposed new ones.[34] This,

however, does not mean that some social and political movements
have not emerged in post-revolutionary Cuba.

My characterization of Cuban society, showing the difficulties
which a political or social movement would encounter, does not deny
that movements can and do exist in Cuba, but points to the constraints on their existence. The apparent resurgence now of social
and political movements could be seen as part of a new strategy for
the development – and survival – of the socialist regime: the presence
of social movements outside the state and its apparatus can be seen as
part of a civil society which, in the final analysis, legitimizes the
political system.

Dissident Groups

There are groups seeking political reforms, particularly in the area of
human rights, which first appeared in 1986 as a reaction to the
rolling-back of the liberalization of the economy. After it became
clear that the government was tolerating the activities of dissident
human-rights groups, the original Comité Cubano por los Derechos
Humanos (CCDH) split and other groups emerged. Now there is a
wide range of political options in terms of dissident groups. There is
the CCDH, hostile to the government and its objectives; the Comité
para la Reconciliación Nacional, which seeks greater political freedom but without directly challenging the government or its objectives; and there is a group which declares itself to be socialist and
'pro-Gorbachev', challenging the government to emulate the example
of Eastern Europe and the Soviet Union.

These groups do not at present have a large following, though they
have become the main political vehicles through which former political prisoners and their families press for opportunities to migrate to
the US. Besides the latter, their membership appears to consist
mainly of intellectuals and artisans, but there is a growing mass of
dissatisfied young people, most of them unemployed, who could
channel their demands for change through these dissident groups.

The Labour Movement

It could be argued that the official trade union organization has in
recent years acted occasionally as a social movement, seeking policy
changes by appealing directly to the population. The unions' control
of a national newspaper, *Trabajadores*, gives them a channel to the

population which they used to criticize government policies in December 1979, when *Trabajadores* launched a campaign not echoed in the PCC daily *Granma*, criticizing corruption among state employees, managers of state enterprises and professionals. This campaign led to changes in official policies and to the large-scale purge which preceded and apparently precipitated the Mariel exodus to the US. In 1986 the unions and *Trabajadores* also led the campaign for the open discussion of cases of corruption and inefficiency which the government was trying to rectify. This was not echoed by *Granma* until its editor was replaced.

These examples may be insufficient to justify the identification of a labour movement, but they certainly show more than the simple existence of a trade union lobby within the state. It reveals at least an ability to promote policy changes, access to a mass audience, and relative autonomy from the state.

The Church and the Church-related Movement

It is around the Church that the greatest evidence for the existence of a social movement can be found. Since the government began a dialogue with the Catholic bishops in 1985, the Church has been playing a major role as the catalyst for a movement of the laity and of intellectuals; some of the latter are not practising Catholics, but they see in the Church, in the *movimiento eclesial*, or the Church as a community, a vehicle for presenting the case for a pluralistic society, without giving up the social achievements of post-revolutionary Cuba or siding with the US and the anti-Castro groups of the exile community.[35]

This has become undoubtedly the most successful social movement in recent years. The bishops have been able to obtain the release of hundreds of political prisoners and, through their links with US bishops, have managed to get Washington to reverse its policies and grant entry visas to former prisoners and their families. Close links with the US Church have involved Cuban bishops visiting the US and several groups of US Church dignitaries going to Havana. These contacts have not only added to the legitimacy of the Church, but also have contributed to defuse some of the tension between Havana and Washington.

The improvement in relations between Church and state has resulted in changes within the PCC, with the establishment of a department for relations with churches and the elimination of atheism from the PCC programme.[36] The Church has reciprocated by treading a careful path, refusing to join in US campaigns against the government and reprimanding human-rights groups for the unauthorized use of churches for their meetings, yet refusing to join Protestant churches in their defence of the government.

The Church, in its broadest sense, constitutes a large, national movement, able to conduct non-liturgical meetings and to publish newsletters; the state radio and television are also dedicating more space to Church news. The Church, in brief, is developing into a social movement which, while advocating the case for a more open civil society, seeks reforms without proposing a power alternative.

CONCLUSION

The collapse of the communist governments of the Soviet Union's East European allies and the emergence of political pluralism in that region pose the question whether or not we can expect any major political change in Cuba. This is not only a matter of the demonstration effect which changes in Eastern Europe can have in Cuba and of the preparations different state institutions and PCC factions are likely to undertake in anticipation, but also a matter of the probable decline in economic support East European members of COMECON can give Cuba. Trade links are not going to disappear overnight, but non-communist-led East Germany and Czechoslovakia are less likely to adopt a favourable attitude towards the needs for manufactured goods of a government closely associated to those they replaced and unable to pay for its requirements in hard currency; the state of the East European economies leaves little room to accommodate Havana's requirements. Whether the Cuban government reaches a *modus vivendi* with its new COMECON partners or whether it reaches out to Western Europe and Japan for help, any arrangement is likely to include pressure for change, or at least a defence of the space already allowed to the Church and to dissidents.

Some changes in the Cuban political scenario – minor as they are – show an awareness of these external pressures.[37] By themselves, though, such changes do not allow us to anticipate much beyond a process of political evolution gradual enough not to put at risk the ruling party's hegemony. It is impossible to anticipate whether or not external pressures – particularly on the economy – might have the effect of significantly accelerating that process.

Otherwise, the only factors which could have any major effect on political arrangements are a change in the country's leadership or an end to Washington's embargo. At present, the former looks unlikely, barring President Castro's death, but the latter would just require a unilateral act on the part of an enlightened US administration. Barring either event, US hostilities will continue to provide a justification for Cuba to remain a society-at-arms.

NOTES

1. Nikki Miller and Laurence Whitehead, 'The Soviet Interest in Latin America', in Robert Cassen (ed.), *Soviet Interests in the Third World* (London: Sage, 1985), pp.114–39.
2. The nationalist troops following Carlos Manuel de Céspedes after his 1868 call for independence from Spain became known as *mambises*, originally a pejorative term used by the Spaniards, but one the insurgents adopted with pride. Jose Martí launched in 1895 another insurrection, from exile in the US, helped by two *mambí* generals, Antonio Maceo and Máximo Gómez. See Fernando Portuondo, *Estudios de Historia de Cuba* (Havana: Editorial de Ciencias Sociales, 1973), pp.71–150; and Julio Le Riverend, *José Martí: Pensamiento y Acción* (Havana: Editora Política, 1982), pp.129–48.
3. The Communist Party was known as Partido Socialista Popular (PSP) until 1961 when it merged with the Movimiento 26 de Julio and Directorio Revolucionario to form the Organizaciones Revolucionarias Integradas. On PSP and Batista's control of the unions see Hugh Thomas, *Cuba or the Pursuit of Freedom* (London: Eyre and Spottiswoode, 1971), pp.972–88; and Peter Marshall, *Cuba Libre* (London: Victor Gollancz, 1987), p.41.
4. Sergio Aguirre, *Eco de Caminos* (Havana: Editorial de Ciencias Sociales, 1974), pp.291–306; Julio Le Riverend, *Historia Económica de Cuba* (Havana: Editorial Pueblo y Educación, 1974), pp.445–6; Hortensia Pichardo, *Documentos para la Historia de Cuba* (Havana: Editorial de Ciencias Sociales, 1973), Vol. I, pp.422–91; Instituto de Historia del Movimiento Comunista y la Revolución Socialista de Cuba, *El Movimiento Obrero Cubano* (Havana: Editorial de Ciencias Sociales, 1975), Vol. I, pp.17–138; Eduardo Dimas, 'La Imprenta y el Movimiento Obrero Gráfico en Cuba', in *Los Obreros Hacen y Escriben su Historia* (Havana: Editorial de Ciencias Sociales, 1975), pp.181–222; and Gerald Poyo 'The Anarchist Challenge to the Cuban Independence Movement', in *Cuban Studies*, Vol. 15, No. 1 (1985), pp.29–42.
5. Aguirre, *op. cit.*; Dimas, *op. cit.*; Central de Trabajadores de Cuba (CTC), *Panorámica de la Historia del Movimiento Obrero Cubano* (Havana: CTC, 1977); Sergio Guerra, *Cronología del Movimiento*

Obrero y de las Luchas por la Revolución Socialista en America Latina (Havana: Casa de las Américas, 1979).

6. This is well-documented in the literature, but an original interpretation is provided by Miller and Whitehead, *op. cit.* See also Tad Szulc, *Fidel: a Critical Portrait* (London: Hutchinson, 1987), pp.407–30.

7. M. Márquez Sterling, *La Diplomácia en Nuestra História* (Havana: Instituto del Libro, 1967), Chapters 2 and 6; Lynn-Darrell Bender, *Cuba vs United States* (San Juan: Inter American University Press, 1981), pp.1–4; and Thomas, *op. cit.*, p.88.

8. *Latin American Regional Reports: Caribbean*, LARC-85-03, (1985), pp.4–5.

9. Arthur Schlesinger, *A Thousand Days: John F Kennedy in the White House* (Boston: Houghton Mifflin, 1965), p.851.

10. Thomas, *op. cit.*, p.1467; Philip Brenner, *From Confrontation to Negotiation* (Boulder, Colorado: Westview Press, 1988), pp.13–16; Szulc, *op. cit.*; and Peter Bourne, *Fidel* (New York: Dodd Mead, 1986), pp.212–14.

11. Interview with Manuel Sánchez Pérez in Madrid on 6 November 1986. Sánchez claimed that in the late 1970s attendance at militia weekend training deteriorated to a critical level because President Carter was not perceived as a threat and his envoy in Havana, the head of the US interests section Wayne Smith, was 'a big man with a beard, dressed in a *guayabera*, seen often in Fidel's company (and who) was *más bueno que el pan*'. Although Smith was posted to Havana 15 months before the end of the Carter administration, and by then US relations with Cuba had become strained once again, his own rapport with Cuban officials is confirmed in Wayne Smith, *The Closest of Enemies* (New York: Norton, 1987), pp.170–238.

12. Smith, *op. cit.*, pp.198–9. Exiles interviewed in March 1988 expressed frequent complaints about Havana's reluctance to increase the number of telephone links between Cuba and the US and to allow low-cost visit facilities for exiles, who are required to pay for rooms in tourism hotels and not allowed to stay with relatives.

13. Interview with Eugenio Rodríguez Balari, president of the Instituto de Estudios y Orientación de la Demanda Interna, Havana, 30 July 1979.

14. This *rectificación de errores y tendencias negativas* will be subsequently referred to just as the process of rectification. See *Latin American Weekly Report*, LAWR-88-32 (18 August 1988), p.9; LAWR-89-03 (19 January 1989), p.9; and LAWR-89-07 (16 February 1989), p.10.

15. This began with V. Chirkov 'How are Things, Compañeros?' and 'An Uphill Task' in *New Times* (12 January 1987), pp.18–19 and (17 August 1987), pp. 16–17, respectively. In August 1989, the government banned two Soviet publication *Novedades de Moscú* and *Sputnik*, and the official PCC daily *Granma* accused several journalists from the Hungarian papers *Magyar Hemzet* and *Magyar Hirlap* of taking part in an 'anti-Cuban campaign'. *Granma* (4 August 1989), and LAWR-89-34 (31 August 1989).

16. Bender, *op. cit.*, pp.55–6; William LeoGrande, 'Cuban-Soviet Relations and Cuban policy in Africa', in Carmelo Mesa-Lago and June Belkin (eds), *Cuba in Africa* (Pittsburgh: University of Pittsburgh, 1982),

pp.13–50; Edward Gonzalez, 'Institutionalisation, Political Elites and Foreign Policies', in Cole Blasier and Carmelo Mesa-Lago (eds), *Cuba in the World* (Pittsburgh: University of Pittsburgh Press, 1979), pp.22–3; Nelson Valdes 'Revolutionary Solidarity in Angola', in Blasier and Mesa-Lago (eds), *op. cit.*, pp.109–11.

17. In Angola, Cuban troops prevented a pro-Moscow faction of the MPLA from staging a coup against President Agostinho Neto. In Ethiopia, Havana refused to allow its troops directly to participate in the Soviet-backed campaign against the Eritrean and Tigrean liberation movements; indirectly, though, Cuban pilots on air patrols over the Ogaden freed Ethiopian manpower to be used against the rebels. See Carla Anne Robbins, *The Cuban Threat* (Philadelphia: Institute for the Study of Human Issues, 1985), pp.231–2, 255–6. During the Zimbabwean liberation struggle, Havana did not follow the Soviet example in backing just ZAPU and gave also considerable training support to ZANU; this proved a wise policy, as shown by the speed with which the ZANU-controlled government established diplomatic relations with Cuba after independence and their marked reluctance over links with Moscow.

18. LAWR-88-48 (8 December 1988), p.5; LARC-88-10 (8 December 1988), pp.4–5 and LARC-89-10 (19 January 1989), p.2. Also Nicola Miller, *Soviet Relations with Latin America 1959–1987* (Cambridge University Press: Cambridge, 1989), pp.124–5.

19. Several members of the 16-strong Cuban delegation at the 1989 LASA Congress argued that such changes were taking place, without going into details; the changes, though, appear to refer mainly to a more efficient structure for the Communist Party and more active popular participation in the People's Power System, rather than to any form of pluralism. LASA International Congress, Miami, 4–6 December 1989.

20. Thomas, *op. cit.*, p.855.

21. *Granma Weekly Review* (11 May 1980), p.2.

22. Comité Estatal de Estadísticas, *La Economía Cubana* (1987), p.6.

23. Interview with Eugenio Rodríguez Balari, 21 September 1988, Havana.

24. The image of Antonio Maceo, the nineteenth-century nationalist leader, is revered throughout military institutions and often used to justify Cuba's presence in Angola, thus invoking the island's African heritage. See Fidel Castro, Speech on 7 December 1989, in *Trabajadores* (8 December 1989), p.4. Maceo's mother, Mariana Grajales, is taken as a symbol of women's involvement in the nationalist struggle, together with women who played a key part in the 1950s guerilla war, such as Celia Sánchez, Haydée Santamaría, Vilma Espín and Melba Hernández.

25. Until 1959, blacks constituted 13 per cent of Cuban migrants to the US, since that date they represent 5 per cent of Cuban migration and remain, on the whole, outside the exile community; see Susan Greenbaum, 'Afro-Cubans in Exile', *Cuban Studies*, Vol. 15, No. 1 (1985), pp.59–72. A 'poor white' resentment can be seen in some of the interviews with immigrants reported in Geoffrey Fox, 'Race and Class in Contemporary Cuba', in Irving Horowitz (ed.), *Cuban Communism* (New Brunswick, New Jersey: Transaction Books, 1981), pp.309–30.

26. Carollee Bengelsdorf, 'On the Problem of Studying Women in Cuba', in

Andrew Zimbalist (ed.), *Cuban Political Economy* (Boulder, Colorado: Westview Press, 1988), pp.119–36.

27. 'Revolutionary merits' is a factor which has weighed heavily in elections to leading positions or in promotions within the government, to the advantage of those who can claim a background as a guerrilla. See Max Azicri, *Cuba: Politics, Economics and Society* (London: Pinter, 1988), p.54.

28. This is a claim often made by dissidents. My own experience in Cuba – certainly not a systematic one – of visiting friends who are seen as 'dissident', confirms that soon after my arrival a neighbour has appeared with some trivial excuse or other. This, of course, does not indicate a policy and could just be officious curiosity; nevertheless it cannot but be perceived as a form of social control by the recipient.

29. The frequency with which militants could disrupt work schedules and wage policies by standing up in a trade union branch meeting and asking for extra hours or a day's wages to be donated to a worthy cause led the CTC to impose a *de facto* ban on such appeals in 1979.

30. LARC-83-08 (30 September 1983), p.8; *Granma* (28 December 1984), pp.1–4.

31. LARC-86-06 (24 July 1986); LARC-87-08 (1 October 1987), p.2.

32. Some publications, such as *Juventud Rebelde* and *Trabajadores*, have adopted mild forms of investigative reporting, following up consumers' complaints and accusations of corruption and wastage. *Somos Jóvenes* published an issue in August 1987 on prostitution and drugs which ran out of copies and became a prized blackmarket item. *Opina* has made several attempts, since its birth in 1979, at meeting its readers' demands, having had bans slapped on its classified ads and 'lonely hearts' columns.

33. Max Azicri, 'Women's Development Through Revolutionary Mobilisation: a study of the Federation of Cuban Women', in Horowitz (ed.), *op. cit.*, pp.276–308.

34. For instance, the abolition of the peasants' markets in April 1986 can be linked to President Castro's criticisms made, according to him, well before that date, see *El regreso de Fidel a Caracas* (Caracas: Universidad Central de Venezuela, 1989), p.24.

35. LARC-86-05 (13 June 1986), p.5.

36. *Ibid.*

37. Roberto Bahamonde stood as a human rights candidate against the PCC nominee at the March 1989 elections for the local People's Power assembly in San Miguel del Padrón. He lost by 31 votes to 60. LAWR-89-13 (30 March 1989), p.12.

Part III
Territories under
Metropolitan Control

10 Political Subordination and Society in the French Antilles

Michel Giraud

INTRODUCTION

I have been invited to examine the modalities by which social structures in the French Antilles determine political life, but my chapter will, in a sense, tackle the problem from the opposite point of view. This is not out of a taste for paradox, but any study concerning Guadeloupe or Martinique must take into account the basic relation of these islands' continuing political dependency on the colonizing power, France.

As a first premise, I can say that the nature of the determining relationship between social and political organization in the French Antilles is the opposite of that which prevails in most European or North American countries. For this reason, the explanatory models treating the links between social classes and political power for example, resulting from Marxist analysis, as employed for industrial countries, cannot be mechanically applied to Guadeloupe and Martinique. Thus, with a 20-year interval, two analysts, both belonging to these societies, felt the same need to move away from these models.

The first, Frantz Fanon, wrote regarding all colonial situations:

> It is neither the factories, the property, nor the bank account which is the major characteristic of the 'ruling class'. The ruling class, is primarily those who come from elsewhere, those who are different from the indigenous population, 'the others'. . . . In the colonies the economic infrastructure is, at the same time, a superstructure. The cause is the effect: wealth equals white, white equals wealth. For this reason, Marxist analysis should be applied to the colonial problem with a certain flexibility.[1]

The second author, Edouard Glissant, a Martiniquan writer, observes:

An analysis of 'social classes' in Martinique, which instead of following the preestablished schemas, attempted to understand the actual situation [the non-autonomy of the economic circuit] would demonstrate that it is useless to pose social problems in this country *without politicising them* [my italics].[2]

I will therefore attempt to show how Guadeloupe and Martinique's dependency on France determines the structure of these societies, as well as why Antillean[3] political life is centred around the question of the political status of these two islands.

Before proceeding further into the heart of the subject, it would be useful to note the major geographical, historical and demographic landmarks relating to the two French Antillean societies. These islands are located in the south-eastern part of the Caribbean archipelago, and belong to the Lesser Antilles. Guadeloupe is to the north of Dominica, and has a surface of 1780 km^2 while Martinique is situated further south between Dominica and St Lucia and its land surface is 1106 km^2.

Although these islands were 'discovered' by Christopher Columbus just before the turn of the fifteenth century, their real colonization took place on French initiative in 1635. By the second half of the seventeenth century, they had been made into sugar islands, dominated by the slave plantation system. In 1848 slavery was abolished, and after World War II the islands became integrated departments of the French republic (termed *départements d'outre-mer*). The Martiniquan and Guadeloupean populations, a product of the intermingling of European settlers and African slaves, to whom, in the second half of the nineteenth century, were added new immigrants, mainly contract workers from India, represent today a population of just over 300 000 inhabitants on each island.

FROM DEPENDENCY TO DEPENDENCY

Guadeloupe and Martinique as societies were created from nothing out of a totally imported population by the dynamics of French merchant capitalism. About 20 years after the beginning of the French occupation of these two islands, the original inhabitants – the Amerindians – had been totally exterminated or expelled. The slate was wiped clean by colonialism; neither society can go back to a pre-colonial past. As distinct from the case of old European societies, the historical structuration of social groups in the French Antilles is less the result of the intrinsic, autonomous effort of the society itself, resulting from its own internal dynamics, than that of an exterior tutelary power imposing and directing from outside.

Being exclusively organized in terms of the economic interests of the exterior power, French Antillean societies have always been in a situation of total dependency on the mainland. From the earliest stages of colonization, this dependence was controlled by the rule of exclusivity: everything produced in the colonies was destined for the mainland, everything consumed in the colonies came from the mainland and had to be transported by metropolitan ships. The colonies were so totally shaped by their outward-orientated economic system that, for a long time, they could be defined as plantation societies.

In other words, societies whose structure was totally shaped by an institution (the plantation) whose character can be described as totalitarian in that it imposed (even in the case of sectors which it did not directly dominate) its export logic. All real accumulation of capital, and therefore any autocentric development was outlawed. It was from this system that the colonies acquired their major characteristics, notably a very marked social stratification, rendered even more rigid by the fact that class divisions were reinforced by strong colour distinctions which tended to be experienced by the social actors as racial differences.[4] Traditionally it was the big planters and merchants, produce exporters, almost all white,[5] who exercised an exclusive domination over the mass of agricultural workers and small peasants who were all black.[6]

Due to the strength of class and colour prejudice, by which the French Caribbean societies are marked, the middle class – small and middle shopkeepers, professional people and civil servants, teachers, consisting mainly of the descendants of mulattos freed during the time of slavery, did not act as a link between the dominant groups and the popular masses which its median position within these societies, as well as its racial composition, seemed to imply.

Today, the plantation economy is in its death throes. Even the partial application of metropolitan social legislation, resulting from the departmentalization of Martinique and Guadeloupe, has increased the wage costs of French Caribbean agriculture to a ruinous degree. This took place at a time when, due to their entry into the EEC, French Caribbean agriculture was already exposed to heightened international competition, particularly from tropical countries affiliated to the Community. The result was an agricultural crisis: for example, the percentage of the GDP represented by the primary sector and the percentage of those employed in agriculture in Martinique went from 40 per cent in the 1950s to less than 10 per cent today. Sugar production on the island is no longer sufficient to meet local demand. On the other hand, by considerably strengthening state services in these departments, followed by a massive injection of public funds into the economy, the French Caribbean's administrative assimilation to the mainland has made public-sector jobs particularly attractive in Martinique and Guadeloupe, for they carry security of tenure and a cost of living allowance, which brings salaries up to 40 per cent more than metropolitan civil service pay.

Non-productive economic activities have also become extremely worthwhile, especially commercial activities (a field which has proved very lucrative for a number of those formerly belonging to the colonial plantocracy). The result is that people and capital are attracted away from the existing productive sectors, thus limiting the development of alternative activities, especially manufacturing industry. This sector's contribution to the GDP has remained fixed at a ceiling of about 5 per cent over the last 30 years, a level so low that it does not facilitate the absorption of the workforce rendered unemployed by the agricultural crisis. What has been expanded is the tertiary sector: on both the islands this sector accounts for more than 75 per cent of the GDP. Thus an artificial growth has taken place, financed by public funds from the mainland, but creating private profit for mainland commerce, while leading the French Antilles inexorably towards a non-productive consumer society.

While raising the general standard of living for the insular populations, the departmentalization of Guadeloupe and Martinique has reinforced the social inequalities inherited from the colonial past. It has, in fact, led to a situation in which white Creole owners, who have gone into the import–export business on a large scale, are getting richer, middle-class privileges are being consolidated, and the rural masses are increasingly marginalized: they are confronted with the hard reality of growing unemployment – more than 20 per cent of the active French Antillean population is unemployed, thus forcing an increasing number to emigrate. In 1982 the number of people born in the French Caribbean, but resident in mainland France, was 182 000 as compared with only 16 000 in 1954.

Departmentalization has also made the French Antilles increasingly dependent on the mainland: the collapse of traditional agricultural production, which it provoked, means that export earnings in Martinique and Guadeloupe represent as little as 10–15 per cent of import costs, with the difference being settled by credit transfers carried out by the French state. The situation in the French Antilles today is thus typical of the constraints of the colonial pact: they represent captive markets reserved for products manufactured on the mainland.

If the French Antillean plantation society only continues to exist as a shadow of its original glory, the mercantile logic by which it was created continues to flourish, to the extent that a Martiniquan economist has suggested considering the tertiary activities which are developing in his country – supermarkets, the hotel trade, tourism – as 'new plantations'.[7] In the French islands this continuity has guaranteed the reproduction – slightly enlarged – of traditional social structures.

DEPENDENCY, RACE AND CLASS

The non-autonomy of the economic circuit, a direct consequence of these societies' political dependence on France, leads to what Edouard Glissant calls the 'non-functionality of the social classes' in Guadeloupe and Martinique. By this he means their low level of economic, social and political initiative.

> The social classes in Martinique are not essentially the result of a series of conflicts within a system (which would in this case be autonomous) but they result from a series of manipulated conflicts, directed by an overseer, who controls the circuit without entering into it as a 'social participant' – namely French merchant capitalism.

Thus we have a society which has been 'created', and lacks an aristocratic tradition, a national bourgeoisie holding economic power; its 'classes' function only in ways which have been decided for them from outside.[8]

Taking, for example, the case of Martinique, let us examine this situation more closely. The local dominant ethno-class, made up of the white Creole big planters and tradesmen, does not form a separate bourgeoisie, but rather what André Gunder Frank would call a 'lumpen bourgeoisie'. This class is, in fact, still totally dependent on the commercial system set up by the colonial power which created it.

During the slave period, in the exercise of its economic power, this dominant ethno-class was dependent on the metropole for the provision of a servile workforce (controlling neither the price nor the quantity provided), for the distribution of its produce on the European market (having no control over the price), and for the maintenance of its social domination, the forces of law and order being sent by France to put down slave revolts.

In post-slavery times, the Antillen commercial élite remained dependent on French protectionism which, by means of a quota policy, guaranteed outlets for colonial produce and fixed prices on the mainland market. Today, with the collapse of the plantation economy, the continuation of its power is only upheld by the 'recycling', through the import commerce which it controls, of the 'manna' of funds injected by the French state into the overseas departments. As for their political representation, it was appropriated over a century ago by the coloured *'petite bourgeoisie'*, with the active support of the French.

Thus the dependent dominant class only profits, more or less passively, from a system of exploitation which it did not set up, and which it does not really run for its own profit. This explains the absence of a national vocation within the bourgeoisie, which is confirmed by the traditional policy of exporting benefits out of Martinique instead of reinvesting in the country. Throughout Martiniquan history, the rare attempts to escape the handcuffs of the colonial pact, by which they were bound, have proved ineffectual or merely led to a change of tutelary power. Thus in order to escape the consequences of the 1789 French Revolution, which for them were severe – notably in the abolition of slavery, the Martiniquan whites handed the country over to the English who occupied it for about ten years. There is nothing here which can be compared to the autonomism which developed in the Spanish Caribbean islands under particular colonial circumstances, though it is true that they were less deeply marked than the French colonies by the institution of slavery. By its incapacity to distance itself from the mainland power, the dominant Martiniquan ethno-class's room for manoeuvre has always been very limited.

The coloured middle class, principally consisting of professional people, civil servants and managers from the private sector, make up a social élite without any real economic power. Its members' social mobility takes place almost exclusively by means of a selective non-technical education devoted to the humanities.

This education has corresponded to the colonial power's requirements since slavery was abolished in 1848; above all, it needed a class to perpetuate Guadeloupe and Martinique's dependency on France. Once the former slaves had become voters under the Third Republic in 1875, the colonial system could no longer hope to survive by force alone. It was necessary to widen the support base by convincing the Antillean populations of the advantages of remaining part of France, as well as to assure them that these advantages were open to all. With this objective it was essential to reinforce the indigenous coloured pro-French middle class with whom the masses could identify, whose social position and life style would represent the ideal they desired for their children. This was achieved by means of widespread public education along with the promulgation of an assimilationist ideology, which presented the maintenance of the relationship with France as a guarantee of progress.[9] However, the production–reproduction of a middle class in Guadeloupe and Martinique was in no way meant to alter or threaten the foundations of the dependency system, which made the French Caribbean islands captive markets serving the interests of mainland commerce. The preservation of these interests presupposes the non-development of a modern production system on these islands. Thus this middle class was to consist of humanities graduates rather than technicians, and this explains the primacy given to humanities rather than sciences within the Antillean education system.

DEPENDENCY AND POLITICS

As Glissant says, this showcase brown middle class exists only in the representative role which France's assimilationist policy has accorded it.[10] It is by virtue of this role that it has maintained its monopoly hold on French Antillean political representation since the Third Republic. Without a major involvement in economic production, this brown middle class has never been able, nor has it desired, to differentiate itself as a group from mainland policies. If today some of its members want to assume a national vocation, this cannot go beyond wishful thinking, given that they lack the economic means to further their ambition.

These particularities of the 'colonial situation' in the French Antilles are the bases of political life. For, the colonized social formations did not precede colonization but were, on the contrary, a product of it; and the components of these social formations did not and do not possess any structural autonomy in relation to the system of dependency which created them.

For a long time it was very difficult for these Antillean societies to create their liberation from the domination to which they were subjected. This is the opposite of what happened in classical colonial situations, whose victims were colonized on home ground, within the framework of their ancestors' land and culture. Thus, for the Antillean populations, made up of men and women whose ancestors were torn away from their native cultures and who are strangers to pre-Colombian Amerindian history, liberation could not signify a return to a tradition and a pre-colonial order which could be dug up from beneath the layers of colonialism; it could only mean the achievement of equality within the French national system, finally rid of the trimmings of colonialism.

Opposed to the white settlers, who planned to continue their reign in the colony by obstructing this very victory, the nineteenth-century coloured population sought to obtain the equality and progress which they were being denied. They invoked the values of post-Revolutionary France and the rights of man and the citizen, quite naturally calling upon the authority and protection of the distant metropolitan power (which also had an interest in fighting the hegemonic aspirations, however fleeting, of the Creole planters, at a time when mainland beet sugar was undeniably replacing colonial cane). As a result, their demands were for French citizenship. Moreover, with the abolition of slavery decreed by the metropole, the image of France, symbol of freedom, had displaced that of France the colonizer; and French colonialism was to attempt to justify itself by developing assimilationist policies in the French Caribbean. So, under the Third Republic, universal suffrage, political representation of the colonies in the French parliament, and compulsory state education were introduced.

For this reason Antillean political life was, for a long time, and to a large extent still is, confined to the framework of assimilation to the mainland. In this perspective, Guadeloupean and Martiniquan departmentalization in 1946, which represented the sanctioning of this assimilation by plebiscite, should be interpreted not simply as the mainland's answer to the question of decolonization, but as the product of a repeated demand by the colonized peoples. This demand was instigated, at the end of the nineteenth century, by the coloured middle class, but rapidly gained the support of the masses.[11] In fact, the French Antilles' acquisition of departmental status was, with the help of labour struggles, the framework for unquestionable social progress, to which workers are legitimately attached, even if, to use Aimé Césaire's expression, it has proved to be a 'slip knot', which has almost liquidated the plantation economy and which threatens to definitely strangle Antillean identity. In the light of this, the continuing impact of assimilation in the Antilles, which pervades even the lower classes, can be understood. And it is for this reason that Antillean political life today is structured along the same power lines as France, reproducing exactly mainland political cleavages.

Antillean political parties are, for the most part, mere regional structures or even smaller branches of French parties – Rassemblement pour la République, Union pour la Democratie Française, Parti Socialiste, Parti Communiste, diverse Trotskyist groupings.[12] With the exception of the Trotskyists, who represent a tiny minority, they accept the French constitutional game, and do not fundamentally envisage Guadeloupe and Martinique's future outside of France, despite the division between departmentalists and autonomists, who form two major blocs (a separation essentially built up on the basis of the right/left tradition in French political life). That this is true of all the major Antillean political forces, including those that claim to be fighting a situation which they still consider colonial, says a lot for the impact of assimilationism on French Antillean political life.

Under these circumstances, the question of the validity of the autonomist thesis can be legitimately posed. Those in favour of autonomy today are following the same rocky path as the 1946 Antillean left (in large part, they are the same people). The latter praised negritude and demanded political assimilation to France. Did they have a choice?

Today the autonomists desire to preserve their peoples' identity, while maintaining an adherence to France, and to work for their island's autocentric development, without questioning the system of political dependency which denies this development. To top it all, they hope financial help from the power at the centre of the system will continue! Given their knowledge of the past, they have less excuse than their forerunners: is it possible to escape the well-known contradiction of undoing the colonial relation by embracing a 'new look' dependency?

A perfect example of this contradiction has been the unfruitful attempt by the Parti Progressiste Martiniquais (founded by Aimé Césaire in 1956 after a break with the French Communist Party), one of the principal protagonists of Antillean autonomism, to break with the assimilationist tradition. In his famous *Letter to Maurice Thorez*, Césaire pointed out that it is not for the colonized populations to be at the service of communism, but rather for communism to be at their service. Thirty years later, the PPM has become the French Socialist Party's docile ally, and when the left came to power in 1981 they decided to call for a moratorium on the question of the evolution of the Antillean department's political status.

The hopes implied in the Antillean fight for freedom could not remain untarnished by Guadeloupe and Martinique's political integration in France (even if the local promoters saw this as a means towards final liberation, a necessary step). Integration follows its own path: it has resulted in a many-faceted metropolitanization of Guadeloupe and Martinique – absolute economic dependency, totally mimetic education, deep acculturation, in short, self-dispossession. In order to carry out the desire to free themselves from the harness of French colonialism, history has led the Antilleans to adopt Francization, in Roland Suvelor's words 'a cultural project which is at the same time complementary and contradictory to their desire for freedom'.[13] In this way they have been pushed into an impasse. In order to be themselves tomorrow, they have, in the meanwhile, become a little more that which they were not. This is the Antillean paradox: the contradiction appears precisely where one least expects it. For their own ends, the Guadeloupeans and Martiniquans have wanted to absorb European *values*, but they find themselves integrated *to* France. History has turned the joke on them.

CONCLUSION

Is there a way out of this situation? What of independence, which might give Antillean identities a political value, while investing the insular economies with the formal power for autonomous organization? The subject is discussed. It is true that the numerous adverse effects of departmentalization – the breakdown of traditional production systems which is not compensated for by the development of new productive activities, increased unemployment, increased emigration, confusion in the education system – have provoked a certain disillusion in some Antilleans and a strong nationalist sentiment in others. But the majority remain deaf to the call for independence. In the absence of a clear perspective on the future, in the event of gaining independence, they would rather, for want of a better solution, remain 'French' in the hope of preserving the relative material security in which, for the time being, they find a refuge.

However, it is not too late: the colonial enterprise is far from having totally succeeded. But one still has to tell the truth to act accordingly.[14] That French West Indians are still French citizens and that they would – quite legitimately – have chosen to be is by no means fatal. Besides, they are not yet French (in terms of culture) and probably they never will be, even if only because integration (an effort to make a people different from what it is through its own resources) is in itself impossible. French Antilleans are already different in their actions and their capabilities. But it is only through independence that their capabilities will flourish, provided the coloured middle class, whose appetite for political power would only equal their lack of economic power, did not direct this independence towards a Duvalier-style experiment, thus paving the way to neo-colonialism.

NOTES

1. Frantz Fanon, *Les Damnés de la Terre* (Paris: François Maspero, 1974, first edition 1961), p.9.
2. Edouard Glissant, *Le Discours Antillais* (Paris: Editions du Seuil, 1981), pp.112–13.
3. The term 'Antillean' will be used as a synonym of 'Guadeloupean and Martiniquan'.
4. On this subject see my book: *Races et Classes en Martinique* (Paris: Editions Anthropos, 1979).
5. For example, in Martinique, less than 20 years ago, the white Creoles owned more than two-thirds of the arable land, almost all the sugar factories, a majority of the banana plantations, and all the pineapple canning plants, as well as having a monopoly of export commerce.
6. Due to the gathering together of occupations in the rural French Caribbean (a number of peasants also work during the sugar harvest as wage earners on the plantations), salaried agricultural workers and small peasants have never represented two clearly distinct groups. On the absence, in these islands, of a real peasantry motivated by an 'ownership mentality' see G. Lasserre, *La Petite Propriété des Antilles Françaises dans la Crise de l'Économie de Plantations* (Montréal: Centre de recherches Caraïbes, Université de Montréal, 1972) and S.W. Mintz, 'Petits Cultivateurs et Prolétaires Ruraux dans la Région des Caraïbes' in *Les Problèmes Agraires des Ameriques Latines* (Paris: CNRS, 1968), pp.93–100.

Michel Giraud

7. See J. Crusol, *La Croissance Économique de la Martinique depuis la Départementalisation* (Fort-de-France: Centre d'Etudes Régionales Antilles-Guyane, 1971).
8. Glissant, *op. cit.*, p.110.
9. It should be noted that public, secular and compulsory education developed in the French Caribbean at the end of the last century, at the same time and on the same lines, if not to the same extent, as on the mainland.
10. 'The Caribbean élite is characterized by the fact that it is representative rather than exploitative, in other words it is not representative because it has, on its own and through its own effort or by its accomplishments, acquired the right to representation . . . it is representative because the colonizer has invested it with this role; it has been methodically created to take charge and to represent, to the letter, in the theatrical sense of the word, the alienation from which the general population suffers.' Glissant, *op. cit.*, p.210.
11. One should bear in mind that, from the time of their creation, the French Caribbean Communist and Socialist Parties were fervent supporters of this demand, to which at the time, the conservatives, especially the colonial plantocracy, were opposed. In 1946 it was Aimé Césaire, at the time head of the Martiniquan section of the French Communist Party, who formulated the departmentalization law.
12. For example, when, in 1934, the question of founding a communist party in Martinique arose (the PCF's proposal was to help the Martiniquan 'comrades' to structure their own organization), the comrades replied that this was a form of discrimination, and demanded the right to belong to a Martiniquan section of the French party. It was only 25 years later that 'autonomous' Antillean communist parties were formed.
13. R. Suvelor, 'Eléments Historiques pour une Approche Socioculturelle', *Les Temps Modernes* (April–May 1983), pp.441–2.
14. But this is by no means easy, as Edouard Glissant says with regard to the mentality of dependency which in the French Caribbean is encouraged by the 'clientelist' application of mainland social policy: 'The application of Social Security laws in Martinique is certainly done in a general context where these laws 1. are presented, if not experienced as a gift from France and not as a conquest of the Martiniquan workers; 2. they have no correlation with any Martiniquan work policy; 3. consequently they lead the population towards a mentality of organized, officially approved begging,. . . . But the first political party which systematically proclaims these truths, concluding in its programme that the Martiniquans would be better off with less, in a system where they controlled the production and work policies, than being half satisfied in a situation of irresponsibility – would lose any influence it possessed. No political grouping is ready to commit ideological suicide. The answer to any individual who upheld this logic would be, with good reason, that it is clear that he has all that he needs and that he does not need the family benefit allowance to survive. Happy ambiguity.' Glissant, *op. cit.*, p.170.

11 Society and Voting Behaviour in Puerto Rico

Juan M. García-Passalacqua and Jorge Heine

*'The people of Elvira,' Dhaniram said, tightening his belt,
'have their funny little ways, but I could say one thing for them:
you don't have to bribe them twice.'*

V.S. Naipaul, *The Suffrage of Elvira*, 1958

Our understanding of the patterns of interaction between Caribbean societies and their respective polities is a limited one. By and large, we still find ourselves trying to sort out emerging patterns of this interaction at the national level; generalizations and propositions about *Caribbean* electoral behaviour, for example, remain to be made.

What has to be done is to draw out the political implications of the condition of post-plantation societies – the effects, if any, of the common core of the region's historical experience on the concrete political behaviour of Caribbean people. As a step in that direction, this chapter provides an examination of the linkages between Puerto Rican society and electoral behaviour.

For students of Caribbean politics, Puerto Rico is significant. Since the turn of the century a total of 26 general elections have been held on the island – more than in any other Caribbean territory. This provides a rich database, allowing for the identification of patterns that are more difficult to isolate in countries with a more limited exposure to democratic elections. Quite apart from the comparatively long duration of Puerto Rico's electoral experience, the intensity of it is also worth underscoring. Far from being mere exercises in power-shuffling among competing élites with little involvement of the common people, since 1936 elections in Puerto Rico have evolved into veritable 'happenings', the equivalents of the Trinidadian carnival, occasions on which a whole people takes to the streets for much of the second half of each election year, culminating in massive turnouts on election day, turnouts that hover above 80 per cent of registered voters. At present, more than half of the total population votes.

The question as to *why* Puerto Ricans vote as they do is central to our understanding of the interplay between Puerto Rican society and the island's political system. Yet, the available literature on Puerto Rican politics does little to illuminate the interaction between the 'social' and the 'political'. The overwhelming majority of authors have chosen to explain political phenomena in terms of the changing ideological and/or material preferences of the electorate, rather than in terms of the latter's socio-economic background.

The underlying assumption of many of these approaches has been that Puerto Rican voters behave like a maximizing *homo oeconomicus* in a political marketplace. Voters are presumed to 'choose' year in and year out among ideologies, platforms and candidates in ways that maximize the potential benefits likely to accrue to the individual voter as a result of his or her choice at the voting booth.[1] We hereby propose that a much more appropriate analogy than the marketplace is the extended family. Family members do not, as a rule, evaluate their duties to each other using cost-benefit analysis; they discharge them because it is what is expected of them, it is 'what has always been done.' Less important than what is *offered* to the voter in terms of campaign promises is *who the voter is* – where he lives, who his neighbours are, as well as what the various candidates and parties have done for him in the *past*, thus meriting the 'family's' gratitude or resentment. To understand Puerto Rican voting behaviour we must realize that more important than *what* people think is *how* they think and what makes them think that way.

VOTERS AND PARTY SYSTEMS IN PUERTO RICO

The first recorded election in Puerto Rico took place in 1809, to indirectly elect representatives to the Spanish *Cortes*. The franchise, however, was limited to such a small number of people and subjected to such fraud and manipulation by the Spanish colonial authorities that it is difficult to consider any nineteenth-century elections as true expressions of the popular will. As late as 1884, for example, with the island's population close to a million, the total number of registered voters was 2492 – little more than 0.2 per cent of the population. The number also fluctuated wildly – it reached a high of 46 042 in 1873 and declined abruptly to 3674 in 1879, for example – depending on the restrictions imposed by Spanish officialdom. The one significant election to take place in Puerto Rico in the nineteenth century was in 1898, in which a total of 121 573 voters cast their ballots for a wide array of candidates.[2]

After the US invasion of Puerto Rico in 1898, the right to vote for all literate males over 21 was institutionalized.

> But voting was for a long time seen as an obligation to the dominant landowner of the rural community rather than as a personal privilege. Political obligation reflected the hierarchical yet personal character of social relationships which grew out of local economic arrangements. Landowners and sharecroppers, workers and storekeepers, were bound together into a functioning system of political power and patronage. As late as the 1930s voters in rural Cañamelar were still selling their votes for a pair of shoes.[3]

From 1944 to 1968 the island had the equivalent of a 'one-party-dominant' system, under the hegemonic rule of the Partido Popular Democrático (PPD), a populist party founded in 1938 by Luis Muñoz Marín, and favouring 'autonomy', currently known as 'Commonwealth' status. With the victory of pro-statehood Partido Nuevo Progresista (PNP) in 1968, the island entered a new era, in which the two leading parties have tended to alternate in power. The Partido Independentista Puertorriqueño (PIP), of a social democratic ideology, has not managed to get more than 5 per cent of the vote.

Political parties in Puerto Rico have their origins in the emergence of liberal politics in nineteenth-century Spain. The original parties were the Incondicionales (conservative loyalists) and the Liberal Reformistas (liberals). The former disappeared without a trace after the US invasion in 1898; the latter split up into a 'Republican' (profederated statehood) and an autonomist camp in the early years of the twentieth century. The autonomists, in turn, bred a pro-independence party in the 1940s. Commonwealth status, the present political condition, was founded in 1952 under the leadership of Luis Muñoz Marín and his Popular Democratic Party. Its hybrid features – placing it somewhere between a classic colony and a fully sovereign nation state – are very much the product of the autonomist mentality. Programmatic differences between parties respond basically to the three alternative solutions to the colonial condition: independence, autonomy or federated statehood.

As Table 11.1 indicates, the data show a clear-cut correspondence between the relative size of the electorate and the few shifts in the existing party system. Four periods thus emerge: (I) *Hacendado* hegemony (1904–17), (II) the socialist challenge (1917–32), (III) populist hegemony (1936–64) and (IV) the urban challenge (1968–88). A major expansion of the franchise took place between 1928 and 1936, ushering in a new political era. The next massive influx occurred in 1972–76, also leading to another new era.

Electoral change occurs only when 'blocs' of voters abandon one of the traditional parties and move to another, or when new voters register. Between 1902 and 1904 the *republicanos* lost 24 731 votes and the *unionistas* gained 55 108, the latter coming from the opposition and from newly registered voters. Between 1914 and 1971 the *republicanos* lost 22 255 and the *socialistas* gained 34 672, again coming from the other party and from newly registered voters (70 000). Between 1952 and 1956 the *populares* remained relatively static; the *socialistas* lost 21 655 votes and the *independentistas* lost 39 348 while the *estadistas republicanos* gained 87 666. Socialists who left in 1917 rejoined the republican camp four decades later. Between 1964 and 1968 the *populares* lost 113 240, only to regain them in 1972 together with new voters.

Four key political movements have existed: *unionista–liberal–popular, republicano–estadista–novoprogresista, socialistas* and *independentistas*. In all elections in which major political realignments have taken place, 'other' parties have made brief appearances, in effect ushering in each realignment: the Constitucional Histórico in 1924; the Unificación Puertorriqueña in 1940; the Partido del Pueblo in 1968; and the Partido de Renovación Puertorriqueña in 1984.

THE STATE OF THE LITERATURE

The first attempt to provide a comprehensive account of Puerto Rican politics during the first half of the twentieth century is Bolívar Pagán's.[4] In the tradition of Spanish historiography, it focuses basically on party leaders and party platforms. Although no explicit, overarching explanation of island politics is set forth, the unstated assumption is that it is fundamentally this leadership behaviour and the various party programmes and planks that hold the key to the various electoral outcomes.

Robert Anderson, in turn, formalized the traditional three-way contest that has been such a prominent feature of island politics into three distinct categories: personalism, corresponding to the autonomist PPD; patronage, to the pro-statehood Partido Estadista Republicano; and patriotism, to the PIP.[5] Quite apart from the fact that his observations simply refer to politics at the top and are irrelevant for mass behaviour, the difficulty with Anderson's analysis is that his categories overlap and are by no means confined to the party he assigns them to. *Personalismo* is rampant in *all* political parties in Puerto Rico,[6] as is patronage – at least in those parties that have any patronage to dispense. Anderson's attempt to split party followers into each of these different groups thus flies in the face of the evidence that the practices he associates with specific parties are widespread across the political spectrum.

What is needed, therefore, is an explanatory framework for Puerto Rican political culture *in toto*. This is what Henry Wells attempted to do.[7] Wells relied on modernization theory to account for the island's political change. According to him, it was the shift from the deference values of traditional society to the welfare values associated with modern society that explains the tremendous support garnered by the PPD from 1940 to 1968 – a support facilitated by the reliance on that most traditional of popular mobilization tools, a highly charismatic leader. In a sense, though, Wells's analysis explains too much. If 'modernization', understood as the rapid social and economic changes that took place in Puerto Rico from the 1940s to the 1960s, explains the emergence of the PPD as the hegemonic party in those years, how does he account for the steady growth of support for the pro-statehood forces that took place in those years, culminating in the victory of the PNP in 1968? Moreover, according to many of the indicators that are normally used to measure 'modernization' (urbanization, school enrolment, growth of the service sector) the island has continued to 'modernize', yet support for the PPD has declined or stabilized.

Kenneth Farr, in his the *personalismo* theory, has argued that the PPD loss in 1968 was due to Muñoz's failure to institutionalize the party.[8] Although the PPD split that took place under Governor Robert Sánchez Vilella (1964–68) had much to do with the 1968 election outcome, this explanation, like Wells's, has not held up well over time. Since 1972 the PPD has been under the firm rule of a single leader (Muñoz's successor), those who strayed from the party

Table 11.1 Elections and party support in Puerto Rico, 1900–84

Year	Registered	Voters	Unionista Liberal Popular	Republicano Estadista Novo Progresista	Socialista	Independentistas
Hacendado Hegemony: The Limited Franchise						
1900	123 140	58 515	—	58 367	—	—
1902	158 924	111 216	34 605	78 823	—	—
1904	225 262[a]	144 240	89 713	54 092	—	—
1906	187 193	157 668	98 406	43 932	—	—
1908	206 055	158 124	101 033	54 962	—	—
1910	221 816	163 568	100 634	58 572	—	—
1912	204 472	149 645	91 420	58 225	—	—
1914	273 116[a]	204 233	107 519	82 574	4 398	—
The Socialist Challenge						
1917	244 530	174 942	90 155	60 319	24 468	—
1920	268 643	249 431	126 446	63 845	59 140	—
1924	326 093	253 520	132 755	30 286[b]	56 103	—
1928	321 113	256 335	132 826	123 415 (a coalition)		—
1932	452 738[a]	383 722	170 168	110 794	97 438	5 257

The Populist Hegemony

1936	764 602[a]	549 500	252 467	152 739	144 294	—
1940	714 960	568 851	214 857	134 582[b]	87 841[b]	—
1944	719 759	591 978	383 280	101 779	68 107	—
1948	873 085	640 714	392 033	88 819	64 121	66 141
1952	883 219	664 947	429 064	85 172	21 655	125 734
1956	873 842	701 738	433 010	172 838	—	86 386
1960	941 034	796 429	457 880	252 364	—	24 103
1964	1 002 000	839 678	487 280	284 627	—	22 201

The Urban Challenge

1968	1 176 895	918 829	374 040[b]	400 815	—	32 166
1972	1 555 504[a]	1 250 978	658 856	563 609	—	69 654
1976	1 701 217[a]	1 458 034	660 401	703 968	—	83 037
1980	2 071 777	1 609 311	756 889	759 926	—	87 272
1984	1 959 877	1 741 418	813 706	762 546[b]	—	56 788

[a] Increments in the number of registered voters seem to have a significant effect on voting behaviour. Note the following: 1904 (67 000), 1914 (70 000), 1932 (130 000), 1936 (312 000), 1972 (379 000), 1976 (246 000).

[b] In four elections a substantial exodus from one of the parties to short-lived split-off movements had a major impact on the electoral outcome. The 'other' parties obtained the following number of votes: in 1924, 34 576; in 1940, 130 299; in 1968, 107 359; in 1984, 69 807.

Source: Comisión Estatal de Elecciones, Informes: 1900–84.

fold in 1968 have largely returned to it and it has been firmly institutionalized. Yet the party lost both the 1976 and the 1980 elections.

From a longer-term historical perspective, Fernando Bayrón portrays the electorate's division as fundamentally between liberals, conservatives and separatists, his ideological equivalent for autonomists, statehooders and independence supporters. These three currents are supposed to 'synthesize' Puerto Rico's political history. According to Bayrón, each election has thus been, directly or indirectly, a 'plebiscite' between the three classic status formulas.[9] Yet, such labels are inadequate to contend with the realities: the supposedly 'liberal' PPD has steadfastly opposed raising the minimum wage, while the 'conservative' PNP has been the main champion of it. Party dynamics in Puerto Rico have little to do with conservativism or liberalism.

The reduction of voter preferences to ideological status choices as the all-explanatory variable is taken to its ultimate conclusion by José Garriga-Picó.[10] His imposition of the elaborate apparatus of game theory on electoral data ends up by overwhelming the empirical evidence.

An important breakthrough from these traditional approaches relying on the politico-ideological dimension of voting behaviour was made, perhaps unsurprisingly, by several non-political scientists. One of the few attempts to examine the *social* roots of Puerto Rican political behaviour over time has been that of Angel Quintero Rivera.[11] Quintero focuses on the *hacendado* class that emerged in the nineteenth century and on the conflict between *hacendados*, on the one hand, and merchants and professionals on the other. The origins of what would eventually evolve into the dominant party in Puerto Rican politics in the twentieth century are traced to this hegemonic class.

This party, the Partido Autonomista led by Luis Muñoz Rivera, obtained 80.6 per cent of the vote in the 1898 elections, the only ones held with universal male suffrage under Spanish rule. Agricultural workers and peasants gave their support to the class to which they in effect were bound. The *hacendados* 'controlled' more people than the merchants and professionals did, and delivered their vote in considerable numbers.

The 1898 US invasion and ensuing occupation of Puerto Rico disrupted the existing power distribution and opened the doors for the change from the *hacienda* system to a plantation economy.

According to Quintero, the decline of the *haciendas* and the limitation of the franchise to 21-year-old, property-owning males shattered the political power of the *hacendados*. It was precisely among agricultural workers in the *haciendas* that illiteracy was highest.

Quintero argues that the concentration of land in the hands of American absentee corporations led to the creation of a new class of 'sugar proletariat'. It was among these sugar workers that the Socialist Party emerged in 1915. And Quintero conclusively proves the strong correlation between support for the socialists and sugar cane cultivation.[12] The party was strongest in those areas where land was concentrated in large tracts used for sugar production for the *centrales*, mostly on Puerto Rico's coastal plains; it was much weaker in the coffee-producing areas under the *hacienda* system, still prevalent in the mountainous interior of the island.

Quintero's work, in many ways richly suggestive and subtle, has the great merit of highlighting the relationship between social class and political behaviour; it is also fundamental for understanding the rise and fall of the Socialist Party. As can be seen from Figure 11.1, though, if set against the larger picture of twentieth-century electoral behaviour in Puerto Rico, the Socialist Party plays a relatively minor role. And in his latest book Quintero himself admits that he has been unable to find 'any pattern at all' for Unionist Party support, and that all he can say of the Republican Party is that it had an 'urban and professional' nexus.[13] To understand the sources of support for Puerto Rico's major political parties we thus have to turn elsewhere.

Sociologist Marcia Rivera, in a pioneering study of the 1968 elections in San Juan, correlated socio-economic data with voting behaviour, with fascinating findings that ran counter to some of the conventional wisdom at the time.[14] Relying on voting data from the smallest electoral units (the *colegios electorales*), she was able to identify significant emerging trends, from the decline of the PPD vote in urban areas to the start of mixed-ballot voting. Anthropologist Rafael Ramírez, in another study of the 1968 elections, this one of a Cataño slum, established the irrelevance of status politics for the vast majority of Puerto Ricans, and the extraordinary gap between the discourse of politicians (and social scientists!) and that of the common people as far as politics is concerned. He also uncovered the significant effects of urban redevelopment on party identification, confirming the work of another anthropologist, Helen Safa.[15]

But no attempt to provide a diachronic account of the changing patterns of party support over time was undertaken by them. And

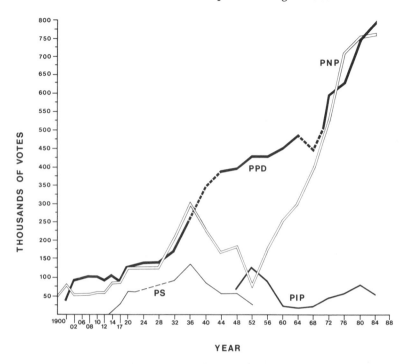

Figure 11.1   Party support in Puerto Rico, 1900–84

even Ramírez's explanation of the switch in support from the PPD to
the PNP in Cataño in 1968 as largely a 'protest', 'throw the rascals
out' vote has not stood the test of time; far from being a one-time
protest vote, the 1968 vote in Cataño signalled the beginning of a
process of secular realignment in Cataño, where the PNP has won all
four elections since.

The first comprehensive attempt to correlate population and
socio-economic change with partisan support in Puerto Rico is thus of
recent vintage. Ibrahim Pérez and María de Lourdes Fernández
examined voting data for all elections from 1952 to 1980 and correlated them with urbanization trends.[16] Their findings trace the rise of
the statehood movement to the island's rapid urbanization. While the
PPD managed to maintain its hegemony in the small rural municipalities of the coast and the mountains, support for the PNP has
emerged with particular strength in the urban metropolitan centres
and in the urban zones of the smaller municipalities. Urbanization, a
more precise variable than the all-encompassing 'modernization',

thus turns out to be a much better instrument to account for the loss of PPD hegemony. Still, for all the correlations computed by Pérez and Fernández, no *explanation* for this correlation between urbanization and PNP support emerges from their study.

METHODOLOGY

Survey research has become the predominant form of inquiry in electoral studies in contemporary political science. This has been fuelled in part by the desire to avoid what W.S. Robinson termed 'the ecological fallacy', a risk incurred in making inferences from any spatial electoral unit to the individual.[17] Leading Caribbean political scientists like Carl Stone and Selwyn Ryan have also relied on extensive opinion surveys to make election forecasts that have often shown to be very accurate.[18]

There is no substitute for a well-designed and rigorously carried out opinion survey. This, of course, is particularly true if our purpose is to extrapolate present opinion to predict future behaviour. However, this is not necessarily the case if we set out to identify the roots of electoral behaviour. For that, the study of aggregate units of analysis may be a more reliable research strategy – the only one, in fact, for pre-survey research days. Whatever its difficulties, moreover, aggregate voting data has some advantages over survey data. It provides evidence of *actual* behaviour (as opposed to *reported* or *announced* behaviour) and it also shows communal patterns of behaviour in ways that are often not apparent in survey data, which has a much more individualistic bias.[19]

In Puerto Rico, the indiscriminate application of survey research techniques that do not take into account the peculiarities of the island's political culture has led to a rather dismal record of inaccurately predicted electoral outcomes (Table 11.2). The record of pollsters in Puerto Rico speaks for itself. To redress the balance in favour of the analysis of aggregate voting data seems to be, therefore, a necessary pre-condition for the development of more reliable survey research instruments.

For these purposes, a useful indicator is the *popularismo* index, a measure of the degree to which support for the PPD, the hegemonic party for much of the past 50 years, in any given electoral unit exceeds or falls below the island-wide support for the party.[20] Although studies pointing out how party support has varied from

Table 11.2   Polls, predictions and election outcomes in Puerto Rico,
1968–84

Year	Source	Prediction	Outcome
1968	*San Juan Star*	PPD wins	PNP wins
1972	*San Juan Star*	'Close electoral battle'	PPD wins by 6%
1976	William Hamilton & Associates	PPD by 9%	PNP by 3%
1980	Clapp & Mayne	PNP by 11%	PNP by 0.2%
1984[a]	Yankelovich, Skelly & White	PPD by 5%	PPD by 3%

[a] The 1984 elections are thus the only ones whose result was more or less accurately predicted by pollsters. But even in the case of the Yankelovich poll, it should be noted that *using the same poll, El Nuevo Día* had forecast on 30 October that the PNP would win by 1%. See *El Nuevo Día* (30 October 1984). Such misuse of polling data has become standard in Puerto Rico.
Sources: *The San Juan Star* (2 March 1968), p.30; (22 October 1972), p.1; (29 October 1976), p.16; (31 October 1980), p.3; *El Nuevo Día* (4 November 1984).

municipio to *municipio* have been fairly common, what has not been done is to examine the available evidence for the smallest units of analysis, the *unidades electorales*.

Since 1976, people in Puerto Rico have voted in such electoral units, set up in the various neighbourhoods. In the 1984 elections, for example, there were 1654 units, with an average of about 1000 voters in each. The number of units in any given *municipio* will vary not only according to population but also with geography. In any given unit, the number of voters can be as high as 3600 or as low as 150. The important point is that such units now match the neighbourhoods in which they are set up, thus making it possible to correlate socio-economic environment with voting behaviour. Before 1976, voters within each precinct were grouped in electoral units in alphabetical order.

Relying on a computerized database of the 1984 election results for all electoral units, we undertook some such correlations. The key premise of this approach, the only one compatible with the extra-ordinary stability of Puerto Rican voting behaviour, is that people vote for reasons other than those normally associated with the democratic process.[21] The relative merits of the different candidates, whether any given administration has been 'good' or 'bad', the promises made to various constituencies, and the 'effectiveness' of media usage and campaign propaganda, though not necessarily irrelevant, seem to be less important than what we have termed the voter's 'communal environment' in determining his or her vote. To put it in its most extreme form, 'how you vote depends on where you live'.

ELECTORAL UNITS IN SOCIETAL SETTINGS

Puerto Rican society is generally described as being among the most homogeneous in the Caribbean. The fact that there is no Creole alternative to Spanish, that Catholicism has traditionally been the religion of the vast majority, and that the number of blacks is smaller than in the rest of the Spanish-speaking Caribbean are all factors that have contributed to this idealized vision of the Puerto Rican people as characterized by a high degree of homogeneity and consensus.

In fact, the opposite is true. Although the island's cleavages may be less immediately apparent than elsewhere in the region, perhaps the most significant feature of Puerto Rican society is its geographic, ethnic, historical, social and economic fragmentation. To the long-standing differences between the capital and 'la isla' (as *sanjuaneros* refer to the rest of Puerto Rico), between the central, mountainous area and the coastal plains, between coffee- and sugar-growing areas, between whites and blacks, we must now add the highly unequal and uneven impact of the accelerated process of economic and social change which the island has undergone over the past half century.

This process has not only systematically highlighted regional differences by favouring San Juan at the expense of the rest of Puerto Rico, and secondary cities such as Ponce and Mayagüez to the detriment of smaller townships; it has also radically increased intra-*municipio* cleavages by introducing the sort of segregated housing patterns that are such a prominent feature of twentieth-century US urban planning and architecture. Yet these are alien to the mixed-use urban settings originally favoured by Spanish officials (still partially evident in places like Old San Juan). Public housing developments, private urbanizations and high-rise condominiums have thus added a new layer of differentiation to an already highly fragmented social order. The way this regional fragmentation is translated into very different patterns of party support throughout the island can be seen in Figure 11.2, where four clear regional clusters emerge.

258

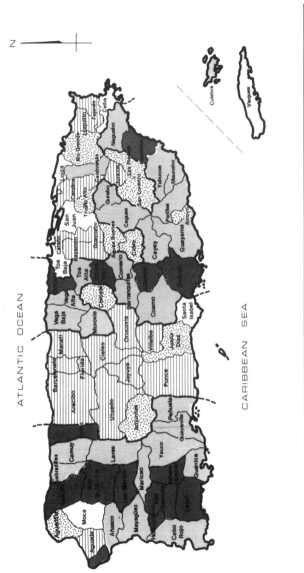

Figure 11.2 Party support by municipio, 1980

THE SOCIAL BASIS OF VOTING BEHAVIOUR

To expose the roots of this highly differentiated electoral behaviour, we will examine three critical factors: urbanization, class and race.

Urbanization

Although the island remained as a largely agricultural one from 1899 to 1940, a period in which the urban population increased from 15 per cent to 30 per cent, the pace of urbanization quickly increased after that. Forty-four per cent of the population was urban in 1960, 62 per cent in 1970 and 66 per cent in 1980. Whereas in 1960 there were only two *municipios* with a population over 100 000, by 1980 there were five of them – all but one of them located in or around the San Juan metropolitan area.

Much of this urban growth, then, has taken place on Puerto Rico's north-east coast, on the corridor that runs from Arecibo all the way to Fajardo, with the San Juan metropolitan area squarely in the middle of it. It is in this area that much of Puerto Rico's industry has settled and where most tourist resorts have been built, thus attracting migrants from the rest of the island.

It is also this area that has become the bastion of the PNP (the pro-statehood movement), although until 1964 the *populares* had never lost a single *municipio* (except San Lorenzo in 1948 and 1960). The PNP, in winning its first gubernatorial election in 1968 also won nine of the ten largest municipalities, mostly around the metropolitan San Juan area. Far from being an anomaly resulting from the division of the PPD in 1968, this was only the beginning of a pattern that would be established over the next four general elections.

As Figure 11.2 shows, the blue banners of the PNP in 1980 extended not only throughout the larger San Juan area, but also as far east as Fajardo and as far west as Arecibo. Of the 21 *municipios* located on Puerto Rico's north coast (of which 19 are predominantly urban and only two rural), incorporating 49 per cent of the island's population, the PNP won 15 and the PPD only six in 1980. Of the remaining 57 *municipios* throughout the rest of the island (of which only 17 are urban and 40 predominantly rural), with 52 per cent of the population, the PNP won only 16 versus the PPD's 41.[22] Among the nine cities that had the largest population increase between 1960 and 1980, only Ponce and Mayagüez were not in the northern corridor; only Mayagüez has remained steadily under PPD control.[23]

This is confirmed by the strong correlation between population and income in the various *municipios*, on the one hand, and support for the PNP on the other (Table 11.3). There is thus little doubt about the correlation between urbanization and PNP support.

Fascinatingly enough, this correlation not only obtains in comparisons between *municipios* but also within them. If we take as our unit of analysis the *barrio* rather than the *municipio*, we will find that the rural/urban cleavage is also reflected quite clearly in markedly different patterns of voting behaviour.

For example, in Puerto Rico's second largest city, Bayamón (which has become, for all practical purposes, a suburb of San Juan), the remaining rural *barrios* still tend to throw their support behind the PNP – reversing almost exactly the voting patterns obtaining in the rest of the locality (Table 11.4). This, of course, tends to suggest the importance of the sociological (as opposed to the purely political) origins of this behaviour; it would seem that although a majority of the rural residents of Bayamón are as available to be co-opted into the extensive patronage network and to receive the many benefits which this, one of the richest and best-managed municipalities is able to bestow on its citizens, they still prefer to vote for the PPD because 'that is the way *jíbaros* vote'.

Class

If urbanization seems to have been one important factor behind the rising support for the PNP, what about the class basis of support for the main political parties? Conventional wisdom has held that the lopsided majorities won by the PPD in the 1950s (65 per cent of the vote in 1952, 67 per cent in 1956) gradually gave way to a much more evenly matched contest with the statehood movement (which increased its support from 10 per cent of the vote in 1952 to 48 per cent in 1976) because Puerto Rico was rapidly increasing its standard of living and becoming a more 'middle-class' society.[24] According to this theory, it was this 'consumerist' middle class, strongly oriented toward the United States and its values that was providing the main impetus for the PER first and the PNP later. While the peasants may well stick to the *populares* and the political heirs of Muñoz, so the theory went, this ever-growing middle class preferred statehood and the 'security' from turmoil and revolution that presumably goes with it to the ambiguities and uncertainties of Commonwealth status.

It was an eminently plausible interpretation, although one not fully

Table 11.3 PNP score by types of *municipio*

Type	Municipio				Per capita Income ($)	Population	PNP score
I	Bayamón, San Juan	Carolina, Caguas	Guaynabo, Toa Baja	Trujillo Alto, Mayagüez	$2 100–4 000	50 000–500 000	3.12
II	Ponce	Aguadilla	Arecibo		$1 525–2 100	50 000–500 000	3.00
III	Hormigueros	Ceiba		Culebra	$2 100–4 000	1 000–23 000	0.66
IV	Naranjito, Toa Alta, Guayama, Canóvanas, Dorado, Humacao, Vega Alta, Río Grande, Cayey, Fajardo, Juncos	Camuy, Vega Baja, Manatí, Cabo Rojo, Cataño, San Germán, Luquillo, Quebradillas, Guayanilla, Las Piedras, Florida	Naguabo, Barceloneta, Gurabo, Aibonito, Añasco, Lajas, Sabana Grande, Moca, Aguada, Lares, Corozal	Cidra, Utuado, Yauco, Salinas, Juana Díaz, Hatillo, Isabela, San Lorenzo, Coamo, San Sebastián, Yabucoa	$1 000–2 100	1 000–50 000	1.15
V	Villalba, Barranquitas, Orocovis, Jayuya	Comerío, Maunabo, Morovis, Peñuelas	Aguas Buenas, Adjuntas, Rincón, Patillas	Vieques, Loíza, Maricao, Arroyo	$1 000–1 525	1 000–23 000	1.43

Source: *Municipio* typology from Comisión para la Revisión de la Ley Municipal, draft report, 'Estudio sobre la revisión de la Ley Municipal', 23 November 1986, pp.II-5–6.
PNP score computed on the basis of the number of elections won by the PNP in each *municipio*'s mayoral election from 1968 to 1984.

Table 11.4   Party support, urban and rural areas, Bayamón, 1980

Urban sector		Rural sector	
PNP	PPD	PNP	PPD
44 395	36 945	5 294	6 521
(50%)	(42%)	(43%)	(53%)

Source: Ibrahim Pérez and María de Lourdez Fernández, 'Análisis cuantitativo de movimientos poblacionales y electorales en Puerto Rico durante las últimas tres décadas' (San Juan: *Análisis*, 1984), p.93.

Table 11.5   Party support and social class in San Juan (%)

	PNP		PPD
	1968	1980	1980
Upper-class areas			
El Condado	58	60	31
Miramar	64	61	30
Lower income areas			
Puerta de Tierra	56	56	37
Barrio Obrero	54	54	39
Llorens Torres	53	56	32
Nemesio Canales	53	61	32
Middle-class areas			
Country Club	48	47	42

Source: As Table 11.4

borne out by the available evidence. The emerging patterns of support for the two major parties are more complex than the 'urban middle class' versus 'poor peasants', distinctions which the conventional wisdom seemed to posit (Table 11.5). The PNP, as seen above, did indeed make major inroads in the urban areas, but its strongest pockets of support were *not* to be found in the middle-class *urbanizaciones*. Rather, it obtained its highest majorities both in the upper-income sectors, such as in beachfront El Condado and in Miramar, a traditional residential neighbourhood of San Juan's bourgeoisie, and in the public housing developments, such as La Perla and Llorens Torres. In the middle-class areas, the vote was much more evenly split between the PNP and the PPD, and substantially higher for the PIP than in the rest of the island.

Voting data from other *municipios*, such as Mayagüez (Table 11.6) confirm that the relationship between support for the PPD, although weakest in the upper-income sectors, is by no means inversely correlated with income in any unilinear fashion; in Mayagüez the poorest *barrio* (Rosario) also has one of the highest PPD indexes, but income becomes a much less useful predictor of party support, once we approach that vast social layer located between the poorest and the high-income sectors.

One useful exercise is to compare and contrast two rather different sets of electoral units, representing population at the lower end of the socio-economic structure. One of these is composed of the *parcelas* (plots of land given by the government); the other is that of the *caseríos* (the public housing developments). What is perhaps most remarkable about the voting pattern of *parcela* and *caserío* dwellers is the consistency of the gap in the PPD vote between both sets of electoral units (Table 11.7). The puzzle is compounded by the ostensible similarities between both groups of voters. The families living in the *parcelas* and in the *caseríos* are among the less privileged sectors of Puerto Rican society and are afflicted by many of the same problems of unemployment, low income and comparatively low education that are such prominent features of the lives of Puerto Rico's poor. Although impressionistic evidence suggests that the *parceleros* are somewhat better off – more likely to have jobs and regular employment than the *caserío* residents. If the relationship between income and PNP support was a more or less direct and unilinear one, we would accordingly expect PNP support among the *parceleros* to be higher than among the *caserío* dwellers. In fact, exactly the opposite is true. A closer examination of the very dissimilar types of settings and habitats in which these two sets of populations find themselves would therefore seem to be warranted.

The *parcelas* emerged as a result of the first 'wave' of projects designed by the ruling PPD in the 1940s and 1950s to deal with Puerto Rico's housing problem. Rather than aiming to provide needy families with a ready-made apartment or single-family home, the low-cost *parcela* programme proceeded on the basis of the governmental transfer of land parcels to qualifying individuals. The houses were built by the owners through a variety of self-help projects, which relied on some government-provided materials, the work of friends and neighbours and other such inputs. The government also provided

Table 11.6 PPD index in Mayagüez by *barrio*, 1980 and 1984

SES ranking	1980			1984			% Rural
	Number of votes	%	PPD index	Number of votes	%	PPD index	
1. Miradero	922	44.38	− 7.51	1 054	42.33	− 8.42	—
2. Río Cañas Abajo	241	45.82	− 6.01	275	43.31	− 7.44	38.1
3. Juan Alonso	385	47.35	− 4.47	434	47.02	− 3.73	27.5
4. Guanajibo	1 984	52.86	+ 1.04	2 160	42.40	+ 1.65	—
5. Algarrobos	1 254	60.43	− 8.61	1 227	55.77	+ 5.02	—
6. Sábalos	1 902	47.58	− 4.24	2 347	46.69	− 4.06	—
7. Mayagüez Arriba	1 775	53.20	+ 1.38	1 800	52.45	+ 1.70	—
8. Quebrada Grande	1 166	57.04	+ 5.39	1 251	54.50	+ 3.75	9.7
9. Pueblo	10 194	51.41	− 0.41	10 254	50.62	− 0.80	—
10. Río Cañas Arriba	218	42.66	− 9.16	265	42.54	− 8.21	100
11. Río Hondo	534	48.95	− 2.88	681	49.89	− 0.86	26.0
12. Sabanetas	1 121	62.52	+10.70	1 186	59.18	+ 8.43	23.8
13. Leguísamo	479	56.02	+ 4.20	509	53.75	+ 3.00	43.5
14. El Limón	348	50.29	− 1.53	358	46.98	− 3.77	100
15. Bateyes	262	52.72	+ 0.89	282	49.56	− 1.19	72.4
16. Quemado	608	53.81	+ 1.98	703	52.54	+ 1.79	20.8
17. Montoso	208	53.75	+ 1.92	228	54.42	+ 3.66	100
18. Malezas	312	55.37	+ 3.50	351	54.25	+ 3.50	100
19. Naranjales	172	50.59	− 1.23	198	49.62	− 1.13	100
20. Rosario	302	60.89	+ 9.06	310	59.96	+ 9.21	100

Source: SES *barrio* ranking derived from 1980 Census data on median family income, % manual workers and number of rooms per house, combined with the authors' own judgement.

Table 11.7   PPD vote in *parcelas* and *caseríos*[a] (1984 elections)

Name	Municipality	% PPD vote
Parcelas:		
Lavadero	(Hormigueros)	67.7
Fortuna	(Luquillo)	65.8
J. Sánchez	(Bayamón)	55.1
Tiburón	(Barceloneta)	54.0
San José	(Toa Baja)	54.0
Imberty	(Barceloneta)	54.0
Stelle	(Rincón)	50.8
Papainí	(Vega Baja)	49.4
Suárez	(Loíza)	48.9
Márquez	(Vega Baja)	48.3
Arroyo	(Florida)	48.0
Verdún	(Guayanilla)	46.6
Vieques	(Loíza)	44.6
Hill Brothers	(San Juan)	43.2
San Isidro	(Canovanas)	42.7
Caseríos:		
Agustín Stahl	(Aguadilla)	53.3
Santiago Iglesias	(Ponce)	48.2
Portugués	(Ponce)	46.7
Dávila Freitas	(Barceloneta)	45.5
Los Mirtos	(Carolina)	45.1
Monte Park	(Carolina)	44.9
Las Dalias	(Carolina)	41.6
Jardines del Monte	(Carolina)	42.6
Ramos Antonini	(Ponce)	41.9
Villa España	(San Juan)	38.9
Llorens Torres II	(San Juan)	38.9
Los Flamboyanes	(San Juan)	38.7
Villa Ponce	(Ponce)	38.7
Santa Marta	(Ponce)	38.6
López Sicardó	(San Juan)	38.5
Los Dominicos	(Bayamón)	38.5
Vista Hermosa	(San Juan)	37.7
Llorens Torres I	(San Juan)	37.5
Los Alamos	(Bayamón)	36.8
Covadonga	(Carolina)	35.0
Jardines del Paraíso	(Carolina)	35.0
Nemesio Canales	(San Juan)	33.4
Sabana Abajo	(Carolina)	26.6

[a] This list includes *all caseríos* and *parcelas* identified as independent electoral units by the Comisión Estatal de Elecciones. There are, of course, many more *caseríos* and *parcelas* throughout the island.
Source: Computed on the basis of Comisión Estatal de Elecciones data.

a minimal infrastructre in the form of roads and utilities, but by and large the *parcelas* are the product of the residents' own effort and community work – the outcome of both individual and collective attempts to resolve a densely populated island's serious housing problem. The result is a community of private homeowners who, whatever their other problems may be, share a pride in place marked by strong community bonds. They have also retained a strong sense of gratitude (*agradecimiento*) and loyalty to the political party that made it possible for them (or their parents and grandparents) to move from the thatched huts of Puerto Rico of the 1930s to the modest but serviceable homes they own today.

The *caseríos*, on the other hand, represent the second, much more ambitious and 'modern' response to the island's housing problem. With a basic design of two- and three-storey walk-ups lumped together in a more or less haphazard fashion, they embody everything that is wrong with Puerto Rico's urban development – fully functional but extremely inhospitable collections of concrete boxes with which few dwellers can identify, let alone be proud of.[25]

Caserío residents do not own the public housing they live in and, in contrast with the *parceleros*, were totally uninvolved in building them. Moreover, the policy frequently followed by the agency that runs them (with the revealing title of Corporation of Urban Renewal and Housing – CRUV) of 'graduating' residents whose income reaches certain levels by steeply increasing their rents, has the perverse effect of increasing the turnover of potential 'community pillars'. The CRUV's policies thus put a premium on staying unemployed, working at cash-only odd-jobs, and engaging in outright illegal activities.[26]

The resulting anomy and *resentimiento* (bitterness) is one in which all pre-existing community webs and loyalty bonds – including support for the PPD – are broken, to be replaced by a much more individualistic, clientelistic, exchange-oriented political culture, in which the PNP has made major inroads. That different neighbourhoods may have radically dissimilar voting patterns is hardly a major finding. What is noteworthy about the severe contrast in the voting behaviour of the *parceleros* and the *caserío* dwellers is how two populations largely drawn from the same socio-economic background, but targeted by two rather different government-sponsored 'solutions' to their housing problem, undergo a process so radically different in their pattern of party identification and allegiance.

Race and Politics: The Case of Loíza

In keeping with the myth of Puerto Rico as a highly homogeneous society, the subject of race and politics is one that has been almost totally ignored by the island's social scientists. Given the absence of systematic studies, it is not possible to make the sort of generalizations that can be made on factors such as urbanization and class. Impressionistic evidence would seem to suggest, however, that black Puerto Ricans, most of whom tend to live on the coastal plains where the sugarcane plantations used to exist, tend to support the pro-statehood parties.

Although no island-wide data on the subject are available, the data for Loíza, the *municipio* with the highest percentage of blacks (58.5 per cent according to the 1950 census – 98 per cent after its division in 1970)[27] confirms that impression. Puerto Rico's only 'black' *municipio* is also the one with the lowest PPD index (−11.2 in 1984) in all of Puerto Rico, and has been so since 1972.[28]

The town of Loíza was founded in 1719. It had two main sectors: the coastal plain populated by slaves working in the cane (known as Loíza Aldea) and the hilly interior populated by peasants working for *hacendados*. In 1910 the municipality's *hacendados* transferred the seat of government from the black sector to the mostly white rural sector (known as Canóvanas). It was not until 1972 that Loíza Aldea was recognized as a separate municipality by a PNP government. The voting pattern since then can be seen in Table 11.8, another instance of *agradecimiento*.

Once again, the stability of political behaviour and the consistency of political adherence of the residents to their anti-*popularismo* stands out. The adherence of black sectors of the population to

Table 11.8   Party support in Loíza, 1972–84

Year	PPD		PNP		PIP	
	Number	%	Number	%	Number	%
1972	2402	(37.5)	3702	(57.9)	278	(4.3)
1976	2441	(33.5)	4504	(61.8)	271	(3.7)
1980	2909	(33.6)	5358	(61.8)	312	(3.6)
1984	4119	(36.7)	6499	(57.9)	254	(2.3)

Source: Comisión Estatal de Elecciones.

pro-American positions and parties has been pointed out by Quintero and explained by the improvement they have enjoyed since 1898, when compared to the treatment blacks received under Spanish rule.

THE DIALECTICS OF 'AGRADECIMIENTO' AND 'RESENTIMIENTO'

Two propositions stand out from the statistical evidence about Puerto Rican voting behaviour. The first relates to the extraordinary stability of this behaviour. The second is that the main political change to have taken place in this behaviour over the past 30 years (the growing support for the pro-statehood parties) has arisen from, and has been closely associated with, the specific type of urban development that has taken place.

In our analysis of the contrasting voting patterns of *parceleros* and *caserío* dwellers, we have already examined the mechanism propelling this change in party identification in the island's urban centres. But what are the sources of the extraordinary stability extant in the electoral behaviour of so many *barrios* and electoral units in Puerto Rico?

Field research in a sample of units including those with the highest PPD indexes and those with the lowest was undertaken to answer that question.[29] These units are among the most remote (and therefore most abandoned by the municipal and Commonwealth governments) in Puerto Rico. The electorate there would have particularly strong reasons to use the right to vote to call attention to their plight. Yet, what emerges from the answers given by informants is a very different picture. Phrases like 'we will continue to vote for the PPD because Muñoz Marín gave us shoes and built roads all the way to here', 'we cannot betray Muñoz' (who retired from the governorship in 1964 and died in 1980) and 'we must keep our party loyalty', came up again and again in those units with the highest PPD index. In Spanish this is called *agradecimiento*.

In units with the lowest PPD indexes, answers tended to be less specific in terms of the reasons for their anti-PPD and pro-PNP stance. Repeated references were made to 'tradition' (defined as 'the way mom and dad have always voted'), although in several cases this 'tradition' was traced to Muñoz's agrarian reform, in which the government 'expropriated land on which our families used to work'. In Spanish this is called *resentimiento*.

Table 11.9 From *arrabal* to *caserío*: adults' preferred political status for Puerto Rico (%)

Political status	Shantytown adults (1959)		Public housing adults (1969)	
	Male	Female	Male	Female
Commonwealth	61.0	61.7	38.2	57.9
Statehood	32.9	21.5	55.9	32.6
Independence	2.4	1.1	0.0	0.0
No report	3.7	15.9	5.9	9.5
Number	(82)	(94)	(68)	(95)

Source: Safa, *The Urban Poor in Puerto Rico* (New York: Holt, Rinehart, 1973), p.75.

In all cases, informants indicated that in the 1988 elections they would vote exactly the same way they had voted in 1980 and in 1984. In this context, what 'tradition' seems to mean is allegiance to a given land tenure system. Voters will support the hegemonic PPD (which for long monopolized governmental power) if land was obtained from it – going back as far as the agrarian reform of the early 1940s. Voters will be against the PPD (and for the PNP) if the family was deprived of land or of a direct link with the land through the expropriation of the landowner for whom the family worked.

This dialectic of *agradecimiento* and *resentimiento* and its close relationship with the land question is especially evident in the contrasting voting behaviour of *parceleros* and *caserío* dwellers. The first remain eternally grateful for that piece of land that changed the family's fortune. The latter not only do not appreciate having been moved from their messy but neighbourly *arrabal* (slum) to the cold, inhospitable surrounding of the *caserío*, but positively resent it – as Safa found out when she re-interviewed many of the same *arrabaleros* ten years later in a *caserío* – (Table 11.9) – and will continue to resent it for the rest of their lives.

But this phenomenon whereby certain major changes in the individual's communal environment tend to have a determinant effect on party identification and political allegiance, fixing it for decades and even passing it on from generation to generation, is by no means confined to *parceleros* and *caserío* dwellers. It is also apparent in the case of black Puerto Ricans (at least to judge from the case of Loíza) and of many other voters throughout the island, for whom the key reference terms on election day are not 'choice' or 'most pressing needs', but 'loyalty' and 'family tradition'. This is the crux of our findings.

The net political effect of these primordial attachments has been to facilitate the hegemony of the political party that expressed the interests of the *hacendado* class first, and its successors later: the *unionistas*, the *liberales*, and the *populares*. Ideologically, this class has opted for *autonomismo* as its preferred status option. And it is indicative of the continuity of this tradition that, much as the founding father of the Unionist Party was Luis Muñoz Rivera, and the founding father of PPD was his son Luis Muñoz Marín, the person most people would identify as the next leader of the PPD is the granddaughter, Senator Victoria ('Melo') Muñoz (Figure 11.3).

THE FRANCHISE AND THE PUERTO RICAN PARTY SYSTEM: ONE LOGIC, NOT TWO

The conventional view on Puerto Rico's political system has recently been crisply stated by Robert Anderson.[30] According to it, change in the one-party-dominant system occurred suddenly in the mid-1960s, propelled, among other things, by the 1967 status plebiscite. The island was also undergoing a process of homogenization, which had started to erase distinctions between rural and urban settings. Politics in Puerto Rico thereafter would be of a 'one-issue' type, with status being the equivalent of what abortion, gun control or other such issues are elsewhere.

Such a view fails to do justice to the mounting evidence that status politics has very little to do with the behaviour of the electorate, that far from becoming homogenized, the island's population is as fragmented as ever, and that the change to a two-party system that took place in 1968 was by no means sudden, but the predictable result of long-term trends in electoral behaviour clearly related to the island's urbanization.

But where does this leave us? Does the increased urbanization likely to take place in a densely populated island mean the heirs of Muñoz are doomed, and that the PNP will inevitably become the hegemonic party in Puerto Rico, much like the PPD from 1940 to 1968? To answer such a question it is necessary to take a step back and look at it from another angle.

The history of voting behaviour in Puerto Rico is very much also the history of the electoral system itself. Given the stability of

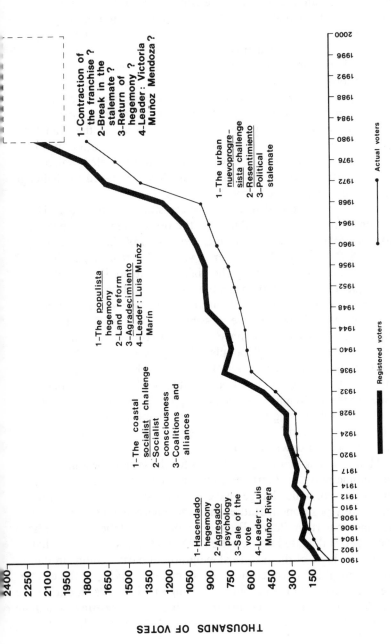

Figure 11.3 Voters, social change and party systems in Puerto Rico

political allegiance, and the strong effects of tradition, major realignments thus only come from tinkering with the system itself – to wit: registering new voters, expanding the franchise, facilitating the registration of split-movements. In the words of a renowned political leader, '*Si no ganamos con las masas, ganamos en las mesas*'.[31]

If we look at Figure 11.3, we will see that each of the four major periods of Puerto Rico's twentieth-century party system was launched not only by preceding changes in the socio-economic structure, but, concomitantly, by major expansions of the franchise. Given the enormous inertia of the Puerto Rican electorate, it is only by the massive addition of new resources into the electoral contest (newly enfranchised voters) that parties have managed to challenge the existing hegemonic party.

In the case of the PNP and its successful challenge to PPD hegemony during the 1968–88 period, the preceding massive urbanization was followed by an enormous expansion of the electorate over the 1968–80 period. The number of voters rose from 1.2 million to 2 million, the result of giving the right to vote to 18-year-olds, the subsequent household to household vote registration drive, as well as of the sheer demographic pressure of the baby-boom generation.

As of 1988, however, the possibilities for any further sizeable expansion of the electorate have effectively come to an end. With full universal suffrage for all people 18 and over and an increasingly ageing population, the number of voters is likely to remain stable. On the other hand, the building boom that took place at such breakneck speed in the 1950s and 1960s came to a halt in the 1970s, as did many of the federal housing programmes that financed so much of Puerto Rico's construction in earlier decades. The process of urbanization has thus slowed down considerably.[32]

All this means that the possibilities for the PNP to become the new hegemonic party in Puerto Rico by the sheer force of demographic and socio-economic changes have been considerably delayed, if not indefinitely postponed. Rather than the emergence of an alternative hegemonic party in Puerto Rico, our model would therefore predict a continued stalemate between the PPD and the PNP. Unless, that is, taking the logic of the historical evolution of party systems in Puerto Rico to its ultimate conclusion, a systematic *shrinking* of the electorate takes place. Since no one can change their minds, reducing the number of voters of 'the other' (to break the existing stalemate between the 'two-minority parties') seems to be indeed the tool being used in 1988 by both parties in a campaign designed to eliminate from the rolls voters identified with the rival party.[33]

WHAT MAKES THEM TICK?: SPATIAL ANALYSIS AND THE BREAKTHROUGH FROM PRIMORDIAL ATTACHMENTS

Studies of Caribbean political sociology have put the twin variables of race and class at the centre of their concern. Without wishing to belittle in any way their importance for our understanding of Caribbean political behaviour, the case of Puerto Rico indicates that two additional (and interrelated) variables have to be considered: one of them is sheer geographical location, the other is urbanization.

In societies sharply divided along ethnic lines like Trinidad and Guyana there may, of course, be a strong overlap between ethnic identity and geographic location. But in other societies of the region, where the ethnic divide is not so stark, more detailed exploration of the patterns of party support and identification at the parish and village level may provide us with important clues for the sources of the primordial attachments that are such an important component of voting behaviour in Puerto Rico.[34]

A voter's communal environment (urban or rural, *parcela* or *caserío*) may be more important than traditional variables like income in predicting his or her behaviour on election day. It is certainly much more significant than whatever candidates happen to utter on the hustings or whatever issues they address on television. The land question may be the key missing link to establish how the local 'tradition' (allegiance to any given political party) came to be in the first place. Urbanization, on the other hand, particularly urban renewal, plays the key role in breaking those primordial attachments and reforging them to new party alliances.[35] Just as with the people of Elvira, destiny seems to knock only once at the door of Puerto Rican voters.

NOTES

1. Thus, even analysts who should know better given their own past research on the subject, tend to take the 'political market paradigm' of voting behaviour for granted. On the 1984 elections, for example,

Marcia Rivera writes: 'The electorate seems to have gone beyond the parties, and if these elections prove anything, it is that a sort of rebellion took place in which voters dismissed the parties' mandates and voted as they really wanted after evaluating alternatives.' Marcia Rivera, 'Las elecciones y el análisis electoral en Puerto Rico', a paper delivered at the Tenth International Congress, Caribbean Studies Association, San Juan, Puerto Rico, 29–31 May 1985, p.17.

2. The only authoritative book on nineteenth-century elections in Puerto Rico is F. Bayrón Toro, *Elecciones y Partidos Políticos de Puerto Rico* (3rd edition; Mayagüez: Isla, 1984); it is the source of these data.

3. Sidney W. Mintz, 'Cañamelar: The Subculture of a rural sugar plantation proletariat', in J. Steward *et al.*, *The People of Puerto Rico* (Urbana, Illinois: The University of Illinois Press, 1956), p.479.

4. B. Pagán, *Historia de los Partidos Políticos Puertorriqueños 1898–1956* (San Juan: private printing, 1972), 2 vols.

5. R. Anderson, *Party Politics in Puerto Rico* (Stanford: Stanford University Press, 1965).

6. H. Wells 'Ideology and Leadership in Puerto Rican Politics', *American Political Science Review*, Vol. XLIX (1955), pp.22–40. For a somewhat different perspective on the subject, see P. Bachrach, 'Attitudes toward Authority and Party Preference in Puerto Rico', *Public Opinion Quarterly*, Vol. XXII (1958), pp.68–73. Based on a survey of UPR students, Bachrach argued that education drove people away from *personalismo*.

7. H. Wells, *The Modernization of Puerto Rico* (Cambridge, Mass: Harvard University Press, 1969).

8. K. Farr, *Personalism and Party Politics in Puerto Rico: The Institutionalization of the Popular Democratic Party* (San Juan: Inter-American University Press, 1973).

9. Bayrón, *op. cit.*, p.7.

10. J. Garriga-Picó, 'Electoral Strategies in the Question of Puerto Rican Studies: An Analysis and Some Projections Using the Theory of Games', CISCLA Working Paper No. 13 (San Germán, PR: Inter-American University of Puerto Rico, 1984).

11. A. Quintero Rivera, *Conflictos de Clase y Política en Puerto Rico* (Río Piedras: Huracán, 1977).

12. *Ibid.*, pp. 117–23.

13. A. Quintero Rivera, *Patricios y Plebeyos: Burgueses, Hacendados, Artesanos y Obreros. Las Relaciones de Clase en el Puerto Rico de Cambio de Siglo* (Río Piedras: Huracán, 1988).

14. M. Rivera, *Elecciones 1968 Puerto Rico* (San Juan: CEREP, 1972).

15. R. Ramírez, *El Arrabal y la Política* (Río Piedras: Universitaria, 1977); also H. Safa, *The Urban Poor in Puerto Rico: A Study in Development and Inequality* (New York: Holt, Rinehart, and Winston, 1973).

16. I. Pérez and M. Fernández, 'Análisis Cuantitativo de Movimientos Poblacionales y Electorales en Puerto Rico Durante los Últimas Tres Décadas' (San Juan: Análisis, 1984).

17. For a good discussion of the subject, see E.W. Austin, J.M. Clubb and M.W. Traugott, 'Aggregate Units of Analysis', in J.M. Clubb, W.H. Flannigan and N.H. Zingale (eds), *Analyzing Electoral History: A Guide*

to the Study of American Voter Behavior (Beverly Hills, California: Sage, 1981).
18. Stone's polls predicted with great accuracy the 1976 and the 1980 election results in Jamaica. Ryan's firm, St Augustine Research Associates, did the same with the 1984 elections in Tobago and in Grenada, as well as with the 1986 general elections in Trinidad–Tobago. Recent articles of theirs using their survey data are S. Ryan, 'New Directions in Trinidad and Tobago,' *Caribbean Affairs'* Vol. I, No. 1 (1988), pp.126–60 and C. Stone, 'Political Change in Jamaica: Life's Better, but the Polls are for Manley, not Seaga', *Caribbean Affairs*, Vol. I, No. 2 (1988), pp.31–46.
19. For a recent analysis of electoral behaviour in the Dominican Republic using aggregate data, see J. del Castillo and W. Cordero, 'El Comporta-miento Electoral Dominicano: un Análisis Comparado de las Elecciones de 1978 y 1981', CISCLA Working Paper No. 15 (San Germán: Inter American University, 1984).
20. The *popularismo* index was developed by Juan Manuel García-Passalacqua in 1968 and has been used since for his election-night television forecasting. In the 1984 elections, it enabled him to announce the final result of the elections at 9 p.m. with a margin of error of 0.04 per cent, four hours before the official results were in.
21. For an earlier, much more preliminary formulation of this approach to Puerto Rican voting behaviour, see J.M. García-Passalacqua, 'Dignidad y Jaibería: Los Paradigmas Políticos Puertorriqueños', *Anales*, Vol. I, Inter American University (1984), pp.9–33.
22. Pérez and Fernández, *op. cit.*
23. On the roots of Mayagüez's exceptionalism, see J. Heine, 'The Last Cacique: Leadership and Politics in a Puerto Rican City', doctoral dissertation, Stanford University (Ann Arbor Michigan: University Microfilms, 1987). This essay partly draws on the arguments and data of 'The Last Cacique'.
24. Partially reflecting this, Farr, commenting on the 1968 election, wrote: 'To the young, middle class urban and suburban voters of metropolitan San Juan, the PPD was apparently outmoded.' Farr, *op. cit.*, p.90.
25. In fact, the *caseríos* have developed a reputation for being veritable breeding grounds for criminals, 'overpopulated, underdesigned experiments in anarchy', as one letter to the *San Juan Star* editor put it, calling for their 'deconstruction'. It is said that poet Luis Palés Matos, Puerto Rico's leading writer of Afro-Caribbean poetry, called then-governor Luis Muñoz Marín to his death bed to ask him for one favour: to honor Palés after his death in whichever may Muñoz saw fit, but *not* by naming a *caserío* after him, as Muñoz had done with two other leading poets, Luis Llorens Torres and Nemesio Canales, names most people today associate with the crime, drugs and general lawlessness rampant in those two San Juan *caseríos*.
26. The yet-to-be-written history of the conception, design, construction and administration of Puerto Rico's public housing developments would make for a fascinating case study of a monumental failure in public policy, a failure that has come to haunt Puerto Rico to this day.
27. Questions related to race were dropped from the US Census in Puerto

Rico in 1960. Statistics on the distribution of the black population in contemporary Puerto Rico are thus unavailable.

28. For a highly informative discussion of Loíza politics, see C. Montalvo, 'Loíza', a paper prepared for the seminar on political analysis (P.S. 4155), taught by the authors in the 1987 fall semester at the University of Puerto Rico, Mayagüez.

29. The high PPD index units selected were in the following *barrios*: Guadiana (Naranjito), Rucio (Peñuelas), Órama (Maricao), Caimito (Juncos), Quebrada (Salinas) and Fortuna (Vega Alta). Those with the lowest PPD index are Capaez (Hatillo), Pedro García (Coamo), Montones (Las Piedras), Jagüez (Rincón), Sierra Alta (Yauco), San Lorenzo (Morovis). Interviews in each of these units were carried out by our students in P.S. 4155 at UPR, Mayagüez in the fall of 1987.

30. R. Anderson, 'Political Parties and the Politics of Status: The Study of Political Organization in Puerto Rico', *Caribbean Studies*, Vol. XXI (1988), pp.1–43.

31. D. Targa, *El Modus Operandi de las Artes Electorales en Puerto Rico* (San Juan: Private printing, 1940) is a collection of examples of the many tricks used at the electoral tables or *mesas*.

32. Secretary of Housing Ariel Nazario has announced that the government of Puerto Rico will 'leave aside the construction of new housing and will concentrate instead on improvements in public housing developments, in rehabilitating existing homes and in physical improvements in the rural communities', *El Nuevo Día* (12 April 1988), p.12.

This announcement followed a $99 million reduction in the Housing Department's budget. Simultaneously, the *parcelas* programme has been stepped up. It took the PPD 20 years to realize that it had been its own disastrous urban renewal and public housing policies that had lain the foundation for the PNP challenge!

33. The number of registered voters whose right to vote has been questioned during the January–May 1988 period is projected to reach 100 000. The fact that most of these are from San Juan, Bayamón, Carolina, Guaynabo and Ponce, the island's largest *municipios* (all PNP bastions) would seem to indicate that the PPD is the most likely beneficiary of this process. See *El Nuevo Día* (16 May 1988), p.16.

34. Cumbersome voting systems in which polling places are not established on a strict residential basis, of course, may preclude any such analysis, as is the case in the US Virgin Islands, for example. One implication of this study is that, whenever possible, electoral systems ought to be streamlined to make such analysis possible.

35. An additional aspect of this reforging is the significant rise in mixed-ballot, independent voters, that in Puerto Rico has gone from less than 1 per cent in 1964 to more than 12 per cent in 1984.

Index

Arrangement is by individual countries, in additional to general subject matter.

Page numbers in **bold** type are those of tables and figures.

288 *Index*

South-eastern Caribbean – *continued*
  European Community, 126
  freedom of expression, 118
  geographical location, 124–8
  government as employer, 124–5
  history, 111–14
  imports, high, 122
  insularity, 112–13, 124–8
  law, rule of, 118
  military, role of, 118
  New Jewel Movement (NJM),
    114–16; *see also* Grenada
  Organization of East Caribbean
    States (OECS), 110
  patronage, 125
  personality cults, 126–7
  politics
    armed insurrection and, 112
    participatory democracy,
      114–16
    party system, 119–21, 127,
    popular representation, 114–16
    population, **111**
    regimes, 21
    Westminster model, 117–19,
      128
  race, 111, 118, 129n
  radicalism, 121
  religion, 116–18
  SCOPE, 126
  size and population, **111**, 124–8
  slavery, 111–12, 121
  Smith, S.A., 117
  social class, 112
  society and politics, 110–12, 112,
    128–9
  South African involvement, 113
  standards of living, 122
  suffrage, universal, 116
  trade unions 114–18
  United States
    and British Virgin Islands, 126
    influence of, 110–11, 112, 122,
      127–9
  West Indies Act (1967), 126
  white population, 112
Soviet Union, 1, 209, 212, 214, 226
Spanish colonialism, 1, 9, **11**, 12, 15
Spanish war (1898), 11

Standing Committee of Opposition
  Parties of the Eastern Caribbean
  States (SCOPE), 126
Stone, Carl, Caribbean politics, 35,
  38, 255
Stubbs, Jean,
  Cuban population, **11**
Suriname, plural-segmented
  society, 7, 9, 12, 17
Suvelor, Roland, French Antilles,
  242
Sylvestre, L., Belizean politician,
  103

Tapia party, Trinidad and Tobago,
  65–6
Tate & Lyle, 88, 89; *see also* Belize
  Sugar Industries Ltd
The Nation, Trinidad and Tobago,
  63
Third World, Caribbean in, 1
Thorp, Rosemary, 20
Toussaint L'Ouverture, General,
  189
Trabajadores, Cuban trade union
  newspaper, 224–5
Transport and Industrial Workers'
  Union, Trinidad and Tobago, 65
Trinidad and Tobago
  Action Committee of Dedicated
    Citizens (ACDC), 64
  Alliance Party, 66
  All Trinidad Sugar Estates and
    Factories Workers' Trade
    Union (ATSEFWU), 55, 65
  Best, Lloyd
    blacks, 48–55, 63–4
    Tapia, 66
  Bryan, Victor, 57
  Butler, 'Buzz', 56
    Party, 54, 56–7
  Capildeo, Dr Rudranath, 60–1,
    62, 64
  Chambers, George, and PNM,
    65–7
  colour, 48–55, 51
  Creoles, 48–55
    Defence Force, 63–4
    hegemony, 62–5